Manufacturing Culture

Victorian Literature and Culture Series

Jerome J. McCann and Herbert F. Tucker, Editors

JOSEPH BIZUP

Manufacturing Culture

VINDICATIONS OF
EARLY VICTORIAN
INDUSTRY

University of Virginia Press
CHARLOTTESVILLE AND LONDON

University of Virginia Press
© 2003 by the Rector and Visitors of the University of Virginia
All rights reserved
Printed in the United States of America on acid-free paper
First published 2003

1 3 5 7 9 8 6 4 2

Library of Congress Cataloging-in-Publication Data

Bizup, Joseph, 1966–
    Manufacturing culture : vindications of early Victorian industry /
Joseph Bizup.
        p.   cm. — (Victorian literature and culture series)
Includes bibliographical references and index.
    ISBN 0-8139-2246-1 (cloth : alk. paper)
    1. Great Britain—Civilization—19th century. 2. Industries—Great
Britain—History—19th century. 3. English literature—19th
century—History and criticism. 4. Great Britain—History—Victoria,
1837–1901. 5. Great Exhibition (1851 : London, England) 6. Industries
in literature. I. Title. II. Series
DA533 .B57 2003
306.3'4'094109034—dc21

                                                          2003009463

For Annmarie and Grace

CONTENTS

ILLUSTRATIONS

ACKNOWLEDGMENTS

IN WRITING this book, I have benefited tremendously from the industry and culture of many friends and colleagues, and I would like to thank them for their support. Patrick Brantlinger, Linda Peterson, and Joseph Roach read drafts of the manuscript in its entirety and helped me to work through my ideas in numerous conversations. Alexander Welsh and Ruth Yeazell offered valuable comments on drafts of several chapters, and Jay Clayton stimulated my thinking about Babbage. Receptive responses to early versions of chapter 1 from Janice Carlisle, Herbert Sussman, and Mark Turner helped me to apprehend the trajectory and implications of my work, while a series of discussions with Sarah Winter, and incisive yet gentle criticisms from Herbert Tucker, contributed greatly to the framing of the whole. Many others, including Nigel Alderman, Timothy Barringer, Ralph Bauer, George Allan Cate, Isaac Cates, Matthew Giancarlo, Edward Hagan, Leigh Harris, Christina Kiaer, Laura King, Eugene Kintgen, Lavinia Lorch, Andrew Miller, Annabel Patterson, Lee Patterson, Vanessa Ryan, Joseph Slaughter, Don Ulin, and Francis Albert Young helped in less formal ways, sharing insights and encouragement that allowed me to write a better book. I owe a special debt of gratitude to James Eli Adams, who has seen more versions of this study than anyone besides its author. His guidance has been invaluable, and I consider myself extraordinarily fortunate to have been his student.

A Victorian Studies dissertation fellowship from Indiana University supported my early research and writing. Two A. Whitney Griswold grants from Yale allowed me to conduct research abroad. A Morse junior faculty fellowship, also from Yale, allowed me to develop my ideas into their current form. I am grateful to both institutions for this support. I would also like to acknowledge the staffs of the Yale University Library, the Yale Center for British Art, the British Library, the National Art Library at the Victoria and Albert Museum, and the Libraries of Columbia University in the City of New York. In particular, Elisabeth Fairman graciously guided me through the Yale Center for British Art's extensive holdings on the Great Exhibition, and Claudia Funke of the Avery Architectural and Fine Arts Library of Columbia University helped with illustrations at a late stage in the manuscript's preparation.

Cathie Brettschneider and the staff at the University of Virginia Press have been supremely patient and supportive. Ruth Melville improved the manuscript with her deft copyediting, and Andrew Marcovy assisted with proofreading.

Chapter 6 draws on material published previously in *English Literature in Transition: 1880–1920* and *Prose Studies.* The illustrations appear through the courtesy of the Yale University Library, the Yale Center for British Art, the Libraries of Columbia University in the City of New York, and the Avery Architectural and Fine Arts Library of Columbia University.

I am grateful, finally, to my teachers, students, and family. My most profound debt is to my wife, Annmarie Caracansi-Bizup, who has been a constant source of strength and inspiration. I dedicate this book to her and to our daughter Grace. Together, they make it all worthwhile.

Manufacturing Culture

Industry as Culture in Nineteenth-Century Britain

IN HIS foundational study *Culture and Society, 1780–1950,* Raymond Williams shows how, over the course of the nineteenth century, "culture" came to serve as a bulwark of defense against the allegedly destabilizing forces of "Democracy" and "Industry." British social critics from Burke to Orwell, he demonstrates, repeatedly looked to culture as both a "mitigating and rallying alternative" to economic and political liberalism and a "court of human appeal" over the practical areas of social life (*Culture and Society* xviii).

Williams identifies Robert Southey's 1829 *Sir Thomas More: or, Colloquies on the Progress and Prospects of Society,* an extended critical dialogue between the ghost of Sir Thomas More and his nineteenth-century interlocutor Montesinos, as one of the earliest texts to employ this soon-to-become-general strategy. In particular, Southey's attack on the early nineteenth-century factory system is predicated upon the principle, fundamental to the emerging ideal of culture Williams examines, that general social conditions can be judged through personal aesthetic response:

> What then shall we say of a system which in its direct consequences debases all who are engaged in it? a system that employs men unremittingly in pursuits unwholesome for the body, and unprofitable for the mind, .. a system in which the means are so bad, that any result would be dearly purchased at such an expense of human misery and degradation, and the end so fearful, that the worst calamities which society has hitherto endured may be deemed light in comparison with it? (Southey 1:170)

The implicit answer to these questions is, of course, that nothing need be said: the factory system damns itself in the stunted beings it creates. Southey's argument, this is to say, proceeds by emblem rather than by example, which is precisely why Macaulay finds it so frustrating. In his review of the *Colloquies,* he chides Southey for judging policy "by the effect produced on his imagination" and asks, "What are all systems, religious, political, or scientific, but opinions resting on evidence more or less satisfactory?" (218,

245–46). Southey, however, regards the sort of public "evidence" Macaulay values as largely irrelevant. In his view, aesthetic feeling leads to social judgments possessing all the certainty and immediacy of physical sensation, and culture and industry remain starkly and obviously distinct. Why is it, he asks, "that every thing which is connected with manufactures, presents such features of unqualified deformity?" (1:174).

As Williams notes, Southey advances a number of claims that have since become familiar staples of the discourse of "culture" (*Culture and Society* 24). As a case in point, Southey adopts a complex posture toward technological progress that continues to inform subsequent social criticism. Southey is no Luddite, but he also refuses to allow rosy anticipations of some happy industrial future to blind him to the contemporary evils wrought by the factory system. To Montesinos's enthusiastic notion that "skill in machinery" will bring "the greatest advantages of science and civilization at the least expense of human labour," More answers, "There is a wide gulph between you and that point" (1:159). To Montesinos's retort that "the benefit will remain after all the evils of the process shall have past away," More charges ominously, "This very manufacturing system, which you regard as introductory to your Utopian era, proves that England has taken no warning" from the example of history (1:160, 161). In *Culture and Anarchy* (1869), Arnold reprises this exchange. Assigning Gladstone the role of Montesinos, Arnold observes how in a recent speech, he "well pointed out . . . how necessary is the present great movement towards wealth and industrialism, in order to lay broad foundations of material well-being for the society of the future." Placing himself in the role of More, Arnold answers: "Now, culture admits the necessity of the movement towards fortune-making and exaggerated industrialism, readily allows that the future may derive benefit from it; but insists, at the same time, that the passing generations of industrialists,—forming, for the most part, the stout main body of Philistinism,—are sacrificed to it" (105). Writing four decades apart, Southey and Arnold issue nearly identical warnings against allowing endlessly deferred hopes of future prosperity to justify the perpetual sacrifice of the present.

Despite such similarities, a crucial difference in tone separates Southey's critique of industry from that of his successors. Although he structures his book as an extended dialogue, Montesinos and More are less distinct personae than complementary vehicles through which Southey expresses his own positions. Throughout, Southey evinces an unshakable conviction in the persuasive power of his appeals. He relies on rhetorical modes that presume agreement and assent, such as the declarative statement and the rhetorical question, and seems to regard his pronouncements as virtually self-evident. In contrast, later critics, such as Carlyle, Ruskin, Arnold, and Morris, adopt oppositional and even antagonistic postures toward their audiences, betraying their deep concern that they will go unheeded. In this light, the baroque rhetorical strategies that characterize high Victorian "sage writing" can be seen as symptoms of an anxiety of rhetorical impotence that afflicts all practitioners of the genre to some degree.[1] If Southey only intermittently invokes culture as an abstraction, it is not merely because he stands near the beginning of the discourse Williams traces; it is also because he perceives little need to justify himself by appealing to an idealized domain of aesthetic values. Arnold's seemingly endless ruminations on what culture is, what culture does, and what culture makes us ask, on the other hand, are equally signs of the concept's maturity and vulnerability.

Yet even Southey occasionally expresses doubts that belie the surety of his rhetoric. At its most excoriating moment, his condemnation of industrial England lapses into lament. The factory system, More intones, "is a wen, a fungous excrescence from the body politic: the growth might have been checked if the consequences had been apprehended in time; but now it has acquired so great a bulk, its nerves have branched so widely, and the vessels of the tumour are so inosculated into some of the principal veins and arteries of the natural system, that to remove it by absorption is impossible, and excision would be fatal" (1:171). Characterizations of the factory system as a threat to the "body" of English society would become a mainstay of early Victorian criticisms of industry, and in subsequent chapters I examine in detail several proindustrial efforts to circumvent these sorts of representations. What I would like to emphasize at this point is rather Southey's sad and angry sense that the cause has already been lost, that it is now too late to excise the cancerous growth.

In Arnold, this worry blossoms into a more disturbing concern that the very concept of culture, as an abstract ideal, has become inextricable from industry. In a telling aside in *Culture and Anarchy*, Arnold finds himself compelled to take explicit issue with the notion that industrialism is a form of culture. An "American defender" of "the English Liberals," he observes, "proposes that we should for the future call industrialism culture, and the industrialists the men of culture, and then of course there can be no longer any misapprehension about their true character; and besides the pleasure of being wealthy and comfortable, they will have authentic recognition as vessels of sweetness and light" (129). Arnold rejects this association out of hand, as an "undoubtedly specious" attempt to counter his substantive social criticisms

3

with mere semantic confusions. "I must remark," he writes, "that the culture of which I talked was an endeavour to come at reason and the will of God by means of reading, observing, and thinking; and that whoever calls anything else culture, may, indeed, call it so if he likes, but then he talks of something quite different from what I talked of" (129).

In thus framing his objection, however, Arnold is engaging in his own bit of rhetorical misdirection. By taking an unnamed American as his primary interlocutor, Arnold implies that the idea of an industrial culture is an alien notion, not indigenous to England. But as we shall see, this idea informs the rhetoric of many prominent English proponents of industry from the second quarter of the nineteenth century forward. Moreover, Arnold himself is being at least a bit "specious" in characterizing the American's idea of culture as simply unrelated to his own. As recent scholarship has emphasized, the Arnoldian concept of culture, although presented as a universal and ahistorical ideal, both took shape in relation to a concurrently emerging "anthropological" notion of culture and contributed in concrete ways to the maintenance of the liberal industrial state.[2] In this light, Arnold's insistence that those who call industrialism "culture" mean "something quite different" from what he means seems less a disinterested effort after semantic precision than a cagey rhetorical maneuver that enables him to dismiss out of hand the "Liberal" position to which he objects.

Paradoxically, I would suggest, the prospect to which Arnold here reacts is itself a product of the broadly Romantic tradition of social criticism he represents. Williams offers ample evidence of the polemical power inherent in the Romantic opposition between industry and culture. My contention is that, in the decades between Southey and Arnold, proponents of industrialism and free trade recognized and actively resisted this power. During the second quarter of the nineteenth century, an identifiable proindustrial rhetoric, predicated upon the subversion of the antithesis between industry and culture, coalesced within two mutually reinforcing bodies of discourse: the contentious debates over the factory system and its social and aesthetic effects, and the extensive discussions of the aesthetic, social, and commercial importance of "design" for British manufactures. Within this pair of discourses, culture was reimagined as a coordinated and complementary development of art, science, and commerce, and automatic manufacture was itself construed as a cultural force or agent. Occasionally these views were advanced directly, but more often they were pursued obliquely, as arguments, images, and metaphors affiliated with the idea of culture were turned to the defense of mechanized industry. Through these sorts of rhetorical appropriations,

Arnold's so-called English Liberals sought to limit the capacity of humanistic or aesthetic culture to serve as a "rallying alternative" to the ideology of industrial capitalism and, more pointedly, to position industrialism itself as a positive moral, social, and aesthetic force. The contrast between Southey's general confidence that culture is inherently incompatible with mechanized industry and Arnold's compulsion to explicitly defend this same position marks a significant shift in nineteenth-century debates over industrialization. This book endeavors to understand that shift by tracing British vindications of industry from the factory debates of the 1830s through the Great Exhibition of 1851, and in so doing to contribute to current scholarship's ongoing contextualization of Williams's "culture and society" tradition.

IF ONE were to accept the argument of *Culture and Society* outright, it might seem that any notion of an industrial culture would have to be dismissed as patently oxymoronic or, at best, as irremediably conflicted. However, we can now recognize Williams's strong thesis itself as a product of the mid-twentieth-century political and intellectual context in which he was working. As Stefan Collini has recently noted, the logic of *Culture and Society* becomes apparent when the book is recognized as Williams's effort to reconcile his dual commitments to social solidarity on the one hand and to humanistic culture on the other. Williams's strategy is to locate himself as the heir to a venerable tradition of thought and feeling that can be viewed as supporting his own oppositional scholarship and politics. The figures he includes in this tradition— Burke, Coleridge, Carlyle, Ruskin, Newman, Arnold, Morris, Lawrence, and Orwell, among others—are not united by any specific ideology or position. What they have in common is that, in retrospect, they may be seen to have contributed to the development of a "nexus of ideas and values" that Williams wishes to recuperate as an alternative to the "bourgeois idea of society" prevailing in his day. Collini argues that it is simply "too reductive" to see the diverse array of writers Williams discusses "as chiefly concerned to articulate a critique of, and alternative to, industrialism." They were not opposed to industrialism specifically but were attempting to find an intellectual and moral position from which "the most 'general' assessments could be made" (23–25).

Collini's judgment is supported by recent scholarship, which has questioned and complicated Williams's argument even as it has continued to testify to his abiding importance and influence. In particular, recent scholarship has raised three compelling objections to Williams's project: first, that he predicates his analysis upon a presumptive dichotomy between the domain of culture and other domains of life; second, that he attributes a false or at least retrospective coherence to what was in fact a heterogeneous and conflicted constellation of discourses; and third, that he vitiates the power of his analysis by identifying too closely with his object of study. These criticisms are valid and appropriate. Williams's laudable social and political agenda may have required a strong narrative of a definite "tradition of English social criticism," but over the past four decades this narrative has come to seem unduly constrictive. Consequently, a number of scholars have responded by documenting the profoundly multivalent and mutable quality of nineteenth-century concepts of culture by tracing the intimate links between the discourse of culture and other political, social, intellectual, and economic discourses, and by demonstrating the role of culture in authorizing and supporting various institutional structures and social practices.

Although they reference Williams only tangentially, Peter Allan Dale's *In Pursuit of a Scientific Culture* (1989), Mary Poovey's *Making a Social Body* (1995), and Catherine Gallagher's *The Industrial Reformation of English Fiction* (1985) all productively complicate the dichotomies on which Williams's narrative is based. Dale argues that "the aesthetic consciousness irresistibly asserts itself in the very midst of the positivist project" of Comte, Mill, and Lewes (30), thus locating a cultural impulse within a strain of high intellectual discourse that was supposed to be irreconcilably opposed to the "culture and society" tradition. Poovey demonstrates the fluidity with which a figure central to this tradition—the image of the "social body"—passed among various social, political, and literary discourses, yoking them all within a broader nationalistic project she calls "British cultural formation." Gallagher, subtly alluding to Williams, notes that the "Condition of England" debates came to a close in the 1860s, when "culture," understood as a pure "realm of values," was opposed to "society," or the "realm of facts" (236). Once culture came to be regarded as an autonomous realm of ethical and aesthetic representation, she holds, it was no longer possible to condemn industrial society for its perverse determinism, its amoral randomness, or its challenges to the "natural" structure of the patriarchal family (264–67). Gallagher thus interrupts Williams's argument almost precisely at its apex, in order to historicize the very dichotomy between culture and society on which it is based.

Other scholars, such as Ian Hunter, David Lloyd and Paul Thomas, and Christopher Herbert, rely explicitly on Williams's fertile opposition between culture and society to motivate their own critical arguments. The very titles of these authors' respective studies—*Culture and Government* (1988), *Culture and the State* (1998), and *Culture and Anomie* (1991)—both acknowledge their debts to Williams and signal the specific nature of their departures from him. Hunter maintains that the emphasis on literature within the "governmental educational apparatus" that evolved over the course of the nineteenth century reflected not a "filtering down" of Arnoldian values but the delineation of literature as "an apparently unstructured domain of experience" through which the development of pupils' moral characters could be supervised and controlled (3, 119–20). Williams, this is to say, had it precisely backward: aesthetic culture does not foster a critical posture toward industrial society; it is the primary vehicle through which educational institutions work to inculcate an ethical subjectivity amenable to a Foucauldian "governmentality" (73–74). Lloyd and Thomas likewise argue that culture "designates not a discursive formation in opposition to society but rather a set of institutions within society at the point of its intersection with the state" (67).[3] Although they praise Williams for recovering an occulted tradition of social criticism, they object to what they see as his problematic identification with his subject and challenge his claim that the idea of culture provides an "immediate basis" for critically engaging industrialization and democratization (11–13). Herbert explicitly positions his genealogy of the modern anthropological and sociological concept of culture as a supplement to and critique of Williams's study. He accepts without reservation two of Williams's major contentions—that the concept of culture entered English social thought in the early nineteenth century, and that the modern sociological concept of culture emerged from an existing literary tradition—but he objects to what he sees as Williams's effort to invest the idea of culture with both a "seemingly unassailable historical coherence" and an unwarranted "moral and philosophical prestige" (22).

Despite such criticisms, this body of work does not so much refute Williams's study as renovate it. In effect, it dislodges his hope that culture can function as a transcendent ideal in order to reconstitute his analysis on a premise more amenable to current theory: that the concept of culture is an immanent product of sustained ideological, intellectual, institutional, and class negotiations. We now see that culture was not and cannot be a "rallying alternative" to industrialism and democracy in any simple sense. We also recognize that although the nineteenth-century discourse of culture purports to treat universal values, it was emphatically a discourse of the middle class. Finally, we understand that the discourse of culture was simultaneously philosophical and rhetorical, theoretical and instrumental. If these generalizations are valid, then there can be nothing absolute or self-evident about the various oppositions (culture and society, culture and democracy, culture and industry) around which the critical tradition Williams addresses was organized. What this meant concretely, in the second quarter of the nineteenth century, was that the idea of culture could be pressed into the service of the very ideology it was purportedly defined against.

THIS PROCESS of appropriation was facilitated by the complicated semantic relationship between the terms *culture* and *civilization* as they were used in the nineteenth century. Although culture was commonly invoked as an alternative to the laissez-faire ethos of industrial civilization, it was not regarded as antithetical to civilization in the same sense as, say, savageness, which from the mid-eighteenth through the mid-nineteenth centuries was *defined* purely as civilization's negation or inversion. Rather, culture functions in Romantic and post-Romantic social criticism in two related but distinct ways. Used narrowly, the term identifies a specific category of moral, aesthetic, and intellectual values that stand in opposition to the dominant values of capitalist civilization, but it also identifies a metacategory that subsumes both of these sets of values and demands their integration. In this more abstract sense, culture connotes not a specific set of values but a state of "harmonious perfection" (Arnold 94–95) that arises from the reconciliation of culture and civilization in their more narrow senses.

It is for this reason that dialectical critics such as Coleridge, Carlyle, and Arnold can appear to endorse one set of values over another while anticipating their ultimate synthesis. In his essay *On the Constitution of Church and State,* for example, Coleridge holds that the English constitution endeavors to balance "two antagonist powers or interests": those of "Permanence," which he associates with those classes bound to the land (whether as property owners or as laborers), and those of "Progression," which he associates with the mercantile, professional, and commercial classes (24–25). Within this scheme, Coleridge identifies culture—the dissemination of which is the task of the "*third* great venerable estate of the realm," the national church—as "the necessary antecedent condition" of this synthesis of contrary interests (42).

Carlyle, in his early essay "Signs of the Times," similarly calls for a "right coördination" of the "Dynamical" and "Mechanical" aspects of human nature, and for "the vigorous forwarding of *both*" (27:73). Carlyle uses the adjectives "Dynamical" and "Mechanical" to contrast internal intellectual or spiritual culture, on the one hand, and external material civilization, on the other. Yet he also recognizes that these two elements are "so intricately and inseparably" intertwined that to define their limits with respect to one another would be impossible, and he holds that favoring one over the other will necessarily have ill effects:

Undue cultivation of the inward or Dynamical province leads to idle, visionary, impracticable courses, and, especially in rude eras, to Superstition and Fanaticism, with their long train of baleful and well-known evils. Undue cultivation of the outward, again, though less immediately prejudicial, and even for the time productive of many palpable benefits, must, in the long-run, by destroying Moral Force, which is the parent of all other Force, prove not less certainly, and perhaps still more hopelessly, pernicious. (27:73)

The parallelism between these two sentences reinforces Carlyle's contention that neither the Mechanical nor the Dynamical should ultimately be subordinated to the other. In particular, his decision to use the word "cultivation," rather than a more neutral alternative such as "development" or "advancement," reinforces his implication that real culture *requires* attention to the outward or Mechanical aspects of life.

Arnold too describes the progress of history as a kind of oscillation between two broad impulses: "Hebraism," which names the "fire and strength" of the "Philistine" bourgeoisie, and "Hellenism," which names the disinterested pursuit of the "sweetness and light" Arnold associates with culture. Yet he also notes that when these forces are placed in opposition to each other, it is most often for the "rhetorical purpose" of advocating one at the expense of the other (164). While Arnold considers "Hebraism" and "Hellenism" to be "in some sense rivals," he also insists that they share the same "final aim" of humanity's "perfection or salvation" and that they are best understood as potentially complementary "*contributions* to human development" (163–64, 171). The general "perfection of human nature" that is the aim of culture in fact requires their mutual development and ultimate reconciliation (112). From this perspective, Arnold's endorsement of Hellenism, like Carlyle's endorsement of the Dynamical, is not an absolute position but a prescription for the present time.

Furthermore, none of the major social critics of the nineteenth century (with the possible exception of Ruskin) saw technological progress as an evil in itself. Rather, they objected to what they perceived as England's disproportionate concern with material advancement and its neglect of the more important "inward" aspects of life. Carlyle, of course, repeatedly recognizes the sublime power and achievement of industry, even as he decries the "mechanical" character of his age. Regarding the mechanical and chemical discoveries of the day, Southey's Sir Thomas More asserts, "You cannot advance in them too fast, provided that the moral culture of the species keep pace with the increase of its material powers" (1:206). Similarly, when Coleridge opines that "a nation can never be a too cultivated, but may easily become an over-civilized race" (49), he understands excessive civilization in relative rather than absolute terms. Coleridge never posits a state of material achievement beyond which humanity should not advance, but he does insist that such advancement must be preceded by an at least commensurate development in culture. Moreover, the term *civilization* has a shifting valence for Coleridge that precludes it from being treated simply as culture's antithesis. In insisting on "the permanent *distinction,* and the occasional *contrast,* between cultivation and civilization" (49), he both differentiates culture from civilization and recognizes the possibility of their reconciliation in principle. In Coleridge's own terms, they are *permanent* opposites (like the forces of Permanence and Progression) but only *occasional* contraries, which implies that under proper conditions they may join together in harmonious synthesis.

Neither is Arnold averse to material progress, so long as it is subordinated to the pursuit of an inner mental and spiritual perfection. Admittedly, he often appears to treat material civilization as the antithesis of culture— "The idea of perfection as an *inward* condition of the mind and spirit is at variance with the mechanical and material civilisation in esteem with us" (95)—but such statements are best interpreted not as absolute pronouncements but as hyperbolic responses to what Arnold perceives as an imbalance in England's national values:

> Faith in machinery is, I said, our besetting danger; often in machinery most absurdly disproportioned to the end which this machinery, if it is to do any good at all, is to serve; but always in machinery, as if it had a value in and for itself. What is freedom but machinery? what is population but machinery? what is coal but machinery? what are railroads but machinery? what is wealth but machinery? what are, even, religious organisations but machinery? (96)

As this series of questions suggests, by "faith in machinery," Arnold does not mean simply the high Victorian sense of security and optimism fostered by England's industrial preeminence. Rather, he is objecting to a more basic tendency to value means over ends, or even to efface the distinction between them altogether. While Arnold clearly sees the inner perfection that is culture's object as an intrinsic good, he also argues that the pursuit of culture is "particularly important" at the present time. The "whole civilisation" of the "modern world," Arnold observes, is "mechanical and external, and tends constantly to become more so" (95). Culture has such a "weighty part to perform" in England precisely because it is in England that "that mechanical character, which civilisation tends to take everywhere, is shown in the most eminent degree." Culture's crucial "function" is to provoke and sustain a countervailing meditation on ends: "But what *is* greatness?—culture makes us ask" (95, 96). From this perspective, culture is not incompatible with material civilization but provides an ethical context for it.

PACE ARNOLD, nineteenth-century proponents of industry seldom called industrialism culture directly, but they did pursue a number of indirect rhetorical strategies designed to imply such an association, such as asserting the superior "culture" of the industrial sectors of society, demonstrating their own cultural competence through judicious literary or historical allusions, or repeatedly using metaphors of "cultivation" to describe the expansion and growth of British industry and industrial society. In a lecture entitled "The Relations of Manufactures to Science and Art," for example, the liberal reformer Sir James Kay-Shuttleworth (James Phillips Kay before his 1842 marriage to Janet Shuttleworth) contends that the "first fruits of civilisation are the results of culture" (*Thoughts* 94). Although the word "culture" in this context primarily means cultivation or development, its nominal form and its association with "civilisation" implicitly blur the Romantic distinction between outward material progress and inward personal growth. For Kay-Shuttleworth, culture is not antithetical to civilization; it is the means through which the "fruits" of civilization may be realized. In a separate address to the Kendal Working Men's Club, he presents himself as an embodiment of this process. After attributing England's prosperity to free trade, self-improvement, and the nation's democratic constitution, he self-consciously positions himself between the competing ideologies underlying English Romanticism and liberal capitalism. Invoking Coleridge, Wordsworth, Southey, and Arnold, among others, he asserts that he has chosen in his own life "a middle course" between "the philosophic calm of a purely contemplative life" of the Lake District and "the turmoil of incessant action and growth" of the industrial north (*Thoughts* 57–59). Whether or not one accepts Kay-Shuttleworth's self-representation, the mere fact that he identifies this "middle course" as a viable ideological synthesis works to undermine the opposition between civilization and culture around which the Romantic critique of industrial society was organized.

The technical consultant and proindustrial propagandist Dr. Andrew Ure likewise plays on the semantic slippage between "culture" and "cultivation" to equate the expansion of industry with the general advancement of civilization. In the preface to his infamous apology for the factory system *The Philosophy of Manufactures* (1835), he insists that if Britain is to maintain her supremacy in trade, she must "diligently promote moral and professional culture among all ranks of her productive population" (vii). Throughout the treatise, he endeavors to counter Tory and Romantic ambivalence toward mechanized industry by using images of cultivation to describe the expansion of British industry. He applauds steam engines for allowing the "rich fields of industry to be cultivated to the utmost" (29) and figures concentrations of capital as a kind of fertilizer, which can enable an industry to prosper in regions that have "not the most congenial soil for its growth" (70). Against this background, Ure counters Southey's characterization of the factory system as "a fungous excrescence from the body politic" (277) with his own image of industry as a kind of cultivation:

> Could a metaphor have proved anything, a more appropriate one might have been found, in the process of vegetable and animal generation, to illustrate the great truth, that Providence has assigned to man the glorious function of vastly improving the productions of nature by *judicious culture,* and working them up into objects of comfort and elegance with the least possible expenditure of human labour—an undeniable position which forms the basis of our Factory System. (278, emphasis added)

Pushing his rebuttal further, Ure maintains that the locus of aesthetic and intellectual "culture" in fact lies with the manufacturing sectors of society. Noting that literature finds its principal patrons among the manufacturing rather than the agricultural classes, he asks pointedly, "Which, then, is the moral and intellectual population?" (278).

The liberal journalist William Cooke Taylor uses a similar image to open an 1849 article in the *Art-Journal* entitled "On the Cultivation of Taste in the Operative Classes" (11:3–5):

> If a farmer should bestow extraordinary care on the cultivation of patches in his ground, tending and watching these favoured spots with the most eminent agricultural skill and the most sedulous anxiety for the development of all their resources, but should wholly neglect the rest of his fields, leaving them to be overgrown with weeds or choked with rushes, we should unhesitatingly say that his course was one involving a large expenditure with almost a certainty of producing no adequate return. The course that would be condemned in the farmer, is precisely that which the British Empire has adopted with regard to National Education generally, and Artistic Education in particular.

In this analogy, the farmer's "fields" map onto the different classes of society, and the "cultivation" of these fields maps onto state-sponsored education. On this basis, we might expect Cooke Taylor to argue for the artistic education of *all* classes: just as the farmer should cultivate the whole of his fields, so the state should educate the whole of its population. Yet he does not make this claim. Instead, he abandons his agricultural metaphor after a single paragraph to pursue a very different line of argument governed by a very different metaphor: the "scale of society."

Cooke Taylor's specific complaint is that the state is courting grave "social dangers" by educating the "lower classes" (by whom he means the nonworking poor and rural laborers) while it neglects the "operative classes" immediately above them. These alleged "dangers," however, are not analogous to those which confront his hypothetical farmer. If the farmer were to devote assiduous attention to a small portion of his fields while neglecting his other holdings, he would waste his effort and resources, but he would still receive some return. Cooke Taylor, however, considers efforts to elevate the taste of the lowest social orders by furnishing them with the rudiments of a literary and aesthetic education not simply wasteful but positively harmful to society as a whole: "Nothing could be more dangerous to society than for the middle classes to find their position perilled and their social relations dislocated by the upheaving of an educated pauperism from beneath." A more prudent course, he maintains, would be to focus on "elevating the taste of the artisan" only, an endeavor he promises will bring a number of concrete moral, social, and commercial benefits. Cooke Taylor's entire argument depends upon an ideological presumption—that social stability requires the maintenance of a strict hierarchy among the classes—at odds with his initial representation of social classes as patches in a field. Whether or not he is conscious of this inconsistency is beside the point. His agricultural metaphor, like Kay-Shuttleworth's contention that the "first fruits of civilisation are the results of culture," or Ure's call for the "rich fields of industry to be cultivated to the utmost," participates in a new proindustrial rhetoric dedicated to affiliating industry with the idea of culture. The rhetorical task confronting liberal proponents of industry was to make this association seem self-evident, since then the idea of culture as a "rallying alternative" to industry would itself become logically suspect.

OVER THE past several decades, social historians have given increasingly greater attention to the specifically rhetorical dimensions of the "factory question," shifting their focus from such subjects as the history of legislation to the discourses that provoked and structured what Robert Gray calls the "cultural transformation" surrounding industrialization.[4] In keeping with this development, this book traces the emergence of a new proindustrial rhetoric that crystallized in the second quarter of the nineteenth century around the specific and defining goals of aestheticizing automatic manufacture, on the one hand, and reconciling its processes with the productive and receptive capacities of the body, on the other. To these ends, defenders of the factory system and advocates of the new discipline of design interpreted the actual agents and products of industrial manufacture—whether factory operatives, the "manufacturing population," mechanically replicated "copies," or elaborately crafted "art manufactures"—as concrete emblems of a prior conceptual unity or beauty. So, for example, purportedly healthy operatives were regarded as signs of the greater harmony of the factory, machines and manufactures as manifestations of abstract productive systems, well-wrought designs as representations of an ideal industrial social order.

The first four chapters of this study document a series of attempts to implement this general strategy at different levels of abstraction. Chapter 1, which focuses on efforts to aestheticize the factory system, argues that the debates over the factory system during the 1830s and 1840s took shape as a struggle over the kinds of images and metaphors through which industry and industrial labor could be legitimately represented. Opponents of the factory system sought to stigmatize mechanized industry as an alien and destructive presence within British society through repeated accounts of the bodily injuries caused by industrial labor. In response, prominent defenders of the factory system such as Edward Baines, Andrew Ure, and William Cooke Taylor represented the factory itself as a great "co-operative body" and romanticized its origins by portraying it as the outgrowth of a native English "genius." Chapter 2 contends that Charles Babbage, perhaps the nineteenth century's most sophisticated student of machinery, understood concrete manufactures and manufacturing systems as material signs of an abstract intellectual beauty. While Baines, Ure, and Cooke Taylor drew upon Romantic aesthetic conventions in their representations of the factory system, Babbage reinscribed those conventions within a utilitarian positivism that anticipated the modernist elevation of pure efficiency into an aesthetic ideal. Chapter 3, which concerns representations of the "manufacturing population," identifies the figure of "the savage" as a specific rhetorical link between the discourse on the factory system and the discourse on design. In both cases, this image localizes abiding anxieties within proindustrial discourse over the tension between aesthetic and technical "progress" intrinsic to the idea of an industrial culture. Chapter 4, which addresses the aesthetic response to actual manufactures, interprets the attempts of two early Victorian periodicals, the *Art-Journal* and Henry Cole's *Journal of Design and Manufactures*, to delineate comprehensive theories of design as incipient efforts to frame industry and commerce themselves as agents of aesthetic culture.

Chapter 5 reads what might be called the official or sanctioned commentary on the Great Exhibition of 1851 as a confluence of the various strains of proindustrial rhetoric analyzed in the earlier chapters. Departing from now dominant interpretations of the exhibition as an expression of English nationalism or as an important moment in the genealogy of modern commodity culture, it focuses instead on efforts to fix the event's meaning as a triumphant celebration of what one lecturer, speaking under the auspices of the Society of Arts, calls the "great bond of unity" joining all classes and industries into one harmonious whole (*Lectures* 2:147*). This overt optimism, however, is haunted by an undertone of failure and regret that exposes abiding fissures within the idea of industrial culture at the moment of its material realization. From this perspective, the exhibition seems less a "great and grand Drama," as William Whewell characterizes it (*Lectures* 1:4), than a tragic reenactment of the very conflict between art and industry that early Victorian proindustrial rhetoric is at pains to deny.

At this juncture, a word is in order regarding the parameters of this study. Because my main concern lies with proindustrial appropriations of the language of aesthetic culture, I do not give direct attention to such matters as the rise of particular industries, the institutionalization of art education, or even the actual social conditions that accompanied Britain's industrialization. I do, however, take up these subjects as they inform my analysis of Victorian proindustrial rhetoric. For example, although class is not a primary focus of my study, I touch repeatedly on the issue: in my discussions of Ure's, Baines's, and Cooke Taylor's handling of trade unionism, in my account of Babbage's relations with his engineer Joseph Clement, in my treatment of Redgrave's discussion of ornament in the "Supplementary Report," in my characterization of the Great Exhibition as an effort to provide an imaginary resolution to class tensions, and, most obviously, throughout the whole of chapter 3. Even here, though, my primary aim is not to discern the "true" state of the manufacturing population in the 1830s and 1840s but to show how various representations of that population contribute to different rhetorical agendas.

Moreover, although I have positioned this study as a contribution to the genealogy of the critical tradition Williams traces in *Culture and Society*, I have not attempted to provide a comprehensive account of that tradition's engagement with the strains of proindustrial rhetoric I examine. The reason is not merely that this tradition reaches its maturity decades after the period with which I am primarily concerned (Carlyle's *Past and Present* appeared in 1843, Ruskin's *Unto This Last* in 1862, Arnold's *Culture and Anarchy* in 1869, Morris's *News From Nowhere* in 1890, and Wilde's "The Soul of Man Under Socialism" in 1891). It is also that I believe the best way to elucidate the perhaps surprising sophistication of early Victorian proindustrial arguments—and thus their role in shaping the "culture and society" tradition—is to treat them as worthy of serious study in their own right. If I am correct in noticing a crucial shift in tone between Southey's and Arnold's responses to Britain's industrialization, then the elaborate and diverse vindications of industry that separate these figures warrant direct and sustained critical attention.

Nevertheless, I recognize that for many readers of the Victorian Literature and Culture series, the interest of my work will depend on its immediate relevance to the now canonical line of Victorian prose that runs from Carlyle through Morris. Therefore, in addition to noticing specific conjunctions with this line of work throughout the study, I also use Ruskin, and especially his chapter "The Nature of Gothic," as a coordinating point of reference. Gallagher closes *The Industrial Reformation of English Fiction* by contending that the "politics of culture" of the 1860s supplanted the modes of representation developed in the context of the "Condition of England" debates of the 1830s and 1840s (chap. 9), but Ruskin's explicit recapitulation of and engagement with the primary arguments of earlier proindustrial discourses indicate that this transition was less a process of supersession than a process of generalization, through which the older anti-industrial rhetorics took a more broadly resonant form. Morris, in his 1892 preface to the Kelmscott Press edition of "The Nature of Gothic," identifies the chapter as "one of the very few necessary and inevitable utterances of the century" because of its profound expression of the inextricable connection between art and work (M. Morris 1:292). I likewise see Ruskin's chapter as "necessary" and "inevitable," albeit not entirely in Morris's sense. Ruskin's statement against the "great evil" of industry—or at least a statement like it—was in fact prepared for and demanded by a quarter-century-long effort to yoke the concept of culture to the cause of industry. Conceived and written within a year of the closing of the Great Exhibition, it both recapitulates the issue-specific debates over industrialism that occupied the 1830s and 1840s and anticipates the expansion of these debates into the general reflection on culture Arnold exemplifies. By orienting the arguments of individual chapters with respect to the different elements of Ruskin's pivotal and exemplary condemnation of industry, I hope to suggest the bearing of early Victorian proindustrial rhetoric on the dominant nineteenth-century critical tradition as a whole.

In my final chapter, I flesh out these suggestions by examining in detail Ruskin's and Morris's criticisms of industrial capitalism. Unlike Arnold, Ruskin does not ponder the opposition between culture and industry in the abstract. Instead, he follows Carlyle in particularizing it as a struggle to recover the creative autonomy of "men," who he argues should be neither "morbid thinkers" nor "miserable workers" but "gentlemen, in the best sense" (10:201). Purging Ruskin's ideal of its class affiliation, Morris likewise endeavors to imagine an alternative to commercial society, sustained not by the desire to acquire and consume but by a pervasive, vitalistic "manliness." Neither of these attempts is wholly successful, but their shortcomings should not be attributed solely to personal failures of imagination. They indicate, rather, the broader inability of the critical tradition that includes Ruskin and Morris to claim industry for culture, just as such figures as Ure, Babbage, and Cole claimed culture for industry.

CHAPTER ONE

"One Co-operative Body"

THE RHETORIC OF THE FACTORY SYSTEM

THE DEBATE over the "factory question" in the second quarter of the nineteenth century was as much a contest for rhetorical hegemony as it was a battle over specific material issues. While this debate certainly concerned such matters as factory conditions, hours of labor, and legal reforms, it took shape discursively as a struggle between two competing figures or emblems, which, following Elaine Scarry and Anson Rabinbach respectively, may be called the "body in pain" and the "body without fatigue."

In *The Body in Pain,* Elaine Scarry observes that "the nineteenth-century British factory world is one in which work is described as approaching the condition of pain." In both Marx and his British sources, she notes, industrial labor is associated not simply with the poverty, disease, and exhaustion of the industrial working classes but also with the "more fundamental shattering of the essential integrity of act-and-object in the human psyche," as working bodies are systematically dissociated from the things they create (Scarry 170).

As Scarry's analysis suggests, the figure of the "body in pain" worked to link the concrete physical sufferings allegedly caused by factory labor to more general strains of moral and social critique. Opponents of the factory system vociferously insisted on the deleterious effects of factory labor on operatives' bodies, routinely emphasizing their mutilation and deformation, as well as their figurative enslavement to machinery and uncanny transformation into machines themselves. Richard Oastler, whose landmark letter "Yorkshire Slavery" made him the moral leader of the Factory Movement, uses heightened images of physical distress to portray child labor as worse than black slavery: "Poor infants! ye are indeed sacrificed at the shrine of avarice, *without even the solace of the negro slave;* . . . No, no! your soft and delicate limbs are tired and fagged, and jaded, at only *so much per week,* and when your joints can act no longer, your emaciated frames are cast aside" (Alfred 1:100). The physician Charles Wing cites Dr. James Phillips Kay's comment that the "persevering labour of the operative must rival the mathematical precision, the incessant motion, and the exhaustless power, of the machine" as independent verification of what he terms in his title phrase the "evils of the factory system" (Wing lxxii). Michael Sadler, in his speech of March 16, 1832, moving the second reading of his Ten Hours Bill, catalogues the damaging effects of factory work on the legs, spine, ligaments, knees, and ankles, and then describes the kinds of accidents that frequently befell children in the mills: "drowsy and exhausted, the poor creatures fall too often among the machinery, which is not in many instances sufficiently sheathed, when their muscles are lacerated, their bones broken, or their limbs torn off, . . . or they are sometimes killed upon the spot" (Alfred 1:179). Such rhetoric, by fostering an immediate sense of the factory system's basic evil—whatever political economy might say, it is obviously immoral to work children to the point of permanent physical harm—aimed to provoke in its audience the kind of dramatic conversion experience exemplified by Oastler's own legendary "awakening" to the need for reform.[1]

Yet this rhetoric also furnished a set of images and metaphors that would be taken up within the broader Victorian effort to oppose "culture" to industrial "civilization." In his Colloquies, Southey anticipates this process of generalization by establishing an analogy between the effects of factory labor on individual workers and the effects of the factory system on the nation as a whole. After carefully invoking early nineteenth-century anti-industrial rhetoric's three characteristic tropes—he suggests that the factory's "moral atmosphere" is as "noxious to the soul" as its "foul and tainted air" is to the body, likens the "degradation" of factory operatives to that of "black or brown slaves, working under the whip," and notes that those who use others as "bodily machines for producing wealth" often become mechanical in head and heart themselves—he expands his critique to frame the "manufacturing system" itself as a threat to the "body politic" (1:166, 169–71). In "The Nature of Gothic," Ruskin pursues a similar strategy. His stylized representation of industrial labor, with its tripartite emphasis on the fragmentation, mechanization, and enslavement of the modern worker, both echoes the specific claims and tropes of early anti-industrial rhetoric and elevates the "wasted" and "racked" body of the factory worker into a general and resonant emblem of the moral and aesthetic bankruptcy of industrial society (10:193).

The factory system's defenders inevitably denied that children were being injured in the mills, at least to the extent alleged, and insisted that it was in mill owners' interests to prevent accidents from occurring. Likewise, they dismissed cries of "factory slavery" as politically motivated exaggerations, and they disputed the notion that factory work in any way transforms operatives into machines, arguing to the contrary that automation liberates workers from the tedium of handicraft occupations. The more sophisticated advocates of automatic industry also recognized, however, that such equivocations and rationalizations were not sufficient to counter the general critical potential latent within the Factory Movement's arguments. Therefore, in addition to challenging its substantive charges, they sought to subvert its characteristic rhetorical strategies by evacuating the figure of the debilitated laboring body of its symbolic power. As Anson Rabinbach has argued, industrialization provoked a novel anxiety over bodily fatigue, which was seen as defining both "the limits of the working body" and the threshold "beyond which society could not transgress without jeopardizing its own future capacity for labor." Against this background, the "body without fatigue" came to constitute a peculiarly nineteenth-century utopian ideal in which "maximum productive output" was reconciled with "minimum exhaustion" (Rabinbach 23). Although Rabinbach bases his analysis primarily on sources from the later nineteenth century, the patterns he recognizes are evident earlier in the century as well. Embracing this ideal of the "body without fatigue," certain proindustrial writers not only argued that factory labor fostered bodily health but also self-consciously interpreted healthy operatives as emblems of the factory's greater organic unity.

In such texts as Edward Baines's *History of the Cotton Manufacture in Great Britain* (1835), Andrew Ure's *Philosophy of Manufactures* (1835), and William Cooke Taylor's *Notes of a Tour in the Manufacturing Districts of Lancashire* (1841), this effort to counter the conventions of contemporary anti-industrial rhetoric is at least as great a concern as the effort to refute the Factory Movement's substantive charges regarding the effects of industrial labor.[2] These three texts display a wide diversity: Baines writes a Whiggish history of the cotton industry, Ure a technical treatise, and Cooke Taylor a piece of free-trade propaganda in the guise of a travel narrative. Nevertheless, they each work to counter the Factory Movement's rhetoric by representing the factory as an organic body and the factory system as an expression of English "genius." By thus emphasizing the factory's formal coherence and indigenous origin, Baines, Ure, and Cooke Taylor develop an alternative vision of the factory system amenable to their proindustrial and free-trade agenda. In their view, the factory system was not, as Southey would have it, a dangerous "excrescence" but an integral part of the national social body.

AS EDITOR of the *Leeds Mercury*, the liberal paper that reluctantly published Oastler's letters condemning "Yorkshire slavery," Baines would have been well aware of anti-industrial efforts to portray the factory system as an alien presence in British society. He responds by producing a natural history of cotton manufacture that positions the nineteenth-century factory system as both the inevitable culmination of world historical developments and, more specifically, the outgrowth of a native intelligence and ingenuity. While this strategy manifests itself in a number of ways, it is perhaps most immediately apparent in the many plates and woodcuts that accompany his text. Baines includes a number of schematic drawings of machines, portraits of historically significant industrialists such as Richard Arkwright, Robert Peel, and Samuel Crompton, images of factories set in gentle pastoral landscapes, views of manufacturing processes, and illustrations of different varieties of cotton. In addition, he offers depictions of various Indian handicraft implements and images of ancient women spinning and weaving in the traditional manner. As Robert Gray astutely notes, the effect of this eclectic collection is "to associate an aestheticised nature with the archaeological past and the colonial present, open to appropriation by a progressive modern industrial Britain" (134).[3]

Ure, a practicing industrial consultant and a former professor of chemistry and natural philosophy at the Andersonian University in Glasgow, was inspired to write his treatise in part to correct what he viewed as Baines's unrealistic representations of the factory system. Ure presents his work as a much needed analysis and codification of the principles of industrial production, describing it in his preface as an attempt to "diffuse a steady light to conduct the masters, managers, and operatives, in the straight paths of improvement" and "a specimen of the manner in which the author conceives technological subjects should be discussed" (v–vi). Among nineteenth-century critics of the factory system, however, Ure was regarded not as a reliable authority but as a flagrantly proindustrial propagandist who demanded vigorous refutation. His notoriety derived not merely from his advocacy of the systematic substitution of self-acting machinery for human "hands" but also from the elevated language in which he expresses his utopian vision of total automation. This ideal, Ure suggests, is implicit in the meaning of the word *manufacture* itself, which once connoted hand labor but, by the early decades of the nineteenth century, had come to refer instead to mechanical production. As Ure explains, "Manufacture is a word, which, in the vicissitude of language, has come to signify the reverse of its intrinsic meaning, for it now denotes every extensive product of art, which is made by machinery, with little or no aid of the human hand; so that the most perfect manufacture is that which dispenses entirely with manual labour" (1). Ure reasons from this definition that a "philosophy of manufactures is therefore an exposition of the general principles on which productive industry should be conducted by self-acting machines." He then asserts that the "end" of manufacture is "to modify the texture, form, or composition of natural objects by mechanical or chemical forces, acting either separately, combined, or in succession" (1). In these statements, Ure studiously avoids any reference to human labor, thus replicating in the premises of his philosophy his conception of the "perfect manufacture."

Nevertheless, even as Ure works to eliminate all references to the laboring body from his philosophy, the body returns in the vitalistic metaphors that inform such phrases as "productive" industry and "self-acting" machinery. Ure in fact positions such machinery within a lineage of mechanical contrivances designed to mimic corporeal life: the pigeon of Archytas, the "Android" of Albert the Great, Abbé Mical's singing brass heads, Vaucanson's mechanical flute player, drummer, and duck, and finally Maelzel's chess player (9–10). As this genealogy suggests, Ure's fascination with automated machinery arises as much from its uncanny appropriation of the qualities of organic life as from its technical efficiency.

Only a paragraph later, this tension erupts in dramatic fashion, as Ure praises the cotton mill in rapturously vitalistic terms:

> It is in a cotton mill, however, that the perfection of automatic industry is to be seen; it is there that the elemental powers have been made to animate millions of complex organs, infusing into forms of wood, iron, and brass an intelligent agency. And as the philosophy of the fine arts, poetry, painting, and music may be best studied in their individual master-pieces, so may the philosophy of manufactures in this its noblest creation. (2)

Like an aesthetic artifact, the textile mill integrates a multitude of elements into a coherent, unified whole. The benevolent order of the factory, as Ure envisions it, renders irksome toil a logical impossibility, and in his eyes, all work takes on the appearance of leisure or recreation. He describes factory children as "lively elves" whose labors "seemed to resemble a sport" (301), and he observes that the women who tend the looms of one establishment have acquired the habit "of exercising their arms and shoulders, as if with dumb-bells, by resting their hands on the lay or shuttle-bearer, as it oscillates alternately backwards and forwards with the machinery" (350). The bodies of Ure's factory operatives are not merely "without fatigue": in their healthful vigor, they mirror the harmonious arrangement of the factory itself.

Such fantastic representations have consistently drawn the attention of Ure's commentators, and modern scholars have applied a range of disparaging epithets to his work. Driver describes *The Philosophy of Manufactures* as the most "brassy" early nineteenth-century exposition of the thesis that economic expansion will naturally solve the social problems that accompanied industrialization (430). E. P. Thompson objects to Ure's "Satanic advocacy" of the factory system (*Making* 359). Maxine Berg, commenting on both the style and the content of Ure's argument, characterizes his treatise as an "extraordinary and blatant panegyric in apology for the factory system" (181). These impressions are consistent with those of Ure's contemporaries. Marx calls Ure "the Pindar of the automatic factory" (*Capital* 544). Engels, somewhat less archly, derides him as the "mouthpiece" and "chosen lackey of the bourgeoisie" and decries his "song of praise" over the "slavery of operatives" (189, 211). The physician Charles Wing likens Ure to a one-sided Dante of industry—"Skipping the Inferno, and the Purgatorio, he calls the attention of his readers to the Paradiso of the [factory] system" (li)—while Peter Gaskell notes his propensity to exhibit "that mingling of truth, exaggeration, and poetical description, usually forming a romance" (*Artisans* 319). As this concurrence of opinion suggests, Ure's disconcertingly poetic celebration of the factory system cannot be dismissed as a mere aberration. It is, rather, a particularly vivid instance of a more widespread effort to undermine the rhetoric of the Factory Movement by representing the factory itself as a vast organic body.

Cooke Taylor purports to offer a disinterested account of one man of letters's travels through the industrial north, but in fact his book is a covert piece of Anti-Corn Law League propaganda, which forcefully articulates its free-trade agenda. Writing in the early 1840s, Cooke Taylor holds that factories are *"un fait accompli"* (5), a presumption that both distinguishes his work from many earlier discussions of the factory system and shapes his specific prescriptions for reform.[4] Although he acknowledges the possibility that some "authoritative interference between the employer and the employed" may be necessary in the short term (vii), he consistently maintains that, when properly conducted, factories promote economic prosperity, moral order, and social harmony. Like Baines and Ure, Cooke Taylor is a staunch advocate of free trade. The greatest cause of distress in the manufacturing districts, he argues, is neither the conditions of factory labor nor the speculative overproduction the factory system allegedly encourages but protectionist trade policies that impede the "absorption" of English manufactures by foreign markets. In opposition to those who see the factory system as a source of social "evils," Cooke Taylor argues for its "moral worth and social importance" and contends that the visible capital invested in large, modern mills inevitably leads employers and workers to recognize their common interests (v, 120). The solution to current problems, he concludes, lies not in legislative interference but in the cultivation of a mutual sympathy and an "open" understanding between masters and men (82).

The significance of Cooke Taylor's *Notes* for my purposes lies less in his free-trade thesis than in the way he manipulates the genre of the travel narrative to rhetorical effect. Participating in the 1840s vogue for industrial tourism (evident in various journalistic treatments of the manufacturing districts as well as in the odd practice of keeping visitors' books at mills), Cooke Taylor produces what amounts to a proindustrial conversion narrative, meant to counter the kinds of anti-industrial epiphanies exemplified by Oastler's dramatic conversion to the cause of the "factory children."[5] His epistolary form enables him to project a persona of earnest disinterest and identifies him with his implied audience of humanistically educated readers unfamiliar with the industrial north yet biased against the factory system. By compiling the *Notes* from a series of letters addressed to Dr. Richard Whately, archbishop of Dublin, Cooke Taylor suggests that his text is simply a record of his investigations, uninflected by political considerations. In contrast to Baines and Ure, whose rhetorical authority derives from their claims of scholarly or technical expertise, Cooke Taylor assumes the pose of an impartial observer: "A life spent in retirement, and devoted to literature" (v), he contends, has left him free of partisan prejudices and has thus qualified him to report objectively on the manufacturing districts: "In print as in private," he tells Whately, "I shall state my observations and reflections with perfect freedom and candour, writing as if these letters were designed only for your eye, and as if the public had only got at their contents by peeping over my shoulder" (1).

What follows this assertion, however, is a derivative recollection of his first visit to Manchester, written in the familiar mode of the technological sublime:

> I well remember the effect produced on me by my earliest view of Manchester, when I looked upon the town for the first time from the eminence at the terminus of the Liverpool railways, and saw the forest of chimneys pouring forth volumes of steam and smoke, forming an inky canopy which seemed to embrace and involve the entire place. I felt that I was in the presence of those two mighty and mysterious agencies, fire and water, proverbially the best of servants and the worst of masters; . . . and I resolved to study their effects in order to discover whether they were productive of good or evil, believing them equally potent for either. (1–2)

If Cooke Taylor's account of the beginnings of his interest in industrial Lancashire is more than a little conventional, it nevertheless succeeds in establishing a sense of solidarity with his intended readership. He admits that, like "most strangers" to the region, he "formed at the first an unfavourable opinion of Manchester and the Factory system" (3). Only when he gave up viewing factories "as modes of social existence placed upon their trial" and accepted the factory system as an "established innovation" was he able to begin correcting the "many hasty errors and mistakes" that had colored his early views (2–3). Cooke Taylor's "notes" do not simply record his impressions of the manufacturing districts and their population; they also narrate the shift in perspective he hopes to effect in his readers. "I think it right to point out some of these corrections," he writes, "not because I feel any particular pleasure in the exposure of my own blunders, but because my example may serve to prevent others from falling into similar errors" (2). By downplaying the uniqueness of his experience, Cooke Taylor normalizes his movement from an ignorant bias against the factory system to an enlightened appreciation of its many benefits and thus offers his "conversion" as a model for others.

From this footing, Cooke Taylor proceeds to assail, in a deceptively leisurely manner appropriate to his chosen genre, the rhetorical foundations of British anti-industrial critique. Throughout his letters, Cooke Taylor addresses directly a number of the conventional charges against the factory system: that it leads to injuries and deformities, particularly among child laborers; that it damages workers' general health; that it forces workers to adjust to the enervating and unnatural routines of mechanized labor; that it fosters moral licentiousness; that it destroys domestic relations; that it encourages violence and dangerous forms of political activism such as trade unionism and Chartism. Yet he also engages these claims rhetorically, cannily sidestepping lines of argument damaging to his position and, like Baines and Ure, turning conventionally anti-industrial images and tropes to his own ends.

BAINES, URE, and Cooke Taylor all take pains to refute representations of the factory system as immoral, unnatural, or perverse. Indeed, each of them draws on images of organic development to portray the factory system not only as a natural consequence of social progress but also as a stimulus to national culture. As I noted in my introduction, Ure uses metaphors of cultivation to yoke the idea of culture to the cause of industry. Baines and Cooke Taylor exploit this strategy as well, by treating the factory system itself as a kind of vegetable growth, well suited to British soil.

Cotton manufacture, Baines claims, first developed in India, where it reached a high state of excellence by the fifth century BCE. It then spread throughout Asia, Africa, and America before finally entering Europe in the thirteenth century. Throughout this long period, it remained essentially a handicraft industry, seeing virtually no technological improvements in either spinning or weaving (48–51). Baines accounts for the early rise and subsequent flourishing of cotton manufacture in India in terms of the inherent character and "physical organization" of that country's people. Quoting from James Mill's *History of British India,* he observes that the sedentary occupations of spinning and weaving are well attuned to the typical Indian's "predominant inclination" toward indolence. On this basis, he then ascribes the fine quality of Indian cottons to the "remarkably fine sense of touch possessed by that effeminate people" (74–75). Conversely, Baines attributes the late success of cotton manufacture in England to the unique quality of the English mind. England, he notes, was the last country in Europe (just as Europe was the last of the world's continents) to develop a significant cotton industry, but it soon achieved global preeminence (84). While various factors contributed to this ascent—including geography and natural resources, prevailing domestic social and political conditions, and the advantages accruing to England from other nations' commercial difficulties (85–89)—the chief agent was native English "genius," which in the eighteenth century fostered a "brilliant series of mechanical inventions" that gave a "decisive check" to Indian competition in the industry (53, 55).

Baines naturalizes this commercial rivalry by representing it through a series of agricultural and horticultural metaphors. After its late introduction to Europe, he writes, the manufacture of cotton "existed there like a tropical plant in northern latitudes, degenerate and sickly, till, by the appliances of modern science and art, it suddenly shot forth in more than its native luxuriance, and is now rapidly overspreading the earth with its branches" (10). Just as the attentions of the gardener can encourage the hothouse flower to develop beyond its ordinary limits, so has the stimulus of Anglo-Saxon ingenuity caused cotton manufacture to surpass its former bounds. In addition to justifying English commercial dominance as the natural result of a judicious technological husbandry, such metaphors also rationalize the reciprocal decline of the Indian cotton industry as an inevitable "withering" (54), perhaps hastened by English competition but due fundamentally to the exhaustion of Asian inventiveness: "In Asia, the spirit of invention, so early developed, has lain nearly dormant for thousands of years; the rich soil has degenerated into poverty, from the perpetual sameness of the crops raised upon it; whilst the intellect of Europe, as though invigorated by the fallow of centuries, has received the seeds of Oriental arts and sciences, and brought them to far higher perfection than their native earth" (36). This view, which is in keeping with the prevailing belief that India had once achieved a high level of civilization but subsequently regressed, has a more immediate resonance as well.[6] In the context of debates over the factory question, Baines's contrast serves as an object lesson through which he can justify the supersession of handicraft labor by machinery as a natural consequence of the flowering of English intellect. Unlike the early flourishing of the Indian cotton industry, which Baines attributes to "Oriental" dexterity (9), the new ascendancy of automatic industry is due to the subordination of "hands" to "heads," of manual skill to the masculine "inventive genius of Englishmen" (36). Such associations work not only to stigmatize the Tory-Radical nostalgia for a lost "golden age" of handicraft manufacture as un-English and unmanly but also to reinforce the teleology of Baines's industrial history, in which the systematic elimination of skilled manual labor becomes the irrefutable index of "progress."

Like Baines, Cooke Taylor portrays the factory system as a natural product of English ingenuity, but rather than justifying the factory system in world historical terms, he endeavors to mitigate its threatening strangeness by tracing its roots to England's Saxon past. Much of the tumult over the factory question, he suggests, may be attributed to the factory's seeming novelty, as well as to its status as a dominant symbol of industrial modernity. "The Factory system is a modern creation," he writes in his first letter; "history throws no light on its nature, for it has scarcely begun to recognise its existence; the philosophy of the schools supplies very imperfect help for estimating its results, because an innovating power of such immense force could never have been anticipated" (4). The anxiety Cooke Taylor describes is the cognitive counterpart to the sublimity of the industrial city. Like the "inky canopy" of steam and smoke which seemed "to embrace and involve" the entire city of Manchester (2), the mysterious origin of industrial technologies cloaks them in an uncanny inscrutability: "The steam-engine had no precedent, the spinning-jenny is without ancestry, the mule and the power-loom entered on no prepared heritage: they sprang into sudden existence like Minerva from the brain of Jupiter, passing so rapidly through their stage of infancy that they had taken their position in the world and firmly established themselves before there was time to prepare a place for their reception" (4). Yet this lack of genealogy is only apparent, for if steam engines, spinning jennies, power looms, and the like were certainly "potent novelties"

(4), they were not spontaneous creations but manifestations of powers inherent in the English mind and character. From this perspective, the history
of English industry is coextensive with the history of the English people.

This essential fact, Cooke Taylor holds, has been obscured by historical
circumstance. Because the factory system "took its sudden start at the moment when the entire energies of the British legislature were preoccupied
with the emergencies of the French Revolution," its foundations were "laid
in obscurity" and a teeming industrial population "crept into unnoticed existence" (3 n). In this analysis, mechanized industry's threatening aspect is
very substantially the anxious creation of an established political and cultural elite whose interests lie in the maintenance of existing structures of
power. In Cooke Taylor's words, the "imputed evils" of the factory system
are "much more its misfortune than its fault" (4 n). Specifically, these evils
are the unfortunate by-products of the necessary struggle through which
factories assumed their place "in a land already crowded with institutions:
the force and rapidity with which they developed themselves dislocated
all the existing machinery of society, disturbed its very framework, and
must necessarily produce, as they have produced, a considerable amount of
confusion and suffering until the difficult task of re-adjustment is completed" (4–5). Anticipating Spencer's idea of the "social organism" perpetually
adjusting to changing external pressures, Cooke Taylor figures the turmoil
accompanying the advent of mechanized industry as an ordinary—albeit
"difficult"—process of social assimilation and adaptation. His careful attri-
bution of vital energy to industrial technologies—"they developed themselves"—as well as his implication that these new mechanisms do not differ
in kind from the "existing machinery of society" reinforce his position that
the factory system is not an alien threat to, but an intrinsic part of, English
civilization.

Unlike Ure and Baines, who eagerly anticipate the total automation of
manufacture, Cooke Taylor insists that factories should not be regarded "as
mere abstractions" or considered "apart from the manufacturing population" (6). Although he initially voices conventional fears of the new "masses
of human beings" populating the industrial cities (6), the dominant emphasis throughout the letters is on the manufacturing population's intelligence,
resolve, and moral virtue, qualities they continue to display even in the face
of the most extreme deprivation. Because Cooke Taylor views these positive
traits as aspects of a native character, he denigrates the "men of Manchester"
as being of "mixed race" and specifically limits his praise to the "genuine
Lancastrians" concentrated in outlying towns and rural mills (45).

This unusual affirmation of the Lancastrian character serves Cooke Taylor's agenda in at least three ways. First, by humanizing the manufacturing population, it bolsters his claim that a lasting improvement in social conditions requires increased acquaintance and sympathy among the classes. Second, it enables him to assuage fears of political unrest by maintaining that the vast majority of operatives possess a respect for property and an aversion to violence equal to that of the middle classes.[7] Third and most important, it facilitates his efforts to construct a native genealogy for the factory system by demonstrating its affiliations with Lancashire's geography and cultural history.

In the first of his letters from the Rosendale Forest, Cooke Taylor establishes an affinity between the region's rugged landscape and its hardy population. As he makes his way though that "undulating country" of steep hills and sudden valleys, he looks back on the Norman Conquest and reflects on the resistance given William by landscape and people alike: "Doubtless it was through this part of Lancashire that the Norman William found such difficulty in leading his army from the hills of Yorkshire to his fortress of Chester, when he had destroyed the last relic of Saxon independence, and punished the love of freedom and independence inherent in the Saxon race by devastating with fire and sword the whole tract of country between York and Durham" (52–53). From the vantage point of the present, however, Cooke Taylor can recognize that the conquest devastated neither the landscape nor the character of the "Saxon race." On the contrary, it set in motion a long historical process by which both were transformed from negative agents of resistance into positive agents of production. Quoting the manufacturer Henry Ashworth's observation that in Saxon hands "the sciences of mechanics and chemistry have been applied to manufacturing industry with a practical intelligence previously unknown" (53), he argues that "Saxon independence" had not been destroyed but rather shifted from the political to the economic register. He thus neutralizes the charge that the factory system amounts to a new "Norman Yoke" by emphasizing the ultimately beneficent effects of both the monarchial conquest of the eleventh century and the economic and technological conquests of the nineteenth.

Similarly, Cooke Taylor observes that geographical features that once served only as impediments to invasion have since become sources of productive power. Again he quotes Ashworth, who notes that the very rivers "remembered for the obstructions they *once* presented to monarchial and military aggression, are *now* directed to the propelling of machinery" (54). Ancillary benefits accrue to agriculture as well. Just as Carlyle would later maintain that the West Indies had brought forth nothing but "jungle, savagery, poison-reptiles and swamp malaria" until they were tamed by the "white European" (29:374), so Cooke Taylor contrasts the former "waste" of Yorkshire (in both senses of the word) with its present productive use. From the time of James I, Cooke Taylor notes, land values have risen 41,000 percent, a figure that moves him to echo Milton's "stirring" praise of the English people as "a nation not slow and dull, but of a quick, ingenious, and piercing spirit" (60).

In these ways, Cooke Taylor links the factory system to the cause of progress while simultaneously characterizing opposition to industrialism as retrograde and even savage. Automated textile manufacture, he holds, has civilized England's northern wilds to the benefit, paradoxically, of agricultural interests typically wary of industrialism. Since the populations of industrial towns provide an expanding market for agricultural products, Cooke Taylor can say that "the soil has literally been ploughed by the spindle and sowed by the shuttle and the loom" (54). This image differs from Ure's earlier assertion that steam power allows "rich fields of industry to be cultivated to the utmost" (29) in its denial of its own obvious metaphoricity. Whereas Ure defends automatic industry by likening it to agriculture, Cooke Taylor now asserts agriculture's real dependence on industry.

WHILE THE naturalization of the factory system through metaphors of cultivation and organic growth effectively counters characterizations of automatic industry as somehow unnatural or un-English, it does little to elucidate the specific workings of factories themselves. Therefore, Baines, Ure, and Cooke Taylor supplement this rhetorical strategy by representing the factory as an expansive laboring "body." Baines and Ure in particular make prominent use of this metaphor to portray factories as expansive, integrated systems of production. For Baines, the modern cotton mill is not only a "vast and admirable machine" (147) but also a kind of body in which diverse technological processes coalesce to a single productive end. All its machines "are moving at once," synchronized by their mutual dependence on "the mighty engine" (243), which serves as the heart of the anthropomorphized factory: "[T]he steam-engine stands in the same relation to the spinning machines, as the heart does to the arms, hands, and fingers, in the human frame; the latter perform every task of dexterity and labour, the former supplies them with all their vital energy" (227). Ure similarly imagines a mill's "main-shafting and wheel-geering" as "the grand nerves and arteries which transmit vitality and volition ... to the automatic organs" (32), and he offers a "whole anatomy" of one of the factory architect William Fairbairn's recent constructions, from the "two-fold heart" of its twin steam engines to the "respective positions of the various productive organs in their respective floors" (34). In addition, he likens mechanical malfunctions to injury or disease. When parts are poorly made or improperly aligned, Ure notes, they produce what amounts to chronic disease, so that "nothing can go well, as happens to a man labouring under aneurismal and nervous affections" (32).

Ure surpasses Baines by distilling from the metaphor of the factory body a powerful and intuitive vocabulary for discussing the factory as a complex, integrated system of production. Unlike Baines, who understands the factory only as a "complete series of machinery," Ure articulates a more comprehensive definition that encompasses human operatives as well. "The term *Factory*," he writes, "in technology, designates the combined operation of many orders of work-people, adult and young, in tending with assiduous skill a system of productive machines continuously impelled by a central power" (13). Ure's desire to foreground the factory's status as a total system leads him both to exclude from his definition organizations such as ironworks, dye works, soap works, and brass foundries, "in which the mechanisms do not form a connected series, nor are dependent on one prime mover" (13), and to blur the distinctions between the factory's human and mechanical components. The marked separation between the "many orders of work-people" and the factory's "system of productive machines" erodes when he asserts that a factory "in its strictest sense, involves the idea of a vast automaton, composed of various mechanical and intellectual organs, acting in uninterrupted concert for the production of a common object, all of them being subordinated to a self-regulated moving force" (13–14). As Marx points out in his comments on Ure in *Capital*, these two formulations are hardly identical. In the first case, the focus is the combination of human workers, while in the second, it is the factory automaton itself. Inanimate machines and their living attendants become merely different sorts of "organs" subordinated to the factory's central source of power.[8] From its inception, Ure maintains, the factory system required workers to submerge themselves in the regularity of the machine. Richard Arkwright's "main difficulty" in devising an operable mill lay not in technical areas but "in the distribution of the different members of the apparatus into one co-operative body" (15).

This understanding of the factory as a unified entity composed of various interdependent systems is consistent with the transition from "associationist" to "physiological" conceptions of organisms at the end of the eighteenth and beginning of the nineteenth centuries. Broadly speaking, the predominant explanatory models in scientific and social theory before the end of the eighteenth century were based on mechanistic principles of association. Society was understood simply as an aggregate of individuals, and biological organisms as collections of parts whose movements and configurations could be explained according to the laws of Newtonian mechanics. By the close of the eighteenth century, however, such mechanistic conceptions were giving way to a new recognition—exemplified by Kant's definition of an organism as a whole in which the parts are simultaneously means and ends—of the interdependence of elements within the context of the whole (Shuttleworth 2–3). More narrowly, Ure's views have affinities with contemporary developments in European physiology, which understood the body as an assemblage of discrete functional systems. Although this kind of systematic physiology did not exert a serious influence on English medicine until the middle of the century, it was being taught much earlier at the Edinburgh Medical School, from which Ure received his M.D. in 1801.[9]

However Ure acquired his knowledge of systematic physiology, it clearly structures his understanding of the factory system. Factories, he asserts, "have all three principles of action, or three organic systems; the mechanical, the moral, and the commercial, which may not unaptly be compared to the muscular, the nervous, and the sanguiferous systems of an animal. . . . When the whole are in harmony, they form a body qualified to discharge its manifold functions by an intrinsic self-governing agency, like those of organic life" (55). Ure's ambition is to elaborate a comprehensive conceptual matrix, defining the relationships among the factory's technical, social, and commercial aspects. To that end, he asserts the congruity of four sets of terms: the mechanical, the moral, and the commercial; the muscular, the nervous, and the sanguiferous; the operative, the master, and the state; and labor, science, and capital. In each of these triads, the first two terms pertain specifically to the factory while the third refers to wider political and economic structures.

In general, Ure's correlations hold up well: it is reasonable to describe the mechanical systems of the factory in terms of motive muscular power or to identify the master's managerial authority with the function of the nervous system. The mappings among the sanguiferous system, capital, and the state, however, seem forced, since they violate Ure's governing metaphor of the factory as body. The representation of capital flow as a kind of sustaining sanguiferous circulation makes sense only if this circulation is understood to be occurring within the wider body of society rather than within the immediate body of the factory. Ure's willingness to push his imagery to such a point of incoherence is evidence of the tremendous importance he attributed to linking the figure of the factory body to the established trope of the "body politic" as well as to the alternative image of the "social body" emerging in contemporary treatments of the manufacturing population.[10] These associations are crucial to Ure's wider argument, since they underlie his subsequent representation of factory discipline as a kind of social contract.

As David Lloyd and Paul Thomas demonstrate, nineteenth-century British cultural and pedagogical institutions worked to transform the "individual of civil society" into a "subject of the modern state" by inscribing the production of citizens within a "universal historical narrative of the evolution of humanity from animal or savage to civilized being" (65). Ure attributes precisely this function to the automatic factory, thus identifying it as a cultural agent. Echoing Baines, he draws a correlation between savageness and handicraft labor, identifying the transition from "task-oriented" time to industrial "work-discipline" with the fundamental renunciation of autonomous desire that grounds civilization itself.[11] "When the wandering savage becomes a citizen," Ure notes, "he renounces many of his dangerous pleasures in return for tranquility and protection." In like fashion, "when the handicraftsman exchanges hard work with fluctuating employment and pay, for continuous labour of a lighter kind with steady wages, he must necessarily renounce his old prerogative of stopping when he pleases, because he would thereby throw the whole establishment into disorder" (278–79).

Ure, E. P. Thompson observes, sees the "transforming power" of religious instruction as a chief means of creating docile and disciplined workers (Ure 423–25; Thompson, *Making* 359–62). But he also and more radically invests ordinary rules of factory order with the unassailable authority of religious pronouncements. The conditions of industrial "citizenship" enforce a cognitive hierarchy between the operative, who possesses only a fragmentary knowledge of the factory's operations, and the manufacturer, who is able to observe the workings of the entire system. "Of the amount of the injury resulting from the violation of the rules of automatic labour," Ure writes, the operative "can hardly ever be a proper judge; just as mankind at large can never fully estimate the evils consequent upon an infraction of God's moral law" (279). Flouting the dictates of factory discipline thus becomes elevated into a sort of industrial sin, akin to transgressing divinely ordained commandments.

Within this model of the factory, Ure assigns the disciplinary functions of the state to the steam engine, which he characterizes as both a benevolent despot and "the workman's never-failing friend" (339). He vigorously denies that automation forces workers to match the relentless pace of the machine, insisting that "the way to prevent an employment from being incessant, is to introduce a steam-engine into it" (309). He imagines the factory floor itself as an "airy and salubrious" court in which the "the benignant power of steam summons around him his myriads of willing menials, and assigns to each the regulated task, substituting for painful muscular effort on their part, the energies of his own gigantic arm" (18).[12] Ure finds this ideal most fully realized in large modern mills such as Thomas Robinson's power loom factory in Stockport, the floors of which, as portrayed in an accompanying illustration (see fig. 1), display an almost classical order and spaciousness. The rows of belts connecting the drive shafts that line the ceiling to the looms below resemble a series of fluted columns, while the stack of spindles in the lower left foreground recalls the ruins that, in eighteenth-century art, conventionally symbolize the recovery, revival, or completion of classical civilization. In keeping with this theme, the exchange between the elegantly dressed master and the factory girl seems less managerial than kindly peda-gogical, and the women at the looms seem to possess, as Ure writes, "not a little of the Grecian style of beauty" (350). Such representations both posi-tion the factory as the inheritor of the mantle of culture and allow Ure to appropriate the familiar rhetoric of Tory paternalism, typically employed in opposition to the factory system, to celebrate the factory's utopian social order.

Cooke Taylor duplicates this strategy in his own explication of what he calls "the social economy of a cotton-factory" (109). The use of machinery, he asserts, creates an "equality of conditions" between employer and operative that fosters "equitable relations between them." While the "perishable" nature of labor has traditionally created a "disparity" of power between workers and employers, the large capital investments required for cotton manufacture subject employers to "a portion of the urgency which presses on the operative," since their capital, like the operative's labor, "must be worked or be destroyed" (112). The "social economy" thus created places a premium on such virtues as discipline, attentiveness, and general intelligence. Wages, Cooke Taylor recognizes, constitute only a small—if highly visible—portion of the cost of production. Therefore, he argues, manufacturers stand to make greater gains by improving their machinery and paying a wage commensurate with intelligent and vigilant superintendence. Humanitarian motivations aside, this economic consideration alone should drive manu-facturers to attend to the health and morals of their operatives. "My precise object," Cooke Taylor states, articulating his overarching thesis, "is to show

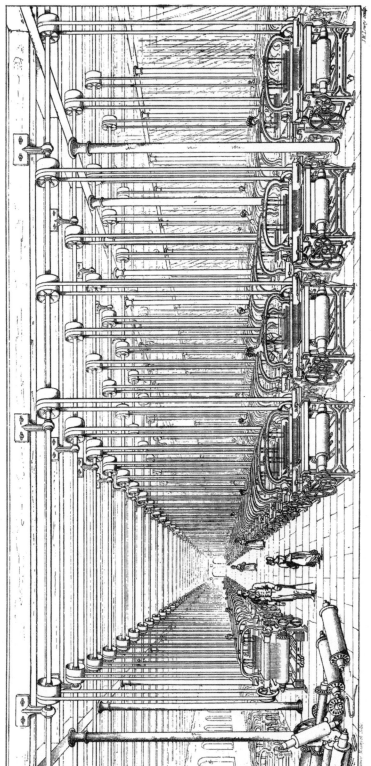

Fig. 1. Power Loom Factory of Thomas Robinson, Esq., Stockport, from Andrew Ure, *The Philosophy of Manufactures.*
(Courtesy of the Yale University Library)

that the factory system directly makes it the interest of the manufacturer that his operatives should not only be good workmen, but good men; and that he is stringently coerced by circumstances to be very attentive to the health, the intelligence, and the morals of the persons he employs" (113). Like Ure, he observes that the "common dependence" of all industrial processes "on one system of machinery" necessarily subjects all persons involved in the mill to a single governing authority: "The steam-engine is the most impartial of arbitrators: it is impassive to bribes, it is insensible of flattery, and it is the common assistant and friend to all" (121).

Cooke Taylor illustrates these claims by appealing to the evidence of the Whitehead mills in the town of Hollymount and Henry Ashworth's mill at Turton. As Gray and others have noted, modern rural mills were frequently put forth as models for emulation. For Cooke Taylor, though, they are also symbols of the factory system's more general contribution to England's domestic culture. A generation ago, he remarks, Hollymount and its environs "were little better than an uncultivated waste," but the town has since been transformed into a virtual "earthly paradise" (66–67, 63). The machinery of the Whitehead mills exhibits the "latest refinements of mechanical ingenuity," but Cooke Taylor gives the bulk of his attention to the "kindness and cordiality" of the proprietors and their devotion to the moral, intellectual, spiritual, and material well-being of their workers. The homes of Hollymount are spacious, clean, and well furnished; most of the men spurn alcohol and have accumulated "considerable sums of money in the savings-bank"; and the factory's children have the benefit of an "elegant and convenient" school, which "could not have cost less than a thousand pounds" (61–63). Cooke Taylor concludes this survey with a lengthy description of Hollymount's Methodist chapel, built by the Whitehead brothers "in the Grecian style," which, like Ure's Grecian beauties, lends the factory system a Hellenic air.

Cooke Taylor praises Henry Ashworth's establishment in similarly laudatory terms, noting for instance that its "dangerous machinery" has been shielded with "great care," so that accidents can result only from "the grossest negligence" or "absolute wilfulness" on the part of the operatives (24–25). Like Ure, he attributes such mishaps to transgressions against the social contract governing the factory's operations, so that even industrial accidents become evidence for the factory system's superior order. What most distinguishes Ashworth's mill, though, is its orchard and garden, which provide Cooke Taylor with compelling emblems for the industrial pastoralism that is his social ideal. "Fruit-trees," he writes, "unprotected by fence, railing, or palisade, are trained against the main wall of the building, and in the season the ripe fruit hangs temptingly within reach of every operative who goes in or out of the mill." Mr. Ashworth's private garden, equally "rich in fruits, flowers, and vegetables," is also "absolutely unprotected," but it too "has never suffered the slightest injury or depredation" (23). Whether the safety of the fruit and produce was due to the operatives' inherent respect for property, as Cooke Taylor contends, or whether it was due to a coercive fear of dismissal, as a reviewer in the *Spectator* surmises, the allegorical associations are unmistakable: Ashworth's mill is a prelapsarian industrial Eden, populated by obedient operatives who have yet to taste the fruit of "insurrection" (329). In its mature state, the factory system fosters a pervasive yet noncoercive social discipline. Operatives are "stringently ruled by their own consent" because they see that "the government they are under works in all its parts for the promotion of their own interests." The true novelty of the factory system lies not in any mechanical innovation but in its refinement of a mode of social organization characterized by this "combination of perfect despotism with perfect freedom" (124).

To THIS point, my analysis has concentrated on the ways in which liberal representations of automatic industry were shaped in response to contemporary critiques of the factory system. By using organic and bodily metaphors to portray the factory system as an inevitable historical development, as a natural fruit of native English intelligence and ingenuity, or as a paradigm of a new social order, Baines, Ure, and Cooke Taylor answer the strong criticisms leveled against mechanized industry by proponents of factory regulation. But what have these liberal apologists to say of the people affected by the factory system, both the operatives living under its disciplinary regime and the handicraft workers displaced by automation? From the early 1830s forward, critics of the factory system contended not only that industrial labor maims and deforms those who perform it but also that it exerts a depressive influence on the general "condition" of the industrial working classes. Liberal advocates of industrialization of course answered these charges directly. They argued that improvements in the design of machinery and factories had greatly reduced the chronic strain on operatives and had all but eliminated accidental injury, and they attempted to show as well that industrial operatives as a group enjoyed a state of health at least as good as that of other segments of the working classes. Such literal responses, however, could do little to soften the emotional impact of the Factory Movement's resonant appeals to images of broken and debilitated laboring bodies. Nevertheless, against the background of what I have called the naturalization of the factory system, and the complementary representation of the factory as a new sort of "co-operative body," liberal proponents of industry such as Baines, Ure, and Cooke Taylor were in fact able to deflect and subvert this evocative strain of anti-industrial rhetoric.

They pursued an array of approaches to this end. Most obviously, they simply contradicted prevailing anti-industrial images of operatives and the working classes. Ure's infamous description of factory children as "lively elves," for instance, is at one level just the negation of Oastler's representation of such children as debilitated, oppressed "slaves." These kinds of representations, it should be noted, are not subject to empirical challenge, because they follow directly from the metaphor of the factory body itself. If the well-run factory has the qualities of a healthy body, its constituent parts or "organs" must participate in that state of health. Reciprocally, healthy operatives function as synecdoches for the greater "health" of the factory as a whole. Within this framework, any injuries that happen to befall individual workers can be dismissed as mere random occurrences that carry no negative implication for the entire system.

More subtly, Baines, Ure, and Cooke Taylor objected on ethical grounds to the purported sensationalizing of the condition of the manufacturing population in anti-industrial polemic. Its exclusive focus on laborers' physical conditions, they argued, discounted these laborers' status as articulate moral agents capable of comprehending and discussing the causes of their conditions. Likewise, they offered alternative explanations for the unemployment of the 1830s and 1840s, arguing that it was not an indication of the so-called evils of the factory system but a negative consequence of restrictions on trade. The crucial point here is not merely that Baines, Ure, and Cooke Taylor sought to counter representations of the working classes that were unfavorable to the factory system, but rather that their broader efforts to define the factory system as an intrinsic part of British culture dictated the particular forms their challenges took.

Ure, who is concerned primarily with the technical details of textile manufacture, represents automatic industry as an unmitigated social boon. He contends that factory workers are generally healthier than their rustic counterparts and that the Malthusian "torpor and brutality" evident in agricultural regions does not exist in industrial areas (384, 354). This disparity, he implies, will only grow as further improvements in machinery continue to increase operatives' wages and capacity for consumption (326). Instead of harming the manufacturing population, Ure concludes, the factory system "is its grand Palladium" (329).

For this reason, he reserves particular spleen for those operatives who participate in trade unions. Within the metaphoric economy of Ure's treatise, trade unions are the negative counterpart to the factory: they are well-ordered social bodies directed toward a destructive rather than productive end. Unions, he writes, "are conspiracies of workmen against the interests of their own order, and never fail to end in the suicide of the body corporate which forms them; an event the more speedy, the more coercive or the better organized the union is" (41). The "machinery of strikes" through which they threaten to "paralyze every mill whose master did not comply with their wishes" (282) is the negation of the productive machinery of the working mill. In contrast to the factory, which recalls the healthy body in its "intrinsic self-governing agency" (55), unions are self-destructive parasites that foster a diseased imbalance in the social body. Strikes, Ure writes, produce an "extraordinary state of things" in which "the inventive head and the sustaining heart of trade" are "held in bondage by the unruly lower members." Moreover, the "destructive spirit" that emerges from this imbalance can manifest itself in acts of violence. During the spinners' "turn outs" in the early 1830s, he continues, "[a]cts of singular atrocity were committed, sometimes with weapons fit only for demons to wield, such as the corrosive oil of vitriol, dashed in the faces of most meritorious individuals, with the effect of disfiguring their persons, and burning their eyes out of the sockets with dreadful agony" (282–83). In relying on images of bodily injury to signify a wider moral culpability, Ure's attack on trade unionism parallels typical denunciations of industrial working conditions. Just as ten-hours advocates emphasized the mutilation and deformation of operatives in the mills, so Ure reads such disfiguring assaults as symbols of trade unions' destructive effects on the greater social body.

Baines, for his part, puts off discussing the "condition of the working classes" until the penultimate chapter of his long *History*. The placement of the chapter is telling, since it suggests that what Engels would later call "the most important social issue in England" (25) is for Baines a final, troublesome matter that must be dealt with before he can launch into his concluding pitch for a free-trade economic policy. Baines's views are what one would expect from a staunch defender of the factory system: that factory labor (long yet light) is no more injurious than most varieties of nonindustrial employment; that real wages are at a historic high and are more than sufficient to support workers and their families; that the social conditions prevailing in the mills do not promote sexual licentiousness; that the provisions of existing and proposed factory legislation are impracticable; that the agitation for a ten-hours bill is a disingenuous effort to secure practical limitations on the hours of adult labor; and finally, that it is nonindustrial workers, exemplified by the handloom weaver, who suffer the severest deprivations.

Baines recognizes that he cannot simply rehearse these conventional claims and hope to be persuasive. Although the whole trajectory of his *History* works to place the large, modern cotton mill at the pinnacle of culture and civilization, he still has to answer the popular belief that industrial operatives suffer debilitating physical harm as a consequence of their labors. One approach Baines takes to this task is to parody the images of exploited and suffering factory children ubiquitous in the Factory Movement's appeals. Quoting favorably James Phillips Kay's opinion that "the present hours of labour do not injure the health of a *population otherwise favourably situated*," Baines objects to the notion that work in the mills "unnaturally taxes flesh and sinews to keep pace with wheels and arms of iron" (450–52, emphasis Kay's).[13] He meets such "hideous caricatures of the effects of factory labour" (453) with a caricature of his own, simultaneously summarizing and mocking conventional condemnations of child labor:

> [I]t is alleged that the children who labour in mills are the victims of frightful oppression and killing toil,—that they are often cruelly beaten by the spinners or overlookers,—that their feeble limbs become distorted by continual standing and stooping, and they grow up cripples, if indeed they are not hurried into premature graves,—that in many mills they are compelled to work thirteen, fourteen, or fifteen hours per day,—that they have no time either for play or for education,—and that avaricious taskmasters, and idle, unnatural parents, feed on the marrow of these poor innocents. (452)

Baines douses such outbursts of indignation with a good dose of cool reason. In answer to those irresponsible orators who, he claims, have relied on "an amplification of detail and a strength of language" to influence those "whose imagination and feelings were much stronger than their judgements," Baines offers his own measured assessment of the condition of factory operatives. He is "far from contending" that factory work is "of the most agreeable and healthful kind," that "there have not been abuses" in the mills, or that legislation is not "justifiable, to protect children of tender years from being overworked" (452, 455–56). Against the background of this elaborate qualification, however, he maintains that although "the hours of labour in cotton mills are long, . . . the labour is light"; that "abuse is the exception, not the rule"; and that Parliament has already "properly interfered to remedy this evil" of "employing children at too early an age, and for too long hours"

(456, 454, 477). In direct contrast to ten-hours advocates, who sought to incite their audiences to moral outrage in rhetoric akin to that of Methodist preaching, Baines's mild tone mirrors the rational order of the factory itself.[14]

A second and more involved approach that Baines uses to great effect is to exploit differential distinctions among the working classes to relativize—and thus temper reactions to—the hard life of the factory operative. Baines opens his chapter with a seemingly conciliatory affirmation of the common humanity of industrial workers. "The workmen who construct or attend upon all these machines," he cautions in almost Dickensian fashion, "are not to be confounded with the machines themselves, or their wear and tear regarded as a mere arithmetical question." On the contrary, they are full members of the social body, "citizens and subjects" who "constitute no mean part of the support and strength of the state" and whose "interests are as valuable in the eyes of the moralist, as those of the classes who occupy higher stations" (434). The purpose of this humanistic gesture, however, is not to foster sympathy for the manufacturing population but to suggest that its condition can be legitimately judged only *in relation* to that of nonindustrial segments of the working class. The appropriate question to ask is "not if the manufacturing population are subject to the ills common to humanity" but "what is the condition of the working classes of the cotton district, *compared with that of the working classes elsewhere?*" (434, emphasis added). As Foucault remarks, the order of the factory is predicated upon the detailed "individuation" and "partitioning" of bodies and machines within a comprehensive rational order (144–45). Baines extrapolates this principle into a rhetorical strategy. By taking the manufacturing population's affinity with all classes as a warrant for making discriminations among the working classes only, Baines dramatically reduces the burden of his argument. To present a favorable view of the factory system he need demonstrate only that the condition of industrial operatives is no worse than that of other sorts of laborers.

This strategy of differentiation directly counters the Factory Movement's reliance on emblematic hyperbole, exemplified by the image of the factory slave. Baines does not attempt to refute this metaphor directly; he simply drowns it in a sea of alternative comparisons: "Colliers, miners, forgemen, cutlers, machine-makers, masons, bakers, corn-millers, painters, plumbers, letter-press printers, potters, and many other classes of artisans and labourers, have employments which in one way or another are more inimical to health and longevity than the labour of cotton mills" (454). The situation of the factory operative, this series implies, is not only not worse than the plight of the most abused class of physical laborer (the plantation slave), it is in fact better than the lot of most sorts of manual workers. It is superior as well, Baines holds, to the conditions of "confinement and exhaustion" that afflict certain classes of "professional men," such as "students, clerks in counting-houses, shopkeepers, milliners, &c." (454). While this further comparison legitimately acknowledges the travails of an emerging white-collar proletariat, it also works in conjunction with Baines's earlier observations to represent factory work as simultaneously the least stressful form of manual labor and the least taxing form of mental labor. Framed in this way, factory work becomes difficult to single out for moral disapprobation.

Yet if such equivocations dull the impact of anti-industrial rhetoric by unduly complicating the field of debate, they do not amount to a positive defense of the factory system, which must ultimately be judged according to its general social and economic benefits. Baines therefore lauds what Kay had called the "enlightened benevolence" of large industrial employers. Contradicting his earlier caution against conflating men and machines, Baines notes with approval that mill owners are coming to have as much concern for "the moral character of their operatives" as they have already demonstrated for "the beauty and efficiency of their machinery." The social health of the factory system, he suggests, is demonstrated by the increasing degree to which it harmonizes individual gain with the general social welfare: "[T]he conviction is strengthening and spreading, that it is eminently the *interest* of a manufacturer to have a moral, sober, well-informed, healthy, and comfortable body of workmen" (483–84). Baines thus perceives an emerging reconciliation between the "imperative duty" of moral obligation and the irresistible compulsion of personal economic "interest," manifest symbolically in the correspondences among a hierarchy of healthy corporeal, technical, and composite social bodies: the body of the individual operative, the body of the factory, and the "body of workmen" as a whole.

The negative counterparts to these healthy industrial bodies are the hand-loom weavers, who have steadfastly resisted the "progress" of mechanized industry and are consequently "the only class that has sunk into distress and degradation" (484). Although Baines claims to sympathize with this distressed segment of the working classes, he also uses the handloom weaver to exemplify the disorderly labor practices subdued by the factory system and to illustrate the futility of resisting inevitable technological "progress." Invoking a crude base-superstructure theory of culture, he asserts that the "history of civilization" is largely the "history of the USEFUL ARTS," which "form the basis of social improvement" by elevating human beings "above abject want," providing them with "comforts and luxuries," and allowing them to "acquire the leisure necessary to cultivate the higher departments of knowledge" (5). The automation of cotton manufacture in particular has set "at liberty a larger proportion of the population, to cultivate literature, science, and the fine arts" (213). By positing such a causal connection between the progress of industrial technologies and the progress of culture, Baines sets up an opposition between the moral and disciplined factory operative (metonymically associated with order, civilization, and culture) and the "reckless and improvident" handloom weaver (metonymically associated with disorder and savageness) (486). These latter associations are made explicit in the description of Manchester's handloom weavers that Baines finds in Kay: "Ill-fed, ill-clothed, half-sheltered, and ignorant—weaving in close, damp cellars, or crowded, ill-ventilated workshops—it only remains that they should become, as is too frequently the case, demoralized and reckless, to render perfect the portraiture of savage life" (485). Kay's equation between handloom weaving and savageness is fortified by his observation that the handloom weavers "consist chiefly of Irish," whom he takes to be Europe's indigenous savages (see chap. 3).

For Baines, this figure of the savage weaver cements the thematic congruence between his historical account of the development of cotton manufacture and his economic explanation for the general distress of handicraft workers in Britain. Both discussions demonstrate that the supersession of hand labor by machinery is natural, inevitable, and ultimately desirable. In this light, the Irish handloom weaver seems an atavistic throwback to a system of manufacture predicated upon an intimate connection between manual skill and production. Just as the "Hindoo weaver . . . has no chance of competing with the power-loom" because of the intrinsic "feebleness and inefficiency of his exertions" (527), so there "can be no reasonable hope" that handloom weavers in Britain "will ever again earn satisfactory wages" (498). The situation is irremediable—"It is the nature of the employment which is the *cause*; the power of the masters to reduce wages is only an *effect*" (500)— and therefore no attempt should be made to rectify it. Indeed, the "course of prudence and true humanity" would be to embrace automation as a kind of civilizing mission and to facilitate the transition of handloom weavers to other sorts of (mechanized) employment (501).

Cooke Taylor's treatment of the working classes is likewise governed by his conviction that mechanized labor generally benefits operatives by reducing fatigue and raising wages. He defends this position by appropriating the characteristic charges against the factory system (that factory labor degrades workers into machines, that it is a kind of slavery, and that it is detrimental to physical and moral health) and applying them instead to nonindustrial modes of production. Unlike Baines and Ure, Cooke Taylor at least admits that the "continuous and unvarying repetition" involved in superintending machinery can "degrade the workman into an automaton" (126), yet he also insists that such degradation is more pronounced in nonmechanized forms of labor. It is "in those branches of industry which are not aided by machinery, but depend chiefly on manual dexterity," he writes, that "the man becomes the machine" (115). Moreover, Cooke Taylor uses the ordinarily anti-industrial analogy between factory labor and black slavery to assert the relative benevolence of large capital. On the authority of Ramón de la Sagra's economic survey of Cuba, he asserts that the slaves of "wealthy planters" are generally far better treated than the slaves of those who endeavor to manage plantations "with small capitals and fictitious credit."[15] His own observations in England similarly suggest that "the equity of the relations between the employers and the employed is disturbed by the want of capital, and not by the command of it" (117). While Oastler and others repeatedly treated the obvious evil of black slavery as a moral benchmark against which to measure the greater evil of the "white slavery" being perpetrated in England's mills, Cooke Taylor parries such appeals by distinguishing between the conditions that obtain on large and on small plantations and then using this difference to illustrate the social dangers of undercapitalization.

When Cooke Taylor takes up the condition of the working classes directly, he counters the Factory Movement's emphasis on the injurious effects of factory labor by simply refusing to address its allegedly sensationalist charges. Like Baines, he attributes the recent "burst of sentimental sympathy for the condition of the factory-operatives" to exaggerated claims regarding the number and severity of accidents in the mills, and he dismisses these claims through parody. Noting that he himself was "for a time fool enough to believe that mills were places in which young children were, by some inexplicable process, ground—bones, flesh, and blood together—into yarn and printed calicoes" and feigning "disappointment at not discovering the hoppers into which the infants were thrown," Cooke Taylor proceeds to argue on economic grounds against the "absurdity" that mill owners care nothing for the welfare of their child workers. On the contrary, "their own obvious interests" serve as guarantors of safety. Accidents, he points out, damage machines as well as people, and "the engineer's bill is considerably heavier than the surgeon's" (25–26).

Cooke Taylor takes a similar approach to the issue of industrial poverty. He protests that unlike other investigators (presumably hostile to the factory system), he will treat the poor not merely as objects of study but as human beings worthy of the dignity of attention: "I will not condescend to appeal, as I well might, to such irrefragable evidence as the haggard form, the sunken eye, the hollow cheek, and the faded lip; I rest my case entirely on the word of the poor man himself: in Lancashire, at least, he does not and he will not lie" (82). Likewise, obliquely acknowledging the genre of industrial tourism his work exemplifies, Cooke Taylor asserts that he has quit the "beaten and ordinary track of investigation . . . to examine the intellectual rather than the physical condition of the Lancashire operatives" (126). Such affirmations of the reasonableness of large mill owners and the "open, candid, and manly" (82) quality of the Lancastrian population not only reinforce the favorable representations of employer and employed that support Cooke Taylor's stance against external regulatory interference in their relations; they also minimize the symbolic significance of the manufacturing population's physical degeneration without denying it as a matter of fact.

Nonetheless, Cooke Taylor's seemingly principled refusal to "condescend" to appeal to the evidence of the body belies the ways in which he, like Baines and Ure, appropriates conventionally anti-industrial metaphors and images to support his free-trade and pro-factory positions. While he heeds "the word" of "the poor man," he also attributes tremendous symbolic significance to the bodies of poor women. In early nineteenth-century discussions of the factory system, representations of the laboring body are often implicitly gendered female, and in such cases the focus almost inevitably comes to rest on the ways in which factory labor unfits women to become wives and mothers, not only by preventing them from developing the skills and moral virtues essential to domestic life, but also by fostering "precocious" sexual appetites and specific physical deformities that interfere with their reproductive capacities. Such treatments employ what Gray identifies as "a platform rhetoric playing on the association of motherhood with 'nature'" to stigmatize factory labor as a threat to the purportedly natural domestic and social order (29).

Cooke Taylor, however, uses such images as emblems of the unnatural economic hardships created by restrictions on free trade. Throughout his letters, he dismisses the notion that the distress of the 1840s is due to a depression in wages caused by overproduction. The problem, he insists, is not low wages per se but the artificial crises created by restrictions on trade. The factory system, like an organism capable of adjusting to environmental changes,

45

"has powers within itself to make an equitable settlement of wages; but in the *absorption* of its production, which must clearly determine the question of employment, the system is subject to the perturbating influence of government and legislation which may either open or close foreign markets" (113, emphasis added). Cooke Taylor supports this opinion with firsthand testimony gleaned from one "very intelligent manufacturer," who attributes "the existing distress" to restrictions impeding the free exchange of English manufactures for foreign agricultural products and raw materials: "[O]ur laws prevented us from receiving the only payment which our customers had to offer, and hence they could not take our goods; *absorption*, therefore, did not keep pace with production" (69–70, emphasis added).

This understanding of trade in terms of "absorption" allows Cooke Taylor to take vignettes of impoverished women struggling to nurse their children as both metaphors and metonymies for the crises of the hungry forties. In a letter from Bolton, he describes one such woman: "She was suckling a wretched infant from a withered breast, and those who witnessed the agonizing scene will never forget how the poor babe writhed on the lap and wrung the nipple with convulsive energies in the desperate attempt to extort that nutriment which the exhausted breast could not afford" (48). In a subsequent letter, he uses a similar image to illustrate the desirability of factory over agricultural work:

> I saw a woman in the very last stage of extenuation suckling an infant, which could scarcely draw a single drop of nutriment from her exhausted breast. . . . On asking why application had not been made to the parish for relief, I was informed that they were persons from agricultural districts, who, on committing an act of vagrancy, would be sent to their parishes, and that they had rather endure anything, in the hope of some manufacturing revival, than return to the condition of farm-labourers, from which they had emerged. (79–80)

Both of these scenes recall the myriad descriptions of women unfitted for motherhood by factory labor that formed such a crucial part of early nineteenth-century anti-industrial rhetoric. Cooke Taylor's intention, however, is not to stigmatize the factory system but to dramatize what he views as the cruel consequences of an erroneous protectionism.

The figure of "absorption"—a process both conceptually abstract and intimately corporeal—sustains this connection. Reflecting on the first of these vignettes, Cooke Taylor writes, "[T]hat suffering mother, that wretched babe, are for ever associated in my mind with the subject [of overproduction]. They afforded proof that deficient absorption and not overproduction was the source of our commercial distress" (48). Commenting on the second, he draws on the language of sanitary reform—cannily reversing the usual characterization of cities as sources of pollution and waste that would be poured out into the surrounding countryside—to make a similar point: "Hitherto the manufacturing towns have absorbed the surplus labourers from the agricultural county; but the drain is now choked, and the stream, driven backwards to its source, threatens a fearful overflow, which may sweep away the very elements of civilisation" (81). Metonymically, these passages depend on a straightforward naming of effect (the "withered" or "exhausted" breast) for cause (the depression of the 1840s). Metaphorically, they are more problematic, since the mapping between the domain of the family and the domain of the economy is overdetermined. One possibility is that the mothers represent English industry and the starving infants those foreign markets artificially kept from absorbing its products. Alternatively, the infants may represent an English industry unable to draw the sustaining "milk" of raw materials from its foreign markets. In either case, the analogies successfully dramatize the crisis of distribution (or "absorption") afflicting both foreign markets and domestic industry, but they fail to capture adequately the corresponding crisis in production. England's warehouses are not "exhausted" but filled with "piles" of textiles "lying idle" (48), just as the industrial districts are overburdened with an idle surplus population. Although all analogies suggest entailments at odds with their primary meanings, the severity of the contradiction in this specific case is significant. Like Ure, whose elaboration of the factory's three "organic systems" is similarly conflicted, Cooke Taylor is driven by the rhetorical imperative of appropriating anti-industrial bodily images to the point of metaphoric incoherence.

IN 1844 Cooke Taylor revisited the factory question in a second pamphlet, entitled *Factories and the Factory System; from Parliamentary Documents and Personal Examination*. As if to compensate for the personal and impressionistic quality of his *Notes*, he eschews the epistolary mode and presents his new pamphlet as an objective exposition of established fact. *Factories and the Factory System*, he announces in his preface, "is neither intended to attack nor to defend the Factory System, but simply to state what that system is; to explain what is its nature and what are its results, so far as they have been yet developed in human experience" (iii). What follows, though, is neither a disinterested attempt to see the factory system as in itself it really is, nor a balanced weighing of views, but a partisan recapitulation of the major claims advanced by proponents of the factory system over the past

decade. Cooke Taylor describes the "capitalist" as a "benefactor of the operative" who "opens to him a field for his labour" (6) and characterizes steam-
powered machinery as "not the tyrant but the slave of the operatives" (12). He
notes that it is in mill owners' self-interest to prevent accidents and disease
(17, 75) and denies charges that factory work causes physical deformities
(64). He disputes the notion that factories contribute to the moral corruption
of female operatives (41–42) and calls "infant labor" a "national blessing"
because it protects children from vice, trains them to industry, and enables
them to contribute to their own support (21–25). He insists that the factory
system should be judged by the conditions prevailing in rural mills, blames
excess population rather than the factory system itself for the "fearful evils"
afflicting industrial towns, and affirms the moral, physical, and intellectual
superiority of operatives to agricultural laborers (39–44, 76–79). Finally, he
contends that although strikes may bring operatives some temporary benefits,
they rarely work to their ultimate advantage, and argues that factory legislation will inevitably damage the cause of labor (94–98).

More significant than Cooke Taylor's rehearsal of these standard positions
is his explicit elaboration of the shaping premise of early Victorian proindustrial rhetoric: that the development of the factory system is consistent
with human nature and coextensive with the progress of civilization. Factories, he writes, are "a result of the universal tendency to association which is
inherent in our nature. . . . They began when the first step was made in civilization, and they must continue until society itself is dissolved in barbarism"
(1). At his most effusive, he portrays the factory system as coextensive with
civilization itself: "[W]e are discussing a system which has accomplished its
establishment in perpetuity, and which must continue to acquire extension
beyond any assignable limits with the general progress of civilization" (111).
Cooke Taylor justifies such grand claims by defining factories and the factory
system in the broadest possible manner:

> A FACTORY, properly speaking, is an establishment where several workmen
> are collected together for the purpose of obtaining greater and cheaper con-
> veniences for labour than they could procure individually at their homes; for
> producing results, by their combined efforts, which they could not accomplish
> separately; and for saving the loss of time which the carrying of an article
> from place to place, during the several processes necessary to complete its
> manufacture, would occasion. (1)

The governing "principle of a factory," he continues, is "that each labourer,
working separately, is controlled by some associating principle, which directs

his producing powers to effecting a common result, which it is the object of all collectively to attain." In contrast to Baines and Ure, who characterize factories as productive series of machines or integrated systems of machinery and human operatives, Cooke Taylor carefully avoids mentioning machinery at all. Instead, he offers a general definition that encompasses most cooperative productive endeavors. Under this rubric, he notes, shipyards and even farms qualify as "species" of factories, since they both depend upon the combined efforts of a number of workers.

Despite this difference, Cooke Taylor is not in fundamental disagreement with Baines and Ure over the nature of the factory. Rather, their separate characterizations of the factory system reflect their different, if still complementary, rhetorical purposes. Baines and Ure emphasize the novel quality of automatic manufacture: the systematic replacement of skilled workers by machines. Cooke Taylor seeks to affirm the factory system's continuity with the whole history of human productive activity. He therefore delineates a category with graded membership that has the modern, automated mill as its central exemplar: "The more the principle of association appears prominent in any species of production," Cooke Taylor writes, "the more rigidly does it become entitled to the name of factory, and the more generally does it receive the name in common parlance" (2).

This elastic conception of the factory facilitates a kind of semantic bait and switch through which Cooke Taylor encourages his readers to make specific inferences favorable to the factory system of their day from general platitudes about the relationship between industry and civilization. He argues, for example, that as "any establishment, in which artisans while working separately from each other still work collectively towards one common mark, is essentially a factory, it follows that the factory system cannot be in itself evil unless all associated industry be likewise evil, a proposition which no man in his senses would venture to maintain" (4). On this basis, he concludes that the factory system "is not only innocent in itself, but a necessary element in the progress of civilization, and a most efficient means of promoting human happiness" (5). Cooke Taylor's reasoning here is not unassailable: imputing evil to the Victorian factory system does not in fact require imputing it to all industry as well. Establishments that are "essentially" factories—in the sense that they are organized according to the principles of "association" and "combination"—may still differ in other significant respects. Because moral valence is not part of Cooke Taylor's definition, he has no warrant for inferring the good or evil of all industry from the single instance of the nineteenth-century factory system. His second assertion is equally deceptive. The "factory system," understood broadly as the cooperative productive association of human beings, may indeed be a "necessary element in the progress of civilization" and the "most efficient means of promoting human happiness," but this does not mean that steam-powered textile mills are similarly essential.

Nevertheless, his remarks are rhetorically effective because they remove the debate over the factory system from the realm of moral principle and place it squarely in the domain of practical consequence. Having established that factories "are founded in [*sic*] right principles," it remains simply "to examine their attendant circumstances" to determine whether they have "perverted" an inherently benevolent system (5). By thus framing the issue, Cooke Taylor ensures that any facts or conditions unfavorable to the factory system may be dismissed as aberrations, subject to correction as automatic industry develops and matures. If this "new industrial system" has "produced many anomalies in its efforts to accommodate itself to institutions previously existing," it is equally true that "the displacements produced by the factory system have been easy of remedy by slightly altering the social machinery" (118). In Cooke Taylor's view, the factory system is not an "excrescence" from the body politic but a model citizen: "[T]he history of the world has been written in vain," he triumphantly concludes, "if it has not taught us that industry has been ever ready to perform its duties when its rights are respected" (118).

CHAPTER TWO

"Beautiful Combinations"

ABSTRACTION AND TECHNOLOGICAL BEAUTY IN THE WORKS OF CHARLES BABBAGE

IN THE companion chapter to "The Nature of Gothic" in *The Stones of Venice* III, Ruskin reinforces the theoretical underpinnings of his condemnation of industrial labor by identifying systematized knowledge as an impediment to free aesthetic expression and receptivity. In a statement that directly attacks the basic premise of the rhetoric of industrial culture, he charges that the Renaissance's "grand mistake" lay "in supposing that science and art were the same things, and that to advance in the one was necessarily to perfect the other." In truth, he counters, art and science are "not only different, but so opposed that to advance in the one is, in ninety-nine cases out of the hundred, to retrograde in the other" (11:47). If Ruskin stops short of finding art and science inherently antithetical, he does hold that advancement in science and manufacture typically entails an aesthetic deterioration. That Leonardo could become a great artist, thinker, and engineer testifies both to the theoretical possibility of integrating these domains and to the extreme difficulty of realizing that possibility in fact.

Ruskin elaborates on this ambivalence toward intellectual knowledge through a pair of contrasting similes that recapitulates in microcosm the overarching antithesis that governs *The Stones of Venice:* "Knowledge is, at best, the pilgrim's burden or the soldier's panoply, often a weariness to them both; and the Renaissance knowledge is like the Renaissance armour of plate, binding and cramping the human form; while all good knowledge is like the crusader's chain mail, which throws itself into folds with the body, yet it is rarely so forged as that the clasps and rivets do not gall us" (11:66). Despite this skeptical posture, Ruskin allows for the pursuit of "science" (a term he uses in its older and more general sense) by those able to wear it lightly. Earlier in the volume, he expresses "the most profound reverence for those mighty men who could wear the Renaissance armour of proof, and yet not feel it encumber their living limbs,—Leonardo and Michael Angelo, Ghirlandajo and Masaccio, Titian and Tintoret" (11:18). As always, Ruskin allows for the exception of genius, which has no need of the concessions he makes to ordinary human limitations.

Ruskin subsequently extends this view to his own day, criticizing contemporary "literary" and "scientific" pedagogy for its inordinate emphasis on the mastery of abstract and esoteric systems of knowledge:

> Our literary work has long been economically useless to us because too much concerned with dead languages; and our scientific work will yet, for some time, be a good deal lost, because scientific men are too fond or too vain of their systems, and waste the student's time in endeavouring to give him large views, and make him perceive interesting connections of facts; when there is not one student, no, nor one man, in a thousand, who can feel the beauty of a system, or even take it clearly into his head; but nearly all men can understand, and most will be interested in, the facts which bear on daily life (16:111–12).

Again, within the context of his dominant skepticism, Ruskin accommodates the rare intellect that can achieve a disinterested and aesthetic appreciation of abstract systemized knowledge. In "The Nature of Gothic," Ruskin rejects the pursuit of "delicate finish" and "refinement of execution" in art and ornament not because they are intrinsically bad but because they are so often purchased at the cost of creative expression: "Always look for invention first," he writes, "and after that, for such execution as will help the invention, and as the inventor is capable of without painful effort, and *no more*" (10:199). In similar fashion, he frames his criticism of nineteenth-century literary and scientific instruction not as a matter of principle but as a pragmatic acknowledgment of most people's limited powers of abstraction.

Charles Babbage was motivated by precisely the kind of intense feeling for the beauty of system that Ruskin finds so rare. Therefore, just as Ruskin recognizes a certain heroism in Leonardo's constant striving after "perfection" even as he laments the waste of this "vain effort" (10:203), so, I believe, he would have given grudging respect to Babbage, whose driving passion was an almost Shelleyan love of intellectual beauty.

TAKEN TOGETHER, Baines's, Ure's, and Cooke Taylor's impassioned defenses of the factory system exemplify a distinct genre of proindustrial writing that matured in the second quarter of the nineteenth century, partly in reaction to sensationalized representations of factories as loci of suffering and moral degradation and partly in response to a growing popular curiosity about the organization of factories and the technical processes involved in manufacture. The most widely read such exposition, however, was not Baines's *History,*

Ure's *Philosophy,* or Cooke Taylor's *Notes* but Charles Babbage's treatise *On the Economy of Machinery and Manufactures* (1832).

Babbage is best known today for devising what amounted to a programmable mechanical computer, but in the 1830s he was also known as a commentator on political economy and the industrial arts. His *Economy* sold three thousand copies upon its publication in 1832, and over the next three years it ran through three subsequent editions and was translated into French, German, Italian, Spanish, Russian, and Swedish (Hyman 122; ed.'s intro., Babbage, *Works* 8:5). The book is divided into two sections. The first grew out of a decade of visits to various workshops and factories in both Great Britain and abroad during which Babbage sought to acquaint himself with "various resources of mechanical art" that might aid him in constructing his Difference Engine. Like other examples of industrial tourism, this section focuses strictly on manufactured objects and technical processes, eliding almost entirely the contributions of human workers.[1] In essence, it amounts to a natural history of the new world of machinery and manufactures, its main aim being to organize the multitude of "curious processes and interesting facts" he observed during his travels into a taxonomy that makes "their general principles and mutual relations" intelligible (8:v–vi). The second section of *The Economy,* which Babbage identifies as a discussion of "the domestic and political economy of manufactures" (8:xxii), complements the first by exploring the broader economic and social consequences of mass production. It is more theoretical in nature, addressing such subjects as the division of labor, the various influences on price, the effects of overproduction, and the invention and application of machinery, and it is the primary basis of Babbage's reputation as an important if unheralded contributor to the development of classical political economy.[2]

Because of *The Economy*'s popularity and influence, it is tempting to treat the work as representative of the genre of proindustrial writing it helped to define. To do so, however, is to risk occluding the study's eccentric brilliance as well as the particular philosophical perspective it reflects. In the course of his career, Babbage engaged in a variety of intellectual and professional pursuits. In addition to designing his calculating engines and writing on industry and political economy, he played a significant role in the founding of several scientific associations, served as a technical consultant to the Great Western Railway, flirted with Radical politics, and indulged a penchant for theological speculation. Most important, Babbage was a serious mathematician with interests in a variety of fields, including analysis, algebra, statistics, the theory of functions, and what would later become known as operations research, cryptology, and game theory.[3] Even more than his intellectual eclecticism, it was Babbage's remarkable power for abstraction, a power amplified and disciplined by his mathematical pursuits, that defined the quality of his thought and most emphatically differentiated him from the typical commentator on manufactures.

The defenses of the factory system put forth by Baines, Ure, and Cooke Taylor are characterized by what the historian Robert Gray calls their "polemical commitment to entrepreneurial liberalism" (133). For all their rhetorical sophistication, the arguments of these works are dictated, ultimately, by the common ideology of their authors. Babbage's *Economy* reflects his similar ideological investments, but it is more fundamentally a manifestation of his general preoccupation with the nature of signification, or what he would come to call the "philosophy of signs" (11:322).[4] Although he is not always rigorous or consistent in the matter, Babbage generally rejects the referential notion of meaning, in which signs (linguistic or otherwise) are taken to be tokens of things in the world, and treats signs as abstract entities that assume meaning in relation to one another. His semiotic ideal was a complete and internally coherent system in which symbols are defined by distinct and unambiguous propositions and can be manipulated according to fixed syntactic rules. He found this ideal most fully realized in the artificial language of mathematics, specifically in the abstract formalism of algebraic calculus. "The multitude of significations which attach to many of the words that compose our ordinary language," he asserts in an early paper delivered to the Cambridge Philosophical Society, "is a disadvantage which is completely removed from that of analysis" (1:372).[5] While an undergraduate at Cambridge, he was a principal agent in the organization of the short-lived Analytical Society, which controversially promoted Leibniz's system of notation for analytical calculus over Newton's, on the grounds of its superior clarity (Hyman 24–28). In the preface to the society's *Memoirs*, Babbage attributes the appeal of mathematics to "the accurate simplicity of its language," observing that an "arbitrary symbol can neither convey, nor excite any idea foreign to its original definitions." Even so, he was troubled by the possibility that this beautiful system could be corrupted, and he insisted that the "immutability no less than the symmetry" of mathematical notation "should be ever guarded with a jealousy commensurate to its vital importance" (qtd. in Hyman 26).[6]

Likewise, Babbage saw the lack of a system of notation capable of describing complex mechanical operations as a significant obstacle to the development of his calculating engines. The relations among their various parts "would have baffled the most tenacious memory," so Babbage set out to devise "a language of signs" through which he could analyze his engines' movements. He attributed to this "Mechanical Notation" a tremendous instrumental power, noting that through this aid, "the Analytical Engine became a reality" (11:86). Similarly, in *The Economy,* Babbage is moved less by the physical presence of machines and manufactures than by what these things embody and represent. In his eyes, machines are not merely ingenious configurations of levers, screws, belts, and gears. They are also material embodiments of abstract concepts and ideas. Manufactures are not "autonomous figures," or commodities in Marx's sense (*Capital* 165). They are signifiers that gesture toward the abstract processes through which they are produced. In *The Economy,* in other words, Babbage does not offer simply a taxonomy of industrial processes or an exposition of economic principles in their application to manufacture; he also endeavors to distill the gritty materiality of industrial manufacture into the sublime rationality of pure mathematics. This drive toward abstraction, rather than his specific anticipation of the computer, is the true source of Babbage's uncanny modernity.

In recent years the connections among Babbage's mathematical pursuits, his conception of the nature of thought and intelligence, his writings on machinery and manufactures, and the broader structure of nineteenth-century industrial society have begun to receive significant scholarly attention. Gordon L. Miller views Babbage's work on his calculating engines as an effort to design an "intelligent machine," which, in turn, would promote the development of "a more rational and intelligent form of society" (70). Mary Poovey treats the factory, as Babbage describes it in *The Economy,* as one emblem of the "modern system of abstraction" which dictates the organization of space—and of bodies in space—in capitalist society (38–40). Simon Schaffer, capitalizing on the multiple meanings of *intelligence,* links Babbage's effort to invest his engines with capacities analogous to human faculties of memory, anticipation, foresight, and vigilance—a project Schaffer glosses as an attempt to make "engines think" (223)—with concurrent struggles over disciplinary surveillance in the factory, the nature of and relationship between intellectual and material property, and the place of skill in industrial production. William J. Ashworth similarly interprets John Herschel and Charles Babbage's mathematical work as an effort to "industrialize the human mind" by disciplining and accelerating the processes of thought (653).[7]

While this body of work convincingly situates Babbage within various nineteenth-century intellectual and social contexts, thus dispelling older notions of him as a prescient visionary or solitary genius, it gives little attention to the aesthetic dimension of his thought. Yet just as Babbage's work on his calculating engines mirrored the disciplinary regime of the factory, so his *Economy* crystallizes a sense of technological beauty nascent in the early nineteenth-century industrial community itself. For Babbage, as for Ure, Baines, and Cooke Taylor, the aesthetic functions to identify industrial manufacture as an integral contribution to British culture. However, while these other advocates of industry draw on Romantic aesthetic conventions to deflect criticisms of the factory system, Babbage pursues the more radical project of subsuming those conventions within his own brand of utilitarian rationalism, arriving finally at a theory of taste in which immediate aesthetic experience is itself subordinated to the pleasure of intellectual analysis. Rather than representing factories as organic bodies or as fruits of an essential national character, he treats mechanical systems as if they were mathematical functions instantiated in wood, leather, and metal. In Babbage's eyes, machines and mechanical systems possess a special kind of beauty, a beauty contingent neither on the formal properties of contemplated objects (the foundation of the School of Design theorists' industrial aesthetic) nor on evidence of personal creative expression (one basis for Romantic and post-Romantic aesthetic critiques of manufacture) but on the abstract efficiency of their operations. For this reason, *The Economy* transcends its generic affiliation with other proindustrial accounts of the factory system to become an early and potent harbinger of the technological aesthetic which would dominate certain strains of early twentieth-century modernism.

IN HER 1851 novel *North and South,* Elizabeth Gaskell captures something of this new aesthetic vision in a conversation between the Reverend Hale, a country parson new to Gaskell's fictionalized Manchester, and Mr. John Thornton, a wealthy young manufacturer. Upon arriving in Milton, Hale experiences feelings typical of those encountering the industrial city for the first time. "After a quiet life in a country parsonage for more than twenty years," Gaskell writes, "there was something dazzling to Mr. Hale in the energy which conquered immense difficulties with ease; the power of the machinery of Milton, the power of the men of Milton, impressed him with a sense of grandeur, which he yielded to without caring to inquire into the details of its exercise" (69). Thornton attempts to enlighten Hale by explaining to him "the magnificent power, yet delicate adjustment" of a steam hammer, but his description merely reminds Hale of "some of the wonderful stories of subservient genii in the Arabian Nights" (80–81).

These contrasting perspectives are broadly emblematic of two aesthetic responses to industrial technology in competition during the first half of the nineteenth century. Hale's impressions are those of an outsider attempting to apprehend an unfamiliar and imposing phenomenon, and as such they have much in common with such images of the technological sublime as Turner's *Rain, Steam, and Speed,* Carlyle's apocalyptic descriptions of the industrial cities, or Dickens's Coketown.[8] Unlike Hale, who is overawed by the sheer energy harnessed by industry, Thornton admires not raw power alone but power applied with minute precision. Moreover, his final emphasis is not on the steam hammer itself but on the hammer's status as a sign of the intellect's power over the physical world. He sees the steam hammer as the "practical realisation of a gigantic thought," as one victory in a "war which compels, and shall compel, all material power to yield to science" (81). Hale is dazzled by the simple "grandeur" (69) of industrial technology; Thornton is moved by the "grandeur of conception" (81) such technology represents.

In the opening paragraph of the first chapter of *The Economy,* Babbage announces the principal features of the aesthetic Gaskell dramatizes in Thornton: a focus on abstract processes and systems, a recognition of efficiency as a predominant criterion of beauty, and—most significant—an understanding of manufactured products as material signs of the processes by which they were produced:

> The amount of patient thought, of repeated experiment, of happy exertion of genius, by which our manufactures have been created and carried to their present excellence, is scarcely to be imagined. If we look around the rooms we inhabit, or through those storehouses of every convenience, of every luxury that man can desire, which deck the crowded streets of our larger cities, we shall find in the history of each article, of every fabric, a series of failures which have gradually led the way to excellence; and we shall notice, in the art of making even the most insignificant of them, processes calculated to excite our admiration by their simplicity, or to rivet our attention by their unlooked-for results. (4)

In the trappings of material culture, Babbage reads the history of its production. An initial survey of individual articles of manufacture—the contents of "the rooms we inhabit" or "those storehouses of every convenience"—leads him to apprehend the progressive development of various manufacturing technologies. He thus invokes an evolutionary model of technological development that aligns his study with contemporary developments in other sciences. Indeed, Babbage was a friend of the geologist Charles Lyell, and his calculating engines may have been one source of inspiration for Darwin

(Hyman 129–30; Schaffer 225–26). The specifically aesthetic implications of this passage may be brought into relief through contrasts with Marx and Ruskin. Unlike Marx, Babbage does not see manufactures as commodities— as "autonomous figures endowed with a life of their own" (*Capital* 165)— but rather as material signs of the evolutionary development of the "processes" by which they were produced. In this sense, Babbage is like Ruskin, who also views manufactures as "signs" of the prevailing conditions of production (10:193). However, Babbage's and Ruskin's interpretations of these signs are diametrically opposed. In treating the "accurate mouldings, and perfect polishings" of the Victorian interior as emblems of a degrading industrial servitude (10:193), Ruskin condemns exactly the simplicity, technical elegance, and precision of execution Babbage admires.

Babbage's appreciation for the efficiency of technological processes recalls Adam Smith's observation in *The Theory of Moral Sentiments* (1759) that the "fitness" of a given contrivance "should often be more valued, than the very end for which it was intended" (179–80). Babbage recognizes, in Smith's terms, that a mechanism's aesthetic appeal derives from the "exact adjustment" of its "means" rather than from its material form or configuration. Like Smith, he regards utility as a necessary precondition for the aestheticization of technological processes. An intricate mechanical process without a use would be a mere curiosity; a process meeting its purpose effectively and simply, on the other hand, is beautiful. Paradoxically, however, although functional utility is an essential precondition for technological beauty, technological processes become beautiful only when their extrinsic functions are superseded, in the minds of their beholders, by the intrinsic "perfection of their effects" and "simplicity of their means" (Babbage 8:182). In other words, they become beautiful when they are contemplated for their own sake, as performances "calculated to excite our admiration by their simplicity, or to rivet our attention by their unlooked-for results" (8:4).

In the first section of *The Economy*, which describes and classifies various machines and techniques, Babbage repeatedly expresses his appreciation for such processes. He writes, for instance, of a "very beautiful process" for wearing down rapids in river beds, of a "very beautiful mode" of casting delicate botanical forms in bronze, and of engraving by pressure as "one of the most beautiful examples of the art of copying carried to an almost unlimited extent" (8:31, 57, 63). In each of these examples, it is the "process" or "mode" or "art" itself (rather than the formal qualities of the machines or the goods they produce) that Babbage finds beautiful. When he does praise specific mechanical "contrivances," he generally admires their functional relationship to larger operations. The best exemplar of such a mechanism, not surprisingly, is "that beautiful contrivance, the governor of the steam-engine," which enables machinery to work with "uniformity and steadiness." Babbage describes a similar device called a "cataract" as "[a]nother very beautiful contrivance for regulating the number of strokes made by a steam-engine" (8:21). In both cases, the beauty he notices arises from the ability of the mechanisms to regulate larger processes flexibly and precisely.

The vaguely Linnaean scheme that organizes the first section of *The Economy* is therefore deceptive, for Babbage is never content simply to classify the myriad manufactures he describes but always seeks to understand them as products of more general technical processes. This concern becomes the explicit subject of the second section of his study, the underlying premise of which is that machines and factories are best understood not as concrete entities but as abstract and mathematically describable systems. This drive to abstraction, which is typical of all of Babbage's work, is fundamental to his two most important contributions to political economy: his clear differentiation between "making" and "manufacturing" and the refinements he proposes to the theory of the division of labor.

The nineteenth-century vision of the factory as an integrated productive system and paradigm of a new social order entailed a substantial reconceptualization of the nature and role of "skill." Cooke Taylor figures the factory system as a prosthesis that compensates for the erosion of manual skill and tactile sensitivity that inevitably accompanies the progress of civilization. It is only through "the continued concentration of mechanical power in mills and factories," he contends, that "British operatives are enabled to compete with those who, like the Hindoos, possessing a more delicate organization, could with the unaided fingers produce a finer texture" of cloth (*Factories* 18). Baines associates automatic industry with a fundamentally new sort of creative power. "Mechanical knowledge," he asserts, "has taught man to substitute for the labour of his own hands, the potent and indefatigable agency of nature," so that "operations which he once *performed*, he now only *directs*" (10). Ure goes a step further, treating the systematic elimination of skilled labor as the explicit goal—rather than a simple consequence—of automatic industry. The guiding "principle of the factory system," he writes, is "to substitute mechanical science for hand skill, and the partition of a process into its essential constituents, for the division or graduation of labour among artisans" (20). The modern factory, in other words, is organized not according to the division of labor, which encourages workers to develop specialized skills, but according to the "equalization of labour, or automatic plan," which dissociates workers from specific technical processes and transforms them into "mere overlookers of machines" (20, 21).

Babbage, in contrast, does not deny the continuing importance of technical skill to manufacture but accommodates it by distinguishing "making" from "manufacturing." He initially differentiates between these two sorts of productive activity by asserting that the former term "refers to the production of *a small*, the latter to that of *a very large number of individuals*," but he subsequently asserts a qualitative distinction as well:

> If, therefore, the *maker* of an article wish to become a *manufacturer*, in the more extended sense of the term, he must attend to other principles besides those mechanical ones on which the successful execution of his work depends; and he must carefully arrange the whole system of his factory in such a manner, that the article he sells to the public may be produced at as small a cost as possible. (8:86)

In one sense, the "maker" and the "manufacturer" might be envisioned as engaging in analogous pursuits but at different levels of abstraction. Just as the "maker" exercises his skill to create a specific article, so the "manufacturer" exercises his "ingenuity" to develop and refine a whole system of production, which subsumes the activities of the solitary "maker." The manufacturer is a maker as well, but of systems rather than of things. In this way, Babbage gives those who conceive of and create abstract systems and economies priority of place over those immediately involved in material processes of production.

In the early 1830s Babbage had strong personal motivation for adopting this position. In 1823, upon the recommendation of Marc Isambard Brunel, Babbage hired the engineer Joseph Clement to construct the first Difference Engine, a machine designed to calculate numerical series automatically. This contract enabled Clement to greatly expand his operation. When he was first engaged by Babbage, he was working out of his kitchen, but over the next several years he transformed his workshop into a leading center of precision machining. By the late 1820s, Clement and Babbage were embroiled in a heated controversy over the ownership of the patterns, drawings, and machine tools connected with the Difference Engine's construction. At the time he was writing *The Economy*, Babbage was also seeking to have the partially completed engine, as well as the plans and specialized tools connected with its construction, transferred from Clement's workshop in Lambeth to a new fireproof building near his own residence on Dorset Street (Hyman 53, 123–35).

As Schaffer has recognized, the conflict between Clement and Babbage stemmed as much from changing conditions of industrial production as it did from the prickly personalities of the principals. Traditionally, skilled artisans maintained personal ownership over the tools of their trades, and machine shops generally operated with little outside supervision. On these grounds, Clement insisted that the specialized lathes and equipment developed in conjunction with the construction of the Difference Engine should be his property, and he viewed the removal of the machine to Babbage's building as a challenge to his status and autonomy as an engineer (Schaffer 213–19). Babbage, for his part, argued that because the calculating engines were the "absolute creations" of his "own mind," he possessed an incontestable "right" to dispose of them "more sacred in its nature than any hereditary or acquired property" (British Library, Additional MSS 40611, fol. 181). The conflict between Clement and Babbage thus touches on the more general question of whether ownership in an industrial society derives (as Clement held) from production and use or (as Babbage maintained) from initial conception and design (Schaffer 210–19).

Babbage's subordination of making to manufacturing emerges directly from this dispute. In 1831, as Babbage was drafting *The Economy of Machinery and Manufactures,* the engineer I. K. Brunel wrote in support of his efforts to take possession of the calculating engine. Commiserating with Babbage, Brunel notes the "inconveniences he is incessantly put to in consequence of the *Maker* being so distant from him" and laments the difficulties caused by "this very distant separation between the superintending and the executing agents." Discounting the formidable technical skills necessary to produce and assemble the machine's individual components, Brunel argues not simply that Clement ought to be brought under Babbage's direct supervisory authority but also that the machine's completion "must require a kind of education from the author" (BL Add. MSS 37186, fol. 186). As in Mary Shelley's *Frankenstein,* it is this intellectual labor that definitively links creature and creator.

In his discussion of the division of labor, Babbage provides a general formulation of the premise underlying Brunel's letter, that the essence of mechanical creation lies in determining "the combinations and dispositions" of parts rather than in individual acts of material production (BL Add. MSS 37186, fol. 186). Babbage, who was named to Newton's former chair as Lucasian Professor of Mathematics in 1828, explains the division of labor in the factory almost as if it were a problem in analytical calculus. According to what has come to be called the "Babbage Principle" of the division of labor, the way to minimize the cost of production is to decompose large tasks into their elemental "processes," many of which can be performed at cheaper rates than the task as a whole, and then to recompose them into a system of production. This procedure reduces the total cost of production by allowing each constituent process to be performed at the lowest possible rate, rather than at the high single rate that would be commanded by an individual skilled workman:

> That the master manufacturer, by dividing the work to be executed into different processes, each requiring different degrees of skill or of force, can purchase exactly that precise quantity of both which is necessary for each process; whereas, if the whole work were executed by one workman, that person must possess sufficient skill to perform the most difficult, and sufficient strength to execute the most laborious, of the operations into which the art is divided. (8:125)

Ure felt that this observation demonstrated Babbage's ignorance about the true nature of automatic industry. In what is clearly a criticism of Babbage, he argues that the preference for employing "merely children" over experienced adult workers "shows how the scholastic dogma of the division of labour into degrees of skill has been exploded by our enlightened manufacturers" (23).[9] Babbage, for his part, was sufficiently unimpressed by Ure to deny his request for a demonstration of the calculating engine (BL Add. MSS 37189, fol. 17). Whatever the rivalry between these two industrial philosophers, the economic validity of Babbage's principle has less relevance for his views on invention and technological beauty than do the mathematical terms of the principle's formulation.[10] The "work to be executed" is understood as an aggregate of various constituent "processes," and the abilities of laborers are represented as infinitely divisible quantities of "skill" and "force." This terminology obscures the material reality of work and the physical presence of human workers, and thus frees the manufacturer to approach the arrangement of the factory as a problem of integration: the total "work to be done" is a sum of various "processes," each of which is itself a function of the variables "skill" and "force."[11]

This analogy between the manufacturer and the mathematician becomes explicit when Babbage extends his discussion to include the division of mental labor. He takes as his model a procedure devised by the French mathematician Gaspard de Prony to produce an extensive set of logarithmic tables. Inspired by Adam Smith's discussion of the division of labor in *The Wealth of Nations*, de Prony hit on the idea "de mettre ses logarithmes en *manufacture* comme les épingles," of *manufacturing* his logarithms like pins (qtd. in Babbage 8:137). De Prony's scheme, as Babbage explains it, was to divide the project into three separate tasks. First, a handful of accomplished mathematicians determined which of the various possible formulas for calculating the necessary functions were most suited to simple numeric calculation. Then, a second group of mathematicians converted the appropriate formulas into specific arithmetic expressions, which, finally, were computed by a large group of clerks. In Babbage's view, de Prony's method "much resembles that of a skilful person about to construct a cotton or silk mill, or any similar establishment." The clerks who performed the actual arithmetic calculations are represented as factory operatives whose activities "may almost be termed mechanical," while de Prony is portrayed as a manufacturer who has "found that some improved machinery may be successfully applied to his pursuit" (8:138). De Prony's project thus demonstrates "that the arrangements which ought to regulate the interior economy of a manufactory, are founded on principles of deeper root than may have been supposed, and are capable of being usefully employed in preparing the road to some of the sublimest investigations of the human mind" (8:135). The ultimate application of these principles is, of course, Babbage's own in the creation of the Difference Engine, which he describes at length following his discussion of de Prony's tables.

Like his distinction between the "maker" and the "manufacturer," Babbage's characterization of the division of labor privileges intellectual over manual creation and in this way challenges traditional Romantic models of aesthetic production, which emphasize individual creative power and the personal connection between creator and creation. Yet this does not mean that Babbage sees invention as a simply mechanical activity. Like William Whewell, John Herschel, and other contemporaries, Babbage rejects the naive Baconian notion that science can proceed through mechanical induction alone and acknowledges the crucial role of creative imagination in scientific and technological investigation.[12] Therefore, even as Babbage insists that many intellectual endeavors may be facilitated by the application of formal and even "mechanical" methods, he also recognizes the crucial importance of individual "ingenuity" and "genius," through which methods and systems are conceived. Indeed, in his later essay on the Great Exhibition, he makes this point directly. "In the fine arts, and in the arts of industry, as well as in the pursuits of science," he writes, "the highest department of each is that of the discovery of principles, and the invention of methods" (10:81).

Since Babbage was firmly convinced of his own extraordinary genius, he had a personal stake in finding a place for individual creative power within the systematic division of labor. But his repeated reflections on the nature of genius were motivated by more than a simple self-congratulatory impulse;

they are consistent with a reduction in the concept's range of application from the late eighteenth to the early nineteenth centuries. During this period, political economy displaced an existing "discourse of genius" that attributed occupational specializations and social divisions to a natural distribution of mental faculties. This older discourse reached its peak with Alexander Gerard's 1774 *Essay on Genius*, but by the beginning of the nineteenth century, the concept of genius was restricted largely to literary and aesthetic discourse (Tenger and Trolander).

The references to genius in Babbage's corpus reflect this narrowing scope. On the one hand, he is reluctant to attribute scientific, technological, or general intellectual advancement solely to the workings of individual minds. In the *Ninth Bridgewater Treatise* (1837), for example, he asserts that we gauge "the intellectual capacity of our race" by "an examination of those productions which have resulted from the loftiest flights of individual genius, or from the accumulated labours of generations of men" (9:4). Although Babbage appears to assign an equal importance to both "individual genius" and ordinary mental "labours," his subsequent observation that these "long-continued exertions" have produced "a body of science . . . surpassing in its extent the creative powers of any individual" subordinates genius to ordinary method and perseverance. The tribute to British inventiveness that opens *The Economy of Machinery and Manufactures* is similarly ambiguous. While Babbage celebrates the "happy exertion of genius," he assigns primary importance to the methodical development of knowledge and expertise through "patient thought" and "repeated experiment" (8:4). On the other hand, he readily affirms the central role of genius in the arts. In his later essay on the Great Exhibition, he argues that the reproduction of works of art enables "genius to be admired by millions whom its single productions would never reach" and describes aesthetic experience as "that admiration which works of genius ever command from cultivated minds" (10:29, 79). Both comments suggest that genius is solely responsible for the best works of art and that one of the main functions of such works is to reveal the genius of their creators.

It is significant, therefore, that the idea of genius enters Babbage's discussion of machinery and manufactures at the precise moment the machine becomes an aesthetic artifact. Throughout his chapter "On Contriving Machinery," Babbage downplays the significance of individual ingenuity and foregrounds the application of specialized knowledge and skills. He describes the invention of new machinery as a methodical process of planning, experimentation, and testing that, like other varieties of scientific investigation, may be facilitated through the division of labor: "The arts of contriving, of drawing, and of executing," he writes, "do not usually reside in their greatest perfection in one individual; and in this as in other arts, *the division of labour* must be applied" (8:186). This rule reflects Babbage's longstanding conviction that science and engineering should be recognized as legitimate professions, a theme he develops at length in his 1830 essay *The Decline of Science* and to which he returns repeatedly in subsequent writings. He laments the "ignorance of the scientific principles, and of the history of their own art" found among amateur "mechanical projectors," and particularly cautions against romanticizing the lone strivings of the "self-constituted engineer," who, "dazzled with the beauty of some, perhaps, really original contrivance" takes up his "new profession" with little sense of the technical expertise and methodical labor necessary for success. Babbage further warns that "the power of making new mechanical combinations is a possession common to a multitude of minds," and he insists that the "great merit" and "great success" of those who achieve eminence for their inventions is "almost entirely due to the unremitted perseverance with which they concentrated upon their successful inventions the skill and knowledge which years of study had matured" (8:186, 187).

Yet despite this celebration of perseverance, expertise, and method, Babbage still attributes the creation of "beautiful" machinery to the workings of genius: "It is however a curious circumstance, that although the power of combining machinery is so common, yet the more beautiful combinations are exceedingly rare. Those which command our admiration equally by the perfection of their effects and the simplicity of their means, are found only amongst the happiest productions of genius" (8:182). This observation is not necessarily at odds with Babbage's portrayal of the development of machinery as a rational, systematic procedure. After all, as in the case of de Prony's logarithmic tables, genius may be responsible for devising specific applications for the division of labor, mental or physical. Nevertheless, while Babbage's appreciation of "beautiful combinations" looks forward to a modernist aesthetic that takes abstract efficiency as a predominant criterion of beauty, he remains unable to account for the creation of such beauty without falling back on familiar Romantic models. The Romantic aesthetic economy still applies, but to the development of technological processes and abstract systems rather than to concrete individual works.

In the final chapter of *The Economy,* a wide-ranging meditation entitled "On the Future Prospects of Manufactures, as Connected with Science," Babbage addresses explicitly a view that runs throughout his treatise, "that the arts and manufactures of the country are intimately connected with the progress of the severer sciences; and that, as we advance in the career of improvement, every step requires, for its success, that this connection should be rendered more intimate" (8:261). This position follows naturally from Babbage's broad understanding of the division of labor, which leads him to see both science and manufacture as subordinate departments of more comprehensive intellectual and economic systems. Since "the division of labour is no less applicable to mental productions than to those in which material bodies are concerned," the best opportunities for advancement in industry "must arise from the combined exertions of all those most skilled in the theory, as well as in the practice of the arts" (8:261). Given this association, Babbage reiterates his contention that "the pursuit of science" should be recognized as a legitimate profession and suggests that "the State" should provide some support to the "cultivators" of its "higher departments," on the grounds that their work contributes to the development of new commercial applications (8:261–62).

Babbage's challenge to the idea that industry has little to learn from science is predicated upon a Baconian sense of the inexhaustible resources of nature and their potential industrial applications. The "crude treasures" of nature do not merely furnish an abundance of raw materials, each of which has the potential to "become the basis of extensive manufactures"; they also offer clues to "other and more valuable principles" that "in their numberless combinations . . . may be destined to furnish, in perpetual succession, new sources of our wealth and of our happiness" (8:265–66). Babbage explains that in contrast to the forces of "molecular attraction" and "gravity," which decrease with distance, the power of knowledge increases with extension, so that "the further we advance from the origin of our knowledge, the larger it becomes, and the greater power it bestows upon its cultivators, to add new fields to its dominions" (8:266). Natural science thus receives sanction as the discipline by which the resources and laws of nature may be "rendered useful to man." Babbage predicts further that "another and a higher science" will come increasingly to control the physical sciences themselves: "It is the science of *calculation* . . . which must ultimately govern the whole of the applications of science to the arts of life" (8:266). This turn is consistent with the drive toward abstraction that characterizes Babbage's thought generally. Just as he identifies the "invention of methods" as the most profound of creative activities and reads manufactures as signs of abstract technological processes, so he sees the material world as ultimately subordinate to pure mathematics, operating through the instrument of the physical sciences.

This utilitarian apology for science and mathematics, however, should not be allowed to obscure Babbage's sincere awe for the sublime inexhaustibility of nature, evident in his repeated recourse to such adjectives as "unlimited," "innumerable," "numberless," "immeasurable," and "countless" (8:265–68). If John Stuart Mill found himself "seriously tormented by the thought of the exhaustibility of musical combinations" (1:149), Babbage labored under no similar anxieties. The "perennial sources of happiness" that Mill finds in the poetry of Wordsworth, Babbage finds in the endless opportunities afforded by nature for scientific inquiry.

The reason for this difference is that Babbage, unlike Mill, understands the expansion of knowledge entirely in relation to its previous limits. Our increasing powers, he explains, "place us at each advance, on some higher eminence, from which the mind contemplates the past, and feels irresistibly convinced, that the whole, already gained, bears a constantly diminishing ratio to that which is contained within the still more rapidly expanding horizon of our knowledge" (8:266). By imagining the domain of knowledge as a vast Cartesian plane, and the knowing mind as occupying a vantage point above it, Babbage conceptualizes scientific progress in terms of a diminishing ratio between the past accumulation of knowledge and the present horizon of possibility. Since each incremental increase enables the mind to ascend yet higher, this horizon is itself always expanding, even as it remains infinitesimal in proportion to nature itself. This complex view entails an intricate mix of optimism and epistemological humility. Even as Babbage celebrates the unlimited powers of the human intellect, he also suggests that it is probable that on some greater scale, human reason is "but, perchance, the lowest step in the gradation of intellectual existence" (8:269).

In such a context, Babbage's proclamations regarding the "continually and rapidly increasing power" (8:266) of knowledge seem less concerned with the subjugation of nature than with the intrinsic development of human intellectual faculties. While Babbage anticipates the increasing "dominion of mind over the material world," he never suggests or even hopes that humanity will attain absolute control over "the creation submitted to its power" (8:268). Ultimately, science is not justified by its utilitarian applications; rather, those applications are merely a means of tracing in the material world the progressive expansion of human intellect. In a broad sense, then, Babbage's account of the mind's advance may be taken as an inflection of what M. H. Abrams identifies as a distinctively Romantic concern with the maturation of human creative power and the unfolding of a "universal history" (225).

More immediately, it may be read as an intervention in an ongoing discussion among Romantic literary figures of the relationship between poetry and science. In a formulation echoed by Hazlitt, De Quincey, Ruskin, and others, Wordsworth asserts a philosophical "contradistinction" between "Poetry" and "Science" (749 n). Yet it would be a mistake to follow John Stuart Mill in interpreting this distinction as a necessary opposition (Carr 247–48). For Wordsworth, science is not so much, as Mill suggests, the "logical opposite" (1:344) of poetry as it is a kindred but lesser form of knowledge. Wordsworth's comparison in the 1802 "Preface" to *Lyrical Ballads* between "the Poet" and "the Man of Science" begins with an assertion of their affiliation, and it is only against this background of similarity that he distinguishes between science and poetry. "The knowledge both of the Poet and the Man of Science is pleasure," Wordsworth asserts, before differentiating between them: "The Man of Science seeks truth as a remote and unknown benefactor; he cherishes and loves it in his solitude: the Poet, singing a song in which all human beings join with him, rejoices in the presence of truth as our visible friend and hourly companion." In Wordsworth's eyes, the knowledge of the poet is universal or "necessary," while that of the scientist is specialized or "personal." Moreover, he describes poetry as inherently communal but science as a solitary pursuit that fosters "no habitual and direct sympathy" between human beings. Such distinctions establish not an "antithesis" but a hierarchy between different modes of knowing. As "the first and last of all knowledge," poetry naturally subsumes the "particular" and "individual" findings of science (752–53).

Wordsworth reinforces this view by presenting poetry as science's successor and mediator: "If the labours of men of Science should ever create any material revolution, direct or indirect, in our condition, and in the impressions which we habitually receive, the Poet will sleep then no more than at present, but he will be ready to follow the steps of the man of Science, not only in those general indirect effects, but he will be at his side, carrying sensation into the midst of the objects of the Science itself" (753). This injunction applies not just to the tangible material transformations produced by industrialization but also to the transformations in consciousness that accompany the development and dissemination of new technologies and scientific theories. One of the crucial tasks of the poet in an era of scientific and technological change is to humanize scientific speculation by leavening it with "sensation" and thereby helping it "to put on, as it were, a form of flesh and blood."

Babbage, a longtime proponent of the professionalization and institutionalization of science in Britain, strenuously objected to this sort of characterization of science as a solitary, arcane, and vaguely inhuman sort of endeav-or. He rejected the image of the "man of science" laboring in isolation and emphasized instead the communal nature of the scientific enterprise. Com-menting on the British Association for the Advancement of Science, an organization he helped to create, Babbage notes that the periodic assembly of independent researchers "always produces an excitement which is favour-able to the development of new ideas."[13] Indeed, he celebrates such gatherings for fostering the very sort of communion Wordsworth so values, calling their "greatest benefit" the "intercourse which they cannot fail to promote between the different classes of society" (8:263). Moreover, Babbage troubles Wordsworth's notion that the scientist "seeks truth as a remote and unknown benefactor" by pointing out that even pure research has practical implica-tions: "The applied sciences derive their facts from experiment; but the rea-sonings, on which their chief utility depends, are the province of what is called abstract science" (8:261). He thus counters romanticized notions of scientific practice by holding up the entire apparatus of British institutional science and emphasizing its critical social and economic importance.

Challenging the general Romantic tendency to privilege sensation over abstract intellect, Babbage inverts the relationship between science and poetry exemplified in Wordsworth's "Preface." Whereas Wordsworth treats poetry as the humanization of science, Babbage presents science as the culmination of poetry. With the development of steam power, he writes, "the imprisoned winds which the earliest poet made the Grecian warrior bear for the protec-tion of his fragile bark" have been "called at the command of science, from their shadowy existence" and made "the obedient slaves of civilized man" (8:268). Likewise, with a nod to Swift and to his own calculating engine, Babbage observes that recent innovations have rivaled the wildest flights of the literary imagination: "[A]s if in mockery of the College of Laputa, light almost solar has been extracted from the refuse of fish; fire has been sifted by the lamp of Davy; and machinery has been taught arithmetic instead of poetry" (8:268). In contrast to Wordsworth, who describes poetry as lending scientific abstractions a palpable "form of flesh and blood," Babbage por-trays science as giving material being to the "unreal creations" of the poetic imagination through an ongoing succession of technological innovations.

Babbage concludes the final chapter of *The Economy* by giving this vindi-cation of science and industry a theological turn. "But if science has called into real existence the visions of the poet," he writes, it has also "conferred on the moralist an obligation of surpassing weight" by having "placed before him resistless evidence of immeasurable design" (8:268). The most influential early nineteenth-century exposition of this thesis is, of course, Dr. William Paley's *Natural Theology.*[14] Paley's speculations are resolutely anthropocentric. The evidence of design he perceives throughout the universe reassures him that humanity is subject to a divine superintendence. "[I]n the first place," he argues, "we can trace an identity of plan, a connection of system, from Saturn to our own globe; and when arrived upon our globe, we can, in the second place, pursue the connection through all the organized, especially the animated, bodies which it supports." In such a universe, humanity has "no reason to fear . . . being forgotten, or overlooked, or neglected" (397). Paley's contemplations of distant planetary bodies thus lead him to the comforting conclusion that humanity occupies a central place in creation.

Babbage's reflections on "human reason," in contrast, lead him to ponder the more general order of the universe:

> For, since every portion of our own material globe, and every animated being it supports, afford, on more scrutinizing enquiry, more perfect evidence of design, it would indeed be most unphilosophical to believe that those sister spheres, obedient to the same law, and glowing with light and heat radiant from the same central source . . . should each be no more than a floating chaos of unformed matter; or, being all the work of the same Almighty Architect, that no living eye should be gladdened by their forms of beauty, that no intellectual being should expand its faculties in decyphering their laws. (8:269)

In essence, Babbage surmises on aesthetic grounds the existence of intelligent, extraterrestrial life. If the "perfect evidence of design" afforded by the material universe implies the existence of an "Almighty Architect," it also implies the existence of a "living eye" capable of being "gladdened" by the "forms of beauty" this Architect has created. Unlike the youthful "gladness" of the poet, as Wordsworth describes it in "Resolution and Independence," the kind of pleasure to which Babbage refers is primarily cognitive. Exploiting the conventional association of vision with mind, he imagines the universal aesthetic faculty in the manner of Emerson's "transparent eyeball," as the "living eye" of a specifically "intellectual being." If Romantic aesthetic theory affirms the primacy of embodied sensation, Babbage subordinates bodily feeling to the more rarefied pleasure of intellectual contemplation. He thus ends *The Economy* as he began it, riveted by mechanical beauty.

In his *Ninth Bridgewater Treatise,* first published in 1837, Babbage himself takes up the burden of "the moralist." This rather disjointed essay (Babbage himself labels it "a fragment") was not a sanctioned contribution to the

Bridgewater series but an answer to Whewell's assertion in the third Bridge-water treatise that mechanical philosophers and mathematicians had no authority to speculate on theological matters. Babbage's treatise is not particularly noteworthy from a theological perspective, but it does have real significance as a further expression of the heightened appreciation for abstract systems that informs his work on the calculating engines and his earlier study of industry. In *The Economy*, the theoretical consideration of this subject is inevitably subordinated to more concrete concerns, but *The Ninth Bridge-water Treatise* (perhaps because of its necessarily speculative nature) gives sustained attention to theoretical issues that are crucial to Babbage's analysis of machinery and manufactures.

In the treatise Babbage defends the theory of creation by design by using an extended analogy between the phenomenal universe and the output of his calculating engines to argue that a mechanistic model of the universe can, in fact, accommodate the evidence of biological and geological change being amassed by the natural sciences. Just as his engines computed mathematical series according to preset rules, so, he speculates, there must exist "some few simple and general principles, by which the whole of the material universe is sustained, and from which its infinitely varied phenomena emerge as the necessary consequences" (9:5). Like his model of the factory, this theological view is predicated upon an ideal of the perfect productive system: one that is self-acting, all-encompassing, infinitely flexible, and infinitely durable. This ideal is itself informed by his lifelong concern with signification. Just as he treats machines as material instantiations of abstract concepts and ideas, and manufactures as signs of the abstract processes through which they were produced, so, in his theological writings, he represents the material universe as a vast assemblage of printed "characters," intended to convey the "truths of natural religion" to those capable of interpreting them (9:xv). In his theology, we hear not only echoes of a nearly antiquated theory of creation by design but also an anticipation of Stephen Dedalus's proclamation: "Signatures of all things I am here to read, seaspawn and seawrack, the nearing tide, that rusty boot. Snotgreen, bluesilver, rust: coloured signs" (J. Joyce 31). This understanding of material creation as an act of semiosis is a principal marker of Babbage's modernity.

Throughout his life, Babbage attributed tremendous value to unambiguous systems of signification, and he was deeply concerned with their potential subversion and decay, whether through intentional deception or through inevitable error. He repeatedly noted the personal and economic costs of faulty or fraudulent information, and he was captivated by the art of deciphering.[15]

Not surprisingly, Babbage was particularly fascinated by wordplay, which he recognized as a kind of limiting case in linguistic signification. At one point in his career, he even began preparations for a treatise on wit, although he ultimately abandoned the project out of fear that it would distract him from "more important enquires" (11:272). While he takes evident pleasure in the well-turned phrase, he also demonstrates an almost morbid preoccupation with the errors and misunderstandings that arise in linguistic communication. He professes a real admiration for jokes that turn on "the intimate meaning of the words employed" but claims to find puns "detestable" (11:272–73). Nevertheless, many of the amusing anecdotes he recounts in his memoir turn precisely on the ambiguities that arise from multiple meanings and similarities of pronunciation. For example, Babbage recalls that while traveling in France with his friend John Herschel, they ordered two boiled eggs apiece for breakfast: "pour *chacun deux.*" The waiter, however, called out to the kitchen, "Il faut faire bouillir *cinquante-deux* oeufs pour Messieurs les Anglais." Babbage was so overcome with laughter at the waiter's "absurd misunderstanding" that he was barely able to explain it to Herschel, who immediately ran to the kitchen to countermand the order (11:145, emphasis added).

This episode is humorous because it is trivial, but in general Babbage was deeply troubled by the propensity of messages to alter during their transmission, and his anxiety in this respect exerted a definitive influence on his theology and philosophy of science. In his memoir, *Passages from the Life of a Philosopher,* he illustrates the problematic nature of religious testimony by likening it to the parlor game "Russian scandal" (or "telephone," as it is now known), which turns to amusement the corruption of a verbal message as it is passed from person to person. His argument hinges on a distinction between divine "revelation," the possibility of which Babbage readily acknowledges, and "human testimony," about which he is profoundly dubious (11:298). Babbage accepts Dr. Johnson's definition of inspiration as "an overpowering impression . . . made upon the mind by God Himself," but he adds that "as such, it is not revelation to any *other* human being" (11:298). As Babbage notes, the term *revelation* is commonly applied not only to direct acts or manifestations of God (its proper meaning) but also to the impressions made by those events on inspired persons, to those persons' accounts of their experiences, to written transcriptions of those accounts, and finally, to translations of those transcriptions into various languages (11:299). As in the game of Russian scandal, every step in this process contributes to the alteration of the original message: "[W]ithout the least want of good faith at any stage, the mere imperfection of language will necessarily vary the terms by which it is described" (11:300). Although verbal communications are most susceptible to such corruption, written accounts are also affected. Manuscript copies by different persons typically contain discrepancies, and even in the case of total agreement, alterations in the meanings of words over time introduce a "perpetual source of doubt as to the exact interpretation" of a given text. Because of the propensity of testimony to decay, Babbage regards the direct observation of nature as the most reliable source of religious knowledge: "The testimony of man becomes fainter at every stage of transmission, whilst each new enquiry into the works of the Almighty gives to us more exalted views of His wisdom, His goodness, and His power" (11:301–2).

On this basis, Babbage speculates in *The Ninth Bridgewater Treatise* that science will eventually succeed revelation as the basis of religious belief (9:47), but his analogy between the universe and the output of his calculating engine locks him into an almost Humean skepticism. If the elements of the material universe are like the mathematical terms generated by his calculating engine, then all that empirical observation can do is document patterns in the phenomenal world. It cannot reveal the laws governing those phenomenal patterns; it can only furnish an always incomplete body of data from which those laws can be provisionally inferred. As in the final chapter of *The Economy*, an acute awareness of the profound limitations of human understanding shadows Babbage's confident faith in the power of science. He recognizes that there is no way to prove absolutely the truth of inferences based on observation alone, and so he is forced to appeal to divine benevolence to guarantee the validity of his empirical method: "In absolute ignorance of any—even the smallest link of those chains which bind life to matter, or that still more miraculous one, which connects mind with both, we can pursue our path only by the feeble light of analogy, and humbly hope that the Being, whose power and benevolence are unbounded, may enable us, in some further stage of our existence, *to read another page in the history of His mighty works*" (9:16, emphasis added).

With this statement, Babbage all but identifies the phenomenal world as a vast tissue of signs. This position follows directly from his analogy between God's creative power and the operation of his own calculating engines. Babbage designed his Difference Engine to eliminate not only errors in calculation but also errors in transcription. In one plan, the engine would feed pieces of movable type to a human operator, who would then assemble them for printing. In a subsequent and better plan, Babbage eliminated the need for manual intervention by having the machine itself impress its results directly onto tablets of soft plaster, which when hardened could be used as molds for casting plates of type (Hyman 54–55). At the core of Babbage's essay lies his conviction that the material universe is similarly constructed. Just as the Difference Engine eliminated errors in transcription by impressing its results on a substrate of plaster, so God eliminates the need for human testimony by impressing religious truth on the substrate of matter: "[T]he truths of natural religion rest on foundations far stronger than those of any human testimony; . . . they are impressed in indelible characters, by almighty power, on every fragment of the material world" (9:xv). Babbage's idiosyncratic comparison between God's creative power and the power of his calculating engine thus converges with the far more canonical image of creation as the Book of Nature.

Just as Babbage represents the unfolding results of preordained laws of creation as a kind of printing, so he also associates the perturbations introduced by free will with speech. In a peculiar digression, he imagines the Last Judgment as a moment of reckoning at which every person would be called to account for the utterances of a lifetime, preserved forever in the reverberating molecules of the atmosphere: "The air itself is one vast library, on whose pages are forever written all that man has ever said or woman whispered. There, in their mutable but unerring characters, mixed with the earliest, as well as with the latest sighs of mortality, stand for ever recorded, vows unredeemed, promises unfulfilled, perpetuating in the united movements of each particle, the testimony of man's changeful will" (9:36). This strange notion, like his other theological views, works by analogy to the calculating engine. Since the engine computed new terms from those which preceded them, it was in principle self-supervising; its final state would reflect every event that occurred over the course of its operation. Similarly, in Babbage's rigorously Newtonian cosmos, the present arrangement of matter serves as a record of everything that has come before. This property enables God to exercise complete surveillance over all human affairs without having to attend to or intervene in them directly. Like Bentham, Babbage holds that writing can mitigate the deficiencies of memory and speech, but he trumps Bentham by envisioning the atmosphere itself as an ideal instrument of disciplinary surveillance, one that is ubiquitous, automatic, infallible, and invisible.[16]

As in his writings on machinery and manufactures, however, Babbage is unwilling to forgo his commitment to the idea of free human will. As Catherine Gallagher has shown, the debates over industrialism that took place during the 1830s and 1840s were riven by contradictory commitments to free will and determinism, commitments that manifest themselves as narrative ruptures within the industrial novel (*Industrial Reformation*, chaps. 1–4). That Babbage's theological speculations, as well as the semiotic theory on which they are based, are similarly conflicted marks them as products of these debates. In the moral universe as in the factory or workshop, Babbage looks to accurate record keeping to guarantee social control, but he also allows for the free play of imagination. If he envisions the ideal factory as a rigorously deterministic system, he also insists on the necessity of inventive "genius," without which innovation could not occur. His theology and his philosophy of science likewise require that human beings be free intellectual agents, capable of independently reading and interpreting the "indelible characters" impressed upon the material world. Although the entire argument of *The Ninth Bridgewater Treatise* is directed against the necessity of divine intervention, Babbage can reconcile his conflicting commitments to determinism and free will only by postulating a benevolent Creator to warrant the veracity of these signs. Ultimately, his elaborate argument for the superiority of empirical science over testimony as a basis of religious belief is based on a simple faith that a divine manufacturer would not attempt to pass off fraudulent goods on an unsuspecting humanity.

In the actual world of nineteenth-century commerce, however, there were no such guarantees. In *The Economy*, Babbage describes at length the dampening effect of fraud and deception on commerce and trade. He observes that the practice of forging the names and marks of reputable makers had, by the 1830s, all but destroyed the export market for British watches. He notes that unscrupulous manufacturers have been known to weave stockings in a uniform width from knee to calf, and then wet and stretch them on frames to give them an appropriate shape (8:98). He cites a parliamentary report attributing the decline of the British lace trade *"more to the making of fraudulent and bad articles, than to the war, or any other cause"* (8:97). His objections, however, are more than merely practical. As I have been arguing, Babbage's admiration for manufactures is predicated upon his (distinctly modern) sense that they exemplify the technological processes through which they were produced and, in this way, facilitate the appreciation of these processes' ingenuity and beauty. In *The Economy*, he expresses such great concern over the prevalence of fraud in manufacture and commerce because it throws into question the semiotic upon which the whole edifice of his progressive, utilitarian program was grounded. He condemns fraudulent articles not because they are inexpensively made but because they are not what they purport to be: "although good to the eye," they are in fact imposters, imitations of higher classes of manufacture (8:97). They thus threaten the commercial order in the same way that the conditions of anonymity and class mobility characteristic of capitalist modernity unsettle traditional social hierarchies.

Such misrepresentations, Babbage recognizes, have a significant effect on price. After acknowledging the standard belief that prices are set by the relation of supply to demand, he proceeds to examine several other factors that influence price, including the durability of goods (8:104–6), the available supply of money (8:107–14), and most insightfully, the cost of verification (8:95–103). Regarding this last factor, Babbage notes that the cost to the purchaser of any article is not simply its price but its price plus the cost of verifying that the article is in fact what the purchaser has contracted to buy. When the quality of an article is evident on inspection, there will be a good deal of uniformity in price at different shops. When such verification is difficult or expensive, however, it can significantly alter the means by which certain articles are produced and distributed, as well as the profit margins on their sale.

Almost twenty years after the first publication of *The Economy,* Babbage revisited this issue in an extended essay on the Great Exhibition entitled *The Exposition of 1851.* Whereas *The Economy* is a forward-looking celebration of industry written out of Babbage's enthusiasm for his own technological project the Difference Engine, this later essay is highly critical in tone, evincing its author's indignation at not being invited to participate in the planning of the exhibition.[17] Nevertheless, *The Exposition of 1851* is an important supplement to *The Economy of Machinery and Manufactures,* since it explicitly elaborates on several issues of crucial importance to Babbage's semiotic of manufacture, including the relationship between the "fine" and the "industrial" arts, the nature of the commodity form, and the role of the intellect in aesthetic appreciation.

Although Babbage discusses a number of the policies instituted by the Royal Commission that governed the exhibition, he is particularly critical of its prohibition against prices. Seeking to placate London merchants worried about their markets, and fearing that the open display of prices would inhibit spectators from receiving more important lessons in technology and taste, the commission adopted an equivocal policy that sought to recognize the importance of price in assessing exhibits while withholding this information from the general public.[18] As Henry Cole reports in the introduction to the *Official Descriptive and Illustrated Catalogue*, "[a]fter much examination and inquiry, the Commissioners resolved that prices were not to be affixed to the articles exhibited, although the articles might be marked as shown for economy of production, and the price stated in an invoice to be sent to the Commissioners for the information of the Juries" (15). Attempting to foster "commercial industry" without encouraging "direct commerce" (Cole, Introduction 1), the commission treated price as a kind of secret knowledge, to be made available only to officially sanctioned observers who could be counted on to use it responsibly. Nevertheless, spectators were implicitly encouraged to inquire about the commercial availability of items on display, and many exhibitors distributed advertisements and price lists (Auerbach 120). Prices, in other words, were treated almost as a kind of pornography, at once shameful yet titillating, extraneous yet captivating, censored yet readily available.

Babbage was incensed by this attitude, which he felt amounted to an official sanction of fraud and deception. In his view, the prohibition did not merely place the interests of a narrow class of commercial "middlemen" over those of consumers (10:58); it also hampered the Great Exhibition's "utility" as a source of technical and economic knowledge. "The price in money," he maintains, "is the *most important element* in every bargain; to omit it, is not less absurd than to represent a tragedy without its hero, or to paint a portrait without a nose" (10:49). Hearkening back to his discussion of "verification" in *The Economy*, Babbage argues that prices convey important information about articles' composition and manufacture. An unexpectedly low price might indicate that an article "had been manufactured in some mode entirely different from that usually practised" or that the material of which it is composed "*could not* be genuine" (10:48). Reliable information about prices in effect allows inferior manufactures to assume a kind of honest humility, since it precludes them from being mistaken for—or masquerading as—better classes of goods.

Conversely, the prohibition against their display at the Great Exhibition greatly impeded the collection of useful knowledge: "The philosopher and the economist, by whose researches and comparisons the public might have been instructed, wander through the lofty avenues and splendid galleries of the Crystal Palace, tantalized by expectations, raised but to be disappointed. They at last are compelled to abandon their mission in hopeless despair, wilfully deprived, by the managers of this industrial feast, of that information on which all their conclusions must ultimately rest" (10:58–59). The ironic consequence of the Royal Commission's embrace of an inappropriate mode of representation was that, by treating the objects on display as if they were products of the fine arts, it transformed what might have been an instructive exhibition into a largely meaningless phantasmagoria, a collection "of little intrinsic use" if still "a very agreeable and splendid show" (10:57). By eliminating an important marker of class distinctions among things, the ban on prices in fact encouraged the very sort of carnivalesque spectacle it was meant to forestall.

In the light of recent critical discussions of the Great Exhibition, however, Babbage's complaint seems also a nostalgic reaction to what might be described as the transformation of "manufactures" into "commodities." A number of scholars have argued that the prohibition against the display of prices reflected and contributed to the general mystification of "things" in commodity culture.[19] If this assessment is correct, then Babbage's protestations notwithstanding, price was simply not the "most important element" in the new, overdetermined notion of the object served up at Cole's "industrial feast." Babbage, though, resisted the exaltation of the commodity form not only because he accepted "exchange" as "the great and ultimate object of the Exposition" (10:49) but also because he perceived that what Thomas Richards calls the "semiotics of commodity spectacle" (38)—in which the order of commodities constitutes a closed system of signification—conflicted with his own semiotic of manufacture. He recognized that the emergence of the commodity form, in liberating manufactures from their modes of production, also precluded them from signifying the technical processes through which they were created. If, as Richards argues, the English response to the revolutionary foment of 1848 was "to begin to confer the privileges of bourgeois individualism on manufactured things" (59), then Babbage wished to keep commodities in feudal thrall to industrial processes of production.

The phenomenon of commodity spectacle, Richards suggests, depends upon the dissolution of the distinction between commercial valuation and aesthetic appreciation. The Great Exhibition, he tells us, contributed to this process by elevating the simple "object of exchange" into "a consolidated image, a visible ideal, and an object of contemplation" (39). Babbage, in contrast, attempts to defend his semiotic of manufacture from the encroachment of commodity spectacle by resisting the erosion of the boundary between what he calls the "fine" and the "industrial" arts. Unlike the School of Design theorists, Babbage does not attempt to reconcile art and manufacture by adducing formal aesthetic principles to govern the "design" of manufactured objects.[20] Instead, he insists that the fine and the industrial arts "are separated by a sufficiently definite line of demarcation" to warrant an exclusively industrial exhibition:

> The characteristic of the fine arts is, that each example is an individual—the production of individual taste, and executed by individual hands; the produce of the fine arts is therefore necessarily costly. The characteristic of the industrial arts is, that each example is but one of a multitude—generated according to the same law, by tools or machines (in the largest sense of those terms), and moved with unerring precision by the application of physical force. Their produce is consequently cheap. (10:29)

This distinction recapitulates the contrast between "making" and "manufacturing" elaborated in *The Economy*. Just as the maker produces only a small number of unique articles, so the fine arts rely on what Walter Benjamin calls an aesthetic of "presence," in which aesthetic value is created by personal expression and the created object's "unique existence at the place where it happens to be" (222). Likewise, just as the manufacturer produces "a very large number" of (ideally) identical articles, so the industrial arts rely upon what may be called an aesthetic of "process," in which manufactured articles achieve their effect by signifying the "unerring precision" of the processes by which they were produced.

In this aesthetic of process, the emphasis is not on the unique identities of individual objects but on "identity" of form replicated across an entire "multitude." It is important to recognize that Babbage is differentiating between categories of techniques or "arts" rather than between categories of objects. This emphasis allows him to circumvent the restrictive parameters that hamper more conventional efforts to distinguish between the fine and industrial arts in terms of utility or form. Unlike Wornum, Redgrave, and other contemporary advocates of design education, Babbage does not champion a "functional" style or condemn the Victorian penchant for elaborate ornamentation, nor does he look to the fine arts for principles of design appropriate to manufactures. This is not to suggest that he views material form as irrelevant to aesthetic judgment but only that he considers it an improper basis for appreciating the industrial arts. With respect to the fine arts themselves, Babbage embraces the neoclassical view that they "idealize nature by generalizing from its individual objects." With respect to the industrial arts, he values form only as *that which is replicated* in the process of manufacture. The beauty of the industrial arts follows from the degree to which they "realize identity by the unbounded use of the principle of copying." His focus is not on the formal qualities of *copies* but on the diverse applications of "the principle of *copying*" (10:29, emphasis added).

This framing of the matter enables Babbage to argue that the fine and the industrial arts are in fact complementary: "The union of the two, enlarging vastly the utility of both, enables art to be appreciated and genius to be admired by millions whom its single productions would never reach; whilst the producer in return, elevated by the continual presence of the multiplied reproductions of the highest beauty, acquires a new source of pleasure, and feels his own mechanical art raised in his estimation by such an alliance" (10:29). The first of these contentions follows from two basic assumptions: first, that maximum utility means the greatest happiness for the greatest number, and second, that a reproduction of a given work of art will elicit the same response as the original. Because reproductions enable a work of art to be experienced by a wider number of people, they must necessarily increase its "utility." This position is a refinement of Babbage's observation in *The Economy* that the economic value of any original depends upon the number of copies it is used to produce. Significantly, one of the main illustrations of this principle in *The Economy* concerns the replication of works of art: the ability to accurately and cheaply reproduce the "figures of the sculptor" through casting, he writes, "promises to give additional value to his productions, and to diffuse more widely the pleasure arising from their possession" (8:72). If in *The Economy* Babbage seems to view (aesthetic) pleasure as something distinct from (economic) value, he comes by 1851 to treat them both as different aspects of the same general quality.

At first glance, Babbage's contention regarding the elevating effect of reproductions of works of art appears to echo a proposition central to the discourse on design—that exposure to fine art will exercise a necessary cultivating influence on manufacturers and the manufacturing population. The artists and critics involved in the Victorian design movement generally found this view highly appealing because, in ratifying the cultural authority of art, it also ratified their own professional status. Babbage, however, is more interested in identifying the ways in which the fine arts can facilitate the appreciation of technological processes. The "new source of pleasure" that arises from the "continual presence" of reproductions is not an aesthetic one in the conventional nineteenth-century sense, since the simultaneous presence of "multiplied reproductions" gives the lie to the fiction upon which that experience depends, "that each example is an individual—the production of individual taste, and executed by individual hands" (10:29). What the simultaneous presence of reproductions does encourage is an appreciation for the "unerring precision" with which an original has been replicated. This sort of pleasure is only enhanced when copies differ in size, because variations in scale emphasize congruities of form. As Babbage explains, "The Venus de Medici itself could not be justly excluded from a purely industrial exhibition—if placed in the centre of a series diminishing on the one side to a statuette of a foot high, and increasing on the other to a figure double her own height." Such a series would have an ancillary importance to the fine arts, by demonstrating "the effect of change of magnitude, when the proportions remain identical" (10:31). The industrial arts thus enable the aesthetic effects of scale to be studied in a way that would be impossible without mechanical reproduction.

Like Prince Albert, Cole, Wornum, and a host of others, Babbage viewed the Great Exhibition as an exemplary opportunity to shape British "taste" with respect to the industrial arts. Where he departs from them is in his insistence that the "pleasure" to be had from the contemplation of the industrial arts is not affective or even moral, but intellectual. It need never be feared, he maintains, that "a knowledge of the *grounds* of that admiration which works of genius ever command from cultivated minds, should diminish the pleasure derived from their contemplation" (10:79). Again recalling the argument of *The Economy*, Babbage asserts that if you explain to a person the "simple means and the beautiful combinations" by which seemingly mysterious technological marvels are brought into being, "you then raise him in his own estimation" by dispelling that false wonder born of ignorance (10:80). This is precisely what Gaskell's John Thornton attempts to do in his conversation with the Reverend Hale. By enlightening him about the operation of the steam hammer, Thornton hopes to instill in him an informed appreciation for the intellectual triumph that great machine represents. Such appreciation, Babbage insists, does not lead to pride or arrogance but rather, as he argues in both *The Economy* and *The Ninth Bridgewater Treatise*, to a profound humility before the "immeasurable design" (8:268) evident in the material universe. The "studious disciple" of technology will ultimately conclude, Babbage holds, that "the only distance which is really *immense*, is that existing between the perfection of the highest work of human skill and the simplest of the productions of nature" (10:80).

This focus on nature's intricate mechanisms fundamentally separates Babbage from Romantic aesthetic theorists like Ruskin who viewed the sort of intellectual appreciation Babbage advocates as a threat to proper aesthetic sensibility. Two years before the opening of the Great Exhibition, Ruskin was prompted by his sense of "the way in which the investigation of strata and structure reduces all mountain sublimity to mere debris and wall-building" to begin an essay entitled "The Uses of Ignorance," which he later aborted (9:xxiii). Ruskin's thesis, it seems safe to presume, was that a culti-vated ignorance could prevent the intellect from interfering with immediate aesthetic "feeling." In a later letter to Charles Eliot Norton, Ruskin applies this notion to his own study of the architecture of Venice. Instead of en-hancing his appreciation for the city, his investigations merely transformed it into "so many 'mouldings.'" "Analysis," Ruskin generalizes, "is an abomi-nable business. . . . One only feels as one should when one doesn't know much about the matter" (9:xxvii–xxviii).

Babbage, for his part, expresses disdain for those who fear the contact of taste "with the more sober powers of reasoning, lest the process of analysis should disenchant its visionary scenes, and dissolve the unreal basis of their delight" (10:80). If the principles of taste are "as general . . . as those which relate to physics" (10:79), they must also be susceptible to the same sort of investigation and analysis. What began as an argument for the compatibility and complementarity of technical knowledge and aesthetic experience becomes in the end an argument for the priority of intellect over affect. In effect, Babbage turns his technological aesthetic inward, taking the analysis of aesthetic experience itself as an additional source of intellectual pleasure:

> Taste united with an intimate knowledge of its principles, and still more if conjoined with the power of eliminating from the fleeting relations amongst the objects of its attention, those resemblances which, when sufficiently mul-tiplied and defined, lead up to the discovery of higher generalizations, confers upon its enviable possessor a double source of happiness; it adds the delight of an intellectual triumph to those romantic feelings which are excited by the beautiful, the lovely, or the sublime in nature, or which are suggested by the most perfect representations of art. (10:80)

Allying himself with a tradition of aestheticism that runs at least through Pater, Babbage defines appreciation as a sort of discrimination, as a process of differentiating the kinds of true associations available to the imagination from the false or accidental conjunctions that arise from mere fancy. However, by insisting that the joys of intellectual triumph can enhance the pleasures derived from the contemplation of the "beautiful," the "lovely" (or pictur-esque), and the "sublime," Babbage also subordinates these central categories of Romantic aesthetic experience to the sense of intellectual triumph that comes from discerning the mechanisms that sustain them. It is this familiar emphasis on abstract systems and principles that connects Babbage's attitude toward taste with his more general views on science, technology, and religion: "In the fine arts, and in the arts of industry, as well as in the pursuits of science, the highest department of each is that of the discovery of principles, and the invention of methods." In each of these three broad areas of human activity, the discovery of methods "surpasses all other discoveries, for it supplies tools for the use of intellect, and enlarges the limits and powers of human reason" (10:81). Babbage here does not simply integrate the arts into his general vision of an accelerating "domain of mind over the material world" (8:35). He also shows art, industry, and science to be complementary spheres of human activity. It is this position, ultimately, that marks him as a chief early proponent of the idea of an industrial culture.

CHAPTER THREE

"A Debilitated Race"

SAVAGENESS IN SOCIAL INVESTIGATION AND DESIGN THEORY

IN HIS 1830 review of Southey's *Colloquies,* the Whig historian and politician Thomas Babington Macaulay writes: "The savages were wretched, says Mr. Southey; but the people in the time of Sir Thomas More were happier than either they or we. Now we think it quite certain that we have the advantage over the contemporaries of Sir Thomas More, in every point in which they had any advantage over savages" (257). Neither Southey's contention nor Macaulay's, of course, really depends upon the actual happiness of primeval "savages." For both writers, the idea of the savage functions rhetorically, as a baseline against which industrial civilization can be measured and judged. Macaulay, in other words, is not disputing Southey on factual grounds. He is objecting to the way in which Southey uses the image of savages to trace an arch of progress and decline that implicitly associates the industrial present with some "wretched," primeval state. Ruskin, in "The Nature of Gothic," also recognizes (at least implicitly) that the overdetermined images of savageness running through treatments of the manufacturing population and discussions of industrial design localize a specific anxiety in early nineteenth-century proindustrial discourse. By taking his most prominent celebration of Gothic "savageness" as the occasion for his first major attack on modern manufacture, he obliquely challenges the basic presumption upon which the entire concept of an industrial culture was predicated: that industrial progress and aesthetic development are not only compatible but in fact mutually sustaining.

Throughout the second quarter of the nineteenth century, proponents of industry had to confront widespread perceptions that automatic manufacture had fostered two serious sorts of decline: a dangerous degeneration of the working classes, evident in their malformed bodies and blunted moral sensibilities, and an equally disturbing deterioration of public taste, evident in the garish ugliness of early Victorian manufactures and in the consuming public's seemingly insatiable appetite for them. Baines, Ure, Cooke Taylor, and Babbage largely sidestep this issue by aestheticizing the *processes* of manufacture. Baines and Cooke Taylor romanticize the factory system by presenting its maturation as a culminating moment in the organic development of the English people. Ure recognizes in factories themselves an organic complexity and unity that rivals that of the finest works of poetry, art, and music. Babbage, more abstractly, emphasizes the intellectual beauty of the techniques and methods he finds embodied in manufactures and mechanical systems. Commentators more directly concerned with mechanized industry's human and material *products,* however, could not similarly avoid the apparent contradiction between industry's continuing progress, on the one hand, and the physical, moral, and aesthetic retrogression it seemed to foster, on the other. Their particular rhetorical challenge was to develop strategies for addressing this problematic disjuncture that did not also entail the wholesale condemnation of industrial capitalism.

Images of savageness became crucial tokens in early Victorian efforts to resolve this conundrum. In studies of the manufacturing population, such images worked to naturalize class distinctions even as they supported various proposals for the "improvement" of the working classes. The "savage" manners and appearance of the working classes—especially those segments rendered apparently superfluous or redundant by the march of industrial progress, such as Irish immigrant laborers or displaced handloom weavers—were presented as both causes and symptoms of the dangerous social decline that had accompanied the rise of automatic manufacture (Berg 137–44). In some cases, such representations served to vindicate mechanized industry by identifying alternative causes for Britain's social crises. In others, they gave expression to an anxiety that the factory system itself was contributing to the apparent degeneration of the working classes. In contemporaneous discussions of the decorative arts, beautifully decorated "savage" arts functioned in a similar dual capacity. From one perspective, they seemed to demonstrate that aesthetic refinement did not correlate with technological sophistication or, even more seriously, that technological progress could in fact encourage aesthetic retrogression. From another perspective, however, they testified both to a universal human desire for beauty and to the existence of universal aesthetic laws through which this desire could be satisfied. If "savage" peoples demonstrated a powerful aesthetic sense, the thinking went, it was because they lived in intimate contact with nature. Conversely, if the taste of "civilized" peoples had been perverted by the rise of industry, it could be restored by distilling from nature a body of objective aesthetic principles applicable to industrial manufacture. The example of savage handicraft productions, therefore, warranted the emerging discourse on industrial design, even as it provided a concrete measure of the aesthetic decline brought on by industrialization.

THESE KINDS of appeals are consistent with the particular function of the idea of savageness in liberal social and economic theory in general, which is to throw into relief the positive qualities of commercial society. In eighteenth-century conjectural history, a "savage state" was postulated as the first of four stages through which all societies pass in their natural evolution toward commercial capitalism. Unless their development were to be artificially arrested or accelerated, it was presumed, societies would emerge from an initial condition of savageness, pass through intermediate pastoral and agrarian stages, and eventually mature into complex commercial civilizations (Meek 2). In classical political economy, which takes this body of thought as one of its main progenitors, the concept of a savage state likewise serves as what one contemporary observer calls "a sort of zero in the thermometer of civilization" (Herman Merrivale, qtd. in Berg 136). It operates as a theoretical horizon of poverty and social chaos against which the inexorable progress of civilization can be gauged. In this capacity, savageness represents not simply the absence of those qualities understood to typify a state of advanced civilization (such as a naturally emergent class structure, an intricate division of labor, and an accumulation of capital reserves) but also the negation of the dialectical reconciliation of discipline and desire upon which commercial capitalism depends. In the savage state, self-enforced renunciation does not culminate in acquisition and consumption. Rather, contradictory yet coexisting drives toward indolence and excess fundamentally preclude the kind of cooperative social action needed to sustain an advanced society. Similarly, the individual savage is viewed not simply as lacking those personal attributes essential to civilized life but as embodying the kind of unfocused and chaotic desire commercial society needs to contain. Images of savages and savageness were thus shaped by the logical demands of the social theories they purportedly illustrated.

Adam Smith, for example, draws selectively on contemporary accounts of Native American peoples to frame his arguments that sympathy and the division of labor are the bases of civilized life (Meek 107–30). In *The Theory of Moral Sentiments,* he describes North American "savages" as possessing an unsettling capacity for "falsehood and dissimulation" which enables them to hide their "desperate" natures behind a mask of "heroic and unconquerable firmness" (205–9). This disjuncture between affect and intention in turn precludes the cultivation of "sympathy" for others, which Smith views as the foundation of moral judgment and social life. In *The Wealth of Nations,* he sketches the social implications of this view, suggesting that civilization is predicated upon the systematic satisfaction of desire through intricate networks of mutual dependence. Providing for even "the very meanest person in a civilized country" requires "the assistance and cooperation of many thousands" (23), and this requirement establishes a fundamental distinction between the conditions of civilized and savage life which overshadows contemporary class differences.

Thomas Robert Malthus likewise appeals to the idea of a "savage state" to justify his principle of population. Malthus presents his *Essay on the Principle of Population* as a neutral exposition of natural economic law (Himmelfarb 101), but he balks at leaving his readers with the impression that this law is the work of a less-than-benevolent Creator. Taking his cue from Pope's *Essay on Man,* he sets out in his penultimate chapter to "Vindicate the ways of God to man" (349). Just as Pope argues that "Whatever IS, is RIGHT" (*Essay on Man* 1:294), so Malthus endeavors to show how the permanent pressure of human want conduces to an ultimate good, the "creation and formation of mind" (353). In this argument, the "savage," who Malthus alleges "would slumber for ever under his tree, unless he were roused from his torpor by the cravings of hunger, or the pinchings of cold" (357), serves as a kind of limiting case, marking the divide between inert matter and living consciousness. The conditions of deprivation and need that characterize the existence of so many, Malthus holds, are in fact essential to the cosmic "process" through which God works "to elicit an aethereal spark from the clod of clay" (353). Within this process, "the wants of the body" serve both as "the first stimulants that rouse the brain of infant man into sentient activity" and as abiding prophylactics against any subsequent regression from this elevated state (356–57). Theologically, the savage state is the state of original sin; it is "the torpor and corruption of the chaotic matter" into which man is born (354). Rhetorically and structurally, it is the negation of Godwin's utopian vision. Whereas Godwin prophesies that "mind will one day become omnipotent over matter" (qtd. in Himmelfarb 103), Malthus hearkens back to an equally idealized state of absolute want to argue that "soul and body are most intimately united" and "grow from infancy together" (354).[1]

The major nineteenth-century political economists follow Smith and Malthus in relying on a postulated savage state to ground their theoretical speculations (Young 35; Berg 137). Although Scottish conjectural history waned in influence with the coming of the nineteenth century, its construction of the savage state as the antithesis of civilized commercial society persisted as one of the framing assumptions of liberal political economy (Meek 219). Nassau Senior, for instance, suggests that the "science" of political economy is applicable only to "civilized society," in which mechanisms of exchange and the division of labor are sufficiently developed. Since the savage rarely has occasion to choose between gratifying immediate wants and exercising the "abstinence" necessary for the accumulation of capital, the "rude state" of society is deemed to be "not perhaps within the scope of Political Economy" (67–69). J. R. McCulloch likewise uses a version of the four-stages theory to support his argument that labor is "the only source of wealth." Contrasting the "extremely barren and unproductive" labor of the savage with the "productive powers" that accrue to societies of "agriculturists and manufacturers," McCulloch contends that the division of labor in these advanced stages both augments wealth and moves individuals to "cultivate and bring to perfection" their particular talents (61–64). Like Malthus, McCulloch figures this impetus as a "vivifying principle" which raises people out of the torpor of the savage state: "A spirit of industry is thus universally diffused; and that apathy and langour which characterize a rude state of society, entirely disappear" (89–90). John Stuart Mill similarly introduces his *Principles of Political Economy* by juxtaposing the "scanty inventory of material wealth" available to the savage with the proportionally greater provisions available in more advanced stages of society. He does not exempt the savage state from the laws of political economy, as does Senior, but treats it, like McCulloch, as a "state of greatest poverty" against which subsequent accumulations of wealth may be assessed (10).

Such contrasts achieve their fullest development in Mill's essay "Civilization," which first appeared in the *London and Westminster Review* in 1836. "The word civilization," Mill begins, "is a word of double meaning," sometimes signifying "human improvement in general"—its dominant eighteenth-century meaning—and at other times signifying "certain kinds of improvement in particular" (18:119). In this latter usage, civilization denotes strictly material improvement, in contradistinction to that combination of moral, aesthetic, and intellectual development coming to be known as "culture" (Young 25–36). By recognizing this distinction explicitly, Mill opens a space for social critique. If the current age is "pre-eminently the era of civilization in the narrow sense," it is not necessarily "equally advanced or equally progressive in many of the other kinds of improvement" (18:119). Rather than identifying the attributes of civilization directly, however, Mill specifies them through negation, as whatever savageness is not. "Whatever be the characteristics of what we call savage life," he writes, "the contrary of these, or the qualities which society puts on as it throws off these, constitute civilization." But savage life is itself characterized as the absence of civilized modes of economic and social organization: "no commerce, no manufactures, no agriculture, or next to none"; "little or no law, or administration of justice"; "no systematic employment of the collective strength of society, to protect individuals against injury from one another" (18:120). Mill thus defines civilization and savageness dialectically, each being the negation or inversion of the other. Like his predecessors, he employs the savage state as a heuristic that enables him to imagine a condition of hyperindividualism unmitigated by voluntary or coerced cooperation. In "savage communities," Mill writes (perhaps employing this phrase, oxymoronic given the terms of his argument, to emphasize the extreme artificiality of his notion of savage life), each person not only "shifts for himself" but displays an actual aversion to social interaction: "[W]e seldom see any joint operations carried on by the union of many; nor do savages, in general, find much pleasure in each other's society. . . . every one trusts to his own strength or cunning, and where that fails, he is generally without resource" (18:120). Against this background, Mill characterizes civilization as an empowering imposition of social discipline. Civilization is a social state "sufficiently perfect" to induce people "to rely for their security mainly upon social arrangements" rather than upon "their individual strength or courage." Mill's characterization of such "discipline" as that "perfect co-operation" which "is an attribute of civilization" (18:122) is a generalization of a view that had informed political economic theory since Smith: that the accumulation of capital depends paradoxically on a self-imposed abstinence, which not only enables acquisition but also authorizes final consumption.

In the intellectual tradition extending from Smith to Mill, the concept of the savage state functions as civilization's conceptual other, illuminating by way of contrast the essential qualities of civilized society. In Smith, it signifies a psychological and social condition characterized by an incapacity for sympathy and the absence of a social division of labor. In Malthus, it represents the primal confrontation between absolute want and absolute indolence out of which civilization arose. In Mill, it means an utter "incapacity" for the kind of "organized combination" upon which civilization depends (18:123). In the second quarter of the nineteenth century, this tradition served as a theoretical framework for an emerging discourse on the state of those mass populations variously called the "poor," the "manufacturing population," or the "working classes." Within this discourse, images of savageness (or sometimes barbarism) are repeatedly called upon to mediate the conceptual relations among bodily desire, working-class bodies, and the greater "body" of society. Liberal observers sympathetic to industry attribute the social problems confronting Britain's industrial towns and cities to the "savage" habits of the lower classes rather than to the factory system itself. Some conservatives, in contrast, emphasize the organic unity of the social body by pointedly refusing to represent the lower classes as savage. Still other, more ambivalent commentators evince a deep anxiety that automatic industry is itself a retrogressive force, pushing the working classes into a paradoxically modern version of a savage state.

These rhetorical dynamics are particularly evident in a group of treatises written by three Edinburgh-educated medical practitioners during the 1830s and 1840s: *The Moral and Physical Condition of the Working Classes* (1832), by James Phillips Kay, a liberal Manchester physician who would later become a prominent champion of a national system of education; *Observations on the Management of the Poor in Scotland, and Its Effects on the Health of the Great Towns* (1840), by William Pulteney Alison, a Scottish poor law reformer and older brother of the Tory historian Sir Archibald Alison; and *Artisans and Machinery* (1836), by Peter Gaskell, a remote cousin of the novelist Elizabeth Gaskell whose work was a major source for Engels's *Condition of the Working Class in England* (1845).[2] Kay, Alison, and Gaskell's common educational heritage facilitates the comparison of their arguments and rhetoric. All three physicians, for instance, were deeply disturbed by the apparent fragmentation of society, which they conceptualized metaphorically as a complex corporate "body," and they each believed that "moral" as well as material factors contributed to the lower classes' susceptibility to disease. Gaskell is generally at a loss at how to address this problem, but Kay and Alison both favor systematic intervention by the state. They both endorse national, bureaucratically controlled systems of poor relief and, in identical language, argue for the necessity of "medical police" to promote health and sanitation (Kay 13; Alison x).[3]

Despite these affinities, the three physicians' divergent political ideologies lead them to adopt distinct approaches to social reform. Kay's liberalism is evident in his dual emphases on self-help and bureaucratic social control. He was an impassioned believer in free trade and held that Great Britain's future prosperity depended upon the continual expansion of commerce. Like Baines, Ure, and Cooke Taylor, Kay insisted that the factory system was not responsible for the social ills afflicting the "great towns." Rather, he attributed the plight of the poor largely to "their own ignorance or moral errors" and held that those who would hope to alleviate it "must depend not alone on elevating them physically, but must seek to produce a strong and permanent moral impression" (5–6). Kay argued that the working classes should be taught the value of domestic economy, social stability, and personal industry through the dissemination of "*correct* political information" (97), and he supported the provision of material relief as an ancillary measure, so long as it was restricted to the "virtuous poor" (45). To this end, he suggested that Manchester and its satellites should be "minutely subdivided" into manageable districts, so that local relief boards could become "minutely acquainted with the character of the inhabitants" (50). Only under such conditions, he believed, could poor relief be administered so that it bolstered rather than discouraged *"the virtuous independence of the working classes"* (51).

Alison advanced an agenda for reform similar to Kay's, but he formulated it as a pragmatic effort to put into practice a modern kind of Tory paternalism. Like Kay, Alison admired the English New Poor Law. He praised as "perfectly reasonable and judicious" its elimination of the use of poor rates to supplement wages, its provision that the able-bodied should receive relief in workhouses only, and its administration by a centralized board to ensure national uniformity, and he advocated the introduction of a similar system in Scotland (35). Alison's support for these apparently liberal measures, however, was based not on a belief in self-help but on a fundamentally conservative sense of the reciprocal obligations among the classes. He regarded "the relief of the poor" as a "religious duty distinctly enjoined in the Holy Scriptures" (iv) and endorsed a legalized system of relief only because he recognized that, given the complexity of modern society, this duty could no longer be fulfilled through the individual actions of members of the higher social orders. Alison did not exempt humanity from Malthus's principle of population, but he did reject the vulgar Malthusian notion that provisions for the poor only lead to greater improvidence. "A certain degree of physical comfort," he held, "is essential to the permanent development, and habitual influence over human conduct, of any feelings higher than our sensual appetites." Where Kay placed primary emphasis on moral education, Alison presented the "relief of physical suffering" as the "preliminary duty" of the philanthropist (73).

Gaskell's perspective is best described as liberal Tory (Berg 64). Although he embraced the principles of political economy, he also felt that rapid industrialization was eroding the social structures on which civilization depends. He vacillated over whether to attribute the condition of the manufacturing population to its own moral failings or to material and social conditions created by industrialism, and consequently found himself unable to advance any practical measures for reform. Instead, he idealized the bygone era of domestic manufacture as a period when conditions of production reinforced the authority of traditional social hierarchies and the patriarchal family, and held fast to a vague hope that increased contact among the classes would restore social harmony.

Since Alison grounds his proposals for reform in a conservative sense that all classes are linked together by historical bonds of rights and responsibilities, he has little incentive to stigmatize the lower orders of society as inherently savage. Rather, he uses the image of savageness to condemn the upper classes' lack of concern for the anonymous poor as a particularly pernicious form of moral callousness. Kay, in contrast, endeavors to deflect blame for the condition of the manufacturing population away from the factory system by assigning it to the brutalizing influence of "savage" Irish immigrants on the native English working class. Gaskell too portrays the moral and physical degeneration of factory operatives as a lapse into savageness, but unlike Kay, he holds the factory system itself largely responsible for this decline. The systematic displacement of adult male workers by machinery, as well as by women and children, he argues, subverts the traditional familial and social bonds upon which "civilization" depends. Drawing on a particular strain of contemporary ethnological theory, which assumed a correlation between whiteness and civilization on the one hand and blackness and savageness or barbarism on the other, Gaskell interprets the condition of factory operatives as an emblem of the broader social retrogression brought on by industrial capitalism.

IF KAY's life was largely dedicated to such matters as sanitation, poor law administration, and national education, he also demonstrated a persistent literary bent, counting among his acquaintances Matthew Arnold, Harriet Martineau, Charlotte Brontë, and Elizabeth Gaskell (Selleck 300–301). Late in life, Kay sought to fulfill his artistic aspirations by publishing two historical novels, *Scarsdale; or, Life on the Lancashire and Yorkshire Border* (1860) and *Ribblesdale, or Lancashire Sixty Years Ago* (1874). The literary merit of these works is negligible, but they have historical value as reconstructions of the social conflicts that followed in the wake of England's industrialization. In *Ribblesdale,* Kay eulogizes the passing of the era of domestic manufacture and poignantly describes the hardships that accompanied the advent of the factory system. In *Scarsdale,* he examines the tumultuous 1830s, providing retrospective insight into his perception of the crucial period in which he first turned his attention to the condition of the urban working classes.

In the first chapters of *Scarsdale,* Kay describes an episode of violent machine breaking in terms that place him squarely on the side of order and discipline, disparaging the "non-resistance doctrine" espoused by some masters and lauding those who would defend their property against unlawful destruction. The confrontation between the mob of desperate handloom weavers and the fortified factory is an expression of the schematic way in which Kay understood industrial social relations generally: as a standoff between the forces of chaos and destruction on the one hand and those of rational and hierarchical order on the other. The only person capable of crossing the divide between these worlds is Oliver, an aspiring physician who, like Kay, has chosen to dedicate his life to the care of the urban poor. Inevitably, young Oliver must ride out to rescue the mill owner's beautiful daughter, who has been caught outside the factory walls. What is significant about this episode is not the rescue itself (which is, of course, successful), but Kay's descriptions of the mob of weavers who oppose the heroic Oliver. As if to suggest that the machine breakers had lost the "singular hardihood, vigour, and manliness" that characterized their ancestors (1:14), he dwells compulsively on their "wild and savage bodies" (1:46), on the way in which they have given themselves over to "the more savage passions" of drunkenness and violence, on the "savage blow" Oliver receives as he attempts to make his way through the crowd (1:64).

The views that give rise to such descriptions are already evident in the social research Kay undertook in the 1830s. In *The Moral and Physical Condition of the Working Classes,* Kay frames his investigations into the lives of the urban poor as a kind of civilizing and sanitizing mission. Just as young Oliver confronts the unruly mob in the service of moral virtue, so Kay takes it as his "duty" to examine society's "ills" in meticulous detail and then to correct the "moral errors" and "imperfect institutions of society" from which they "flow" (8, 5). As Mary Poovey has shown, disease functions as a unifying metaphor in Kay's text, authorizing his investigations as a kind of diagnosis of the maladies afflicting the social body (Poovey 57–58). Yet Kay also recognizes that this collective body comprises a multitude of living bodies, which he arranges along a gradient from savageness to civilization. The metaphor of the social body and the specter of the savage work together to justify his policy of benevolent "sanative interference" (11). For instance, Kay figures the "habitations of the poor" in England's cities both as "mighty wildernesses of building" and as crowds of threatening bodies "which stretch out their arms, as though to grasp and enclose the dwellings of the noble and wealthy" (11). Like Edwin Chadwick, with whom he would later work in his capacity as an assistant poor law commissioner (Selleck 104–41), Kay sees sanitation as an instrument of civilization by which an unruly urban wilderness may be tamed, constrained, and integrated into the larger social body.

Nevertheless, Kay remains ambivalent about portraying the specifically English working classes as savage. Although his observations certainly carry this implication, he refuses to make such a representation directly. Like Adam Smith, he favorably contrasts the circumstances of the poor in civilized societies with the deprivations that are supposed to characterize savage life: "The unsheltered, naked savage, starving on food common to the denizens of the wilderness, never knew the comforts contained in the most wretched cabin of our poor" (78). The dissonance between this statement, which contrasts the savage and the poor, and Kay's earlier characterization of England's slums as mighty wildernesses, which implicitly identifies the two, arises from the multiple ideologies informing Kay's analysis. When he voices middle-class fears of a perpetually threatening working-class population, he figures that population as savage; when he speaks with the voice of English nationalism, however, he embraces this same population as "*our poor.*" Kay reconciles these two perspectives by integrating metaphors of contagion and savageness to frame the Irish—who might be called *their* poor—as a primary cause of the degradation of the English manufacturing population: "The *contagious example* which the Irish have exhibited of *barbarous* habits and *savage* want of economy," he writes, "united with the necessarily debasing consequences of uninterrupted toil, have demoralized the people" (27, emphasis added).

This hybridized representation, Poovey argues, reinforces an emerging English nationalism predicated upon the exclusion of the Irish as alien others (Poovey 65–72). But it also illuminates a structural parallel between Kay's treatment of the Irish and his conception of his own social projects. In addition to identifying the Irish as a primary cause of Manchester's social problems, Kay attributes to them a brutalizing agency that mirrors the civilizing influence of free trade, sanitation, and education. Like other liberal champions of industry, Kay attributes England's prosperity to the domination of nature through the development of human "faculties," the expansion of "knowledge," and the advancement of technical "arts": "[S]cience has revealed her secret laws—genius has applied the mightiest powers of nature to familiar use, making matter the patient and silent slave of the will of man" (79). Kay's investigations into the "ills that fester in secret, at the very heart of society" (8) stem from an analogous ambition to enforce dominion over human nature, to subject the unruly desires of the body to the discipline of moral and religious law. Paradoxically, he construes the "ignorance and pauperism" of the Irish as a similar kind of instrumental knowledge. Just as science has revealed nature's "secret laws"—and Kay, the "secret" ills of working-class life—so the Irish have "discovered, with the savage, what is the minimum of the means of life, upon which existence may be prolonged" (21). In Kay's view, the Irish are not merely a "contagious example" of "barbarous habits"; they are actively instructing the English working classes in what might be called the "secret" art of savageness:

> The paucity of the amount of means and comforts *necessary for the mere support of life,* is not known by a more civilized population, and this secret has been taught the labourers of this country by the Irish. . . . Instructed in the fatal secret of subsisting on what is barely necessary to life—yielding partly to necessity, and partly to example,—the labouring classes have ceased to entertain a laudable pride in furnishing their houses, and in multiplying the decent comforts which minister to happiness. (21–22)

In keeping with the precepts of classical political economy, Kay recognizes the subsistence level as a culturally determined threshold, and he understands the progress of civilization as a gradual refinement of desire. Although he distances himself from the "strong" Malthusian arguments of those who hold that the working classes "are condemned for ever" to lives of poverty and toil, he is nevertheless haunted by a sense of the ephemerality of "the capricious tastes and the imaginary appetites" upon which civilization depends (78–79). The subversive power of the Irish is the antithesis of the civilizing agency Kay attributes to education. By teaching the "secret" of subsistence to the English working classes, the Irish are in fact sharing with them the darker and more dangerous secret of the precarious fragility of civilization itself.

This representation of the Irish enables Kay to reconcile his ideological commitment to industrial capitalism with his professional concern for public health. If the complex of social problems Kay calls the "disease of the body politic" cannot be remedied by any "specific" (76), it can nevertheless be traced to a particular source: the "colonization of the Irish" as a source of cheap factory labor (80). Kay does not scapegoat the Irish while simultaneously legitimizing their use as an economic resource, as might be expected. Rather, he argues against the continued exploitation of the Irish as a shortsighted and ultimately detrimental expedient. Earlier in the century, he observes, English mill owners imported Irish labor without regard for its potentially debilitating long-term effects on English society and commerce. Social factors must enter into even "simple economical" calculations, and on this basis, he maintains that the Irish's negative "influence on civilization and morals" far outweighs any immediate benefit to be had from the "comparative cheapness" of their labor (80). The same commercial considerations that compel the "enlightened capitalist" to attend to the physical and moral health of his operatives require him to maintain the greater heath of the social body by forgoing the immediate advantages of cheap Irish labor.

While Kay advocates "unlimited reciprocity" over "narrow and bigoted exclusion" in "relations of commerce" (85), he objects to a parallel fluidity in the movements of laboring populations. Evincing a typically English fear of colonial contamination, he contends that if commercial reciprocity encourages the "advance of civilization" (85), the equally reciprocal "colonization of the Irish" (80) has had the opposite effect. Early in his treatise, Kay observes that the "colonization of savage tribes has ever been attended with effects on civilization as fatal as those which have marked the progress of the sand flood over the fertile plains of Egypt" (21). He later writes that "the introduction of an uncivilized race does not tend even primarily to increase the power of producing wealth, in a ratio by any means commensurate with the cheapness of its labour, and may ultimately retard the increase of the fund for the maintenance of that labour" (82). Applying these general precepts of history and economics to contemporary Manchester, he portrays the English—in a striking inversion of political reality—as the victims of Irish colonial expansion.

In "proof" of these contentions, he rehearses in detail "the natural progress of barbarous habits" once they are introduced among a civilized people:

The population gradually becomes physically less efficient as the producers of wealth—morally so from idleness—politically *worthless* as having few desires to satisfy, and *noxious* as dissipators of capital accumulated. Were such manners to prevail, the horrors of pauperism would accumulate. A debilitated race would be rapidly multiplied. Morality would afford no check to the increase of the population: crime and disease would be its only obstacles—the licentiousness which indulges its capricious appetite, till it exhausts its power—and the disease which, at the same moment, punishes crime, and sweeps away a hecatomb of its victims. A dense mass, impotent alike of great moral or physical efforts, would accumulate; children would be born to parents incapable of obtaining the necessaries of life, who would thus acquire, through the mistaken humanity of the law, a new claim for support from the property of the public. They would drag on an unhappy existence, vibrating between the pangs of hunger and the delirium of dissipation—alternately exhausted by severe and oppressive toil, or enervated by supine sloth. Destitution would now prey on their strength, and then the short madness of debauchery would consummate its ruin. Crime which banishes or destroys its victims, and disease and death, are severe but brief natural remedies, which prevent the unlimited accumulation of the horrors of pauperism. Even war and pestilence, when regarded as affecting a population thus demoralized, and politically and physically debased, seem like storms which sweep from the atmosphere the noxious vapours whose stagnation threatens man with death. (81–82)

In this long reflection, Kay weaves his governing images of infection and savageness into a Malthusian nightmare of racial degeneration in which the "moral check" operative in civilized society gives way to the "positive checks" of disease, starvation, crime, and war. If physical degeneration and moral decay render this population unfit "producers of wealth," so does a parallel dissipation of desire render them unfit consumers. Instead of stimulating the economy by increasing the demand for what Kay had earlier called "the decent comforts which minister to happiness" (22), they merely dissipate society's capital reserves even as they exhaust their own strength in hopeless efforts to gratify their "capricious appetite." For Kay as for Malthus, what makes an appetite "capricious" is not its basis in bodily desire but its failure to stimulate the higher intellectual, moral, spiritual, and aesthetic faculties. Under Irish influence, Kay envisions the English working classes sinking into the savage state precisely as Malthus defines it: successive periods of tedious and ineffectual labor alternating with periods of absolute indolence and sloth. Kay thus vindicates the factory system, and the liberal ideology it embodied, by identifying the "savage" Irish—rather than the social conditions created by the rapid industrialization of England in the first half of the nineteenth century—as the "chief source of the demoralization, and consequent physical depression of the people" (80).

ALISON'S PRINCIPLED refusal to portray the poor as savage signals his tacit rejection of the liberal justification for an interventionist program of reform represented by Kay. In contrast to Kay, whose emphasis on self-help leads him to favor moral reform over direct material relief, Alison maintains that in an advanced society a legalized system of relief is essential to the cultivation of those "artificial wants" (such as the desire for cleanliness, palatable food, comfortable domestic habitations, and intellectual stimulation) upon which the efficacy of the "moral" or "preventative" check on population depends (Alison 53–54). Like Kay, Alison uses the example of the Irish to develop his argument, but he does not take their impoverished condition as evidence of their intrinsically savage nature, nor does he figure them as a threat to the English working classes. Instead, he contends that the "disparity in prosperity" between Ireland and England demonstrates the efficacy of organized systems of relief. In both countries, he notes, the size of the population is "restrained by the difficulty of obtaining subsistence." In Ireland, the near total absence of a "preventative check of moral restraint" brings the population to "the very verge of the limit which is set by absolute starvation" (48). In England, however, this moral check is so powerful that no significant proportion of the population (excluding Irish immigrants) suffers such deprivation. Alison concludes from this contrast that "below a certain grade of poverty, the preventive check of moral restraint has no power" (49). If, as one of Alison's authorities suggests, the Irish poor are worse than savage, if they blend "most of the evils of civilization with the ignorance, apathy, sloth, and dirty habits of complete barbarism" (4), this condition is not intrinsic to the Irish character but arises from the absence of systematic relief. Indeed, the "same union of reckless improvidence, with extreme destitution" is "uniformly found" among the poor of Scotland and other countries (47–49).[4]

Dismissing as "perfectly visionary and Utopian" (102) the notion that the poor can become self-sufficient, Alison argues that in civilized societies the "higher ranks" have a special duty to provide for the welfare of the lower. He defends this claim on both humanistic and structural grounds. Developing an insight he finds in Walter Scott and Maria Edgeworth, and anticipating George Eliot's well-known dissection of human nature in *Middlemarch,* Alison insists that it is both arrogant and cruel to attempt to differentiate the deserving from the undeserving poor, since the personal circumstances of the poor are shaped at least as much by contingency as by character: "All human characters are mixed, and a very little observation of human life is enough to shew, that whether the better or the worse part of the dispositions of an individual, especially of the lower orders, shall determine his fate, or the character he is to bear in the world, is very often a question decided by contingencies altogether beyond his control" (80). Given this humane perspective, the question becomes not *whether* but *how* to provide for the needs of the poor.

In Alison's opinion, a legalized system of relief is preferable, for practical reasons, to a reliance on voluntary charity. The conditions of anonymity fostered by modern life, he contends, preclude individuals from ascertaining "the real character and wants of those whom they relieve" and opens them up to "a risk of frequent misapplication of their charity" (75). Organized relief under the supervision of paid inspectors would obviate this practical difficulty, and it would ensure the just and uniform distribution of assistance among recipients. Drawing again on the example of Ireland, he observes that although there is "no nation more generous," a sole reliance on voluntary charity has driven the Dublin poor "into a state of destitution and misery which it is painful to contemplate." He notes further that the "voluntary system" currently in place in Edinburgh has proven ineffective in keeping a large segment of the city's population from an "abject destitution and consequent suffering, *wholly unknown to the great body of the richer inhabitants*" and that similar voluntary arrangements have proven equally unsuccessful in Glasgow, Dundee, and Paris (76–77). Despite his Tory leanings, Alison is not so nostalgic as to long for an improbable reintegration of the "two nations," but he also insists that the structural estrangement of the rich from the poor does not release the rich from their obligation to the lower classes. Alison thus finds within the Tory ideology of reciprocal rights and responsibilities a conservative justification for a measure typically associated with the rise of the Victorian welfare state.

Alison illustrates the moral callousness of modern society by comparing the way in which estates are managed in the "civilized" present to the way in which they were governed in the "savage" past. Flouting conventional representations of the Irish as rude and uncivilized, he instead juxtaposes the behavior of upper-class landlords to that of a "savage" Scottish chieftain:

> We shudder at the savage answer attributed to a Highland Chief, when asked what was to become of the numerous families whom he had ejected from his estate to make room for sheep-walks, "Loch Duich is deep enough for them all!" But let us reflect on what happens continually in our own day, and among a people of at least as humane feelings as ourselves: "Ejectment of the peasantry is in the power," says Mr. Revans, "of every person in Ireland from whom they hold their lands, and is freely exercised to satisfy every variety of feeling, by Protestants and Catholics, by Tories, Whigs, and Radicals, equally towards those of their own as of other sects." And when we inquire into the fate of those poor families, unprotected by the law, thrown on the world, where there is no demand for their labour, we have abundance of evidence as to the very frequent result. (61)

Despite their identical practical effects, we abhor the chieftain's disregard for the families on his estate, while we accept as perfectly reasonable modern landlords' exercise of their property rights. Alison's comparison reveals the uncomfortable truth that we are horrified less by the chieftain's actions than by his ability to look coldly upon the imminent deaths of his subjects.

The suffering of displaced Irish peasants provokes no real outrage because it is hidden from view by a curtain of legality. "[T]hey suffer much certainly," Alison quotes one witness as commenting, "but they are soon lost sight of" (61).

The lesson here is clear, but Alison nevertheless feels compelled to state it explicitly: "[I]n an advanced and complex state of society, neither the happiness nor the lives of the great body of the poor have any adequate security from the humane feelings of the higher orders; not because those feelings do not exist, but because their operation is rendered absolutely unavailing by the want of sufficient intercourse between these different classes" (61). While Alison mourns the loss of such intercourse, he also accepts its passing as an inevitability. Therefore, rather than advance some quixotic scheme for recovering a more organic mode of social life, he adopts the pragmatic strategy of recasting the personal moral obligation of the privileged to care for the poor as a kind of consumption. Unlike Marx, Alison does not decry the alienation that accompanies the production of commodities under commercial capitalism, but he does challenge "productive labourers and the higher ranks" to accept the responsibilities as well as the rewards of their privileged social positions. The "order of things" in "civilized" society, he maintains, demands that they contribute to the maintenance of the indigent and unemployed, persons "of whom, individually, they know as little as of the workmen whose hands have prepared for them the various luxuries which they daily consume" (63). The social status these higher classes enjoy, Alison recognizes, is as much a commodity as the goods they consume. The maintenance of the poor is "*the price which they pay* for all the advantages and enjoyments which they derive from the complex and artificial, but to them highly favourable, state of society in which they live" (63, emphasis added). Alison's concern is that commercial civilization not spawn a new and quintessentially modern form of savageness among the upper classes, characterized not by conflict, scarcity, and want but by willful neglect of a distressed population too easily ignored.

IF ALISON succeeds in positing a conservative alternative to Kay's diagnosis of industrial society's "ills," Gaskell dramatizes the self-consuming quality of Kay's rhetoric in his own inability to formulate a coherent response to the social crises that accompanied mechanized industry. *Artisans and Machinery* is a reissue, with some slight changes, of Gaskell's 1833 treatise *The Manufacturing Population of England*, a study of the condition of the working classes very much in the mode of Kay. Since Gaskell refers to Kay only in the second version, it seems likely that he had no knowledge of Kay's similarly titled work when he first drafted his study. The clear affinities between Kay's treatise and Gaskell's should therefore be attributed to their participation in a common discourse and their common standing as professional men rather than to direct influence.

The major effect of Gaskell's 1836 revision, in fact, is to reposition his study as a response not to Kay but to Ure, whose *Philosophy of Manufactures* appeared in 1835. Gaskell acknowledges Ure's authority on strictly technical and economic issues, and he accepts some of his observations regarding the condition of factory operatives as well,[5] but he emphatically rejects Ure's claims regarding the social benefits of the factory system. Charging that in his enthusiasm for automatic industry, Ure "has overlooked the human agent except in so far as it forms a subordinate part in his great drama of steam and machinery" (133), Gaskell puts forth his own melodrama of social, moral, and physiological degeneration. Noting that automated machines "are yet in their infancy" (333), he prophesies that machinery will soon supersede human labor in both agriculture and manufacture, thus rendering the working classes not merely redundant but dangerous in their redundancy. Gaskell answers Ure's representation of the factory as an ideal social body governed by "the benignant power of steam" by observing wryly that like "other potent genii, steam occasionally puts off its gentle docility, blowing up factories, steam-boats, &c. &c." (318 n). Like an overheated boiler, he warns, England is threatened "not by force or competition from without, but by the pressure from within" (321).

This challenge extends implicitly to Kay as well, since he holds a position similar to Ure's. Kay's argument in *The Moral and Physical Condition of the Working Classes* is structured by two basic propositions: first, that "[m]oral and physical degradation are inseparable from barbarism," and second, that "[c]ivilization . . . is most powerfully promoted by commerce" (78). He keeps these propositions in force sheerly by dint of his ideological commitment to liberal capitalism. If the working classes in Manchester appear to be sinking into a state of savageness or barbarism, then this decline must be due to *"foreign and accidental causes"* rather than to the material conditions created by the factory system itself (78). Like Kay, Gaskell uses images of savageness to express his anxiety over the apparent decline in the "health and morals" of the working classes, but even as he echoes Kay's rhetoric, he calls into question the unreflective equation between commercial and social welfare on which it is based. While Kay comforts himself by attributing the decline of the manufacturing population to such extrinsic causes as an influx of immigrant labor, Gaskell pursues the more unsettling possibility that it stems from the systematic destruction of the domestic sphere by the factory system itself.

Gaskell views the latter half of the eighteenth century as the pinnacle of civilization, as a "golden times of manufactures" when the conditions of production reinforced personal morality, patriarchal authority, and social hierarchy (12). Identifying the progress of civilization with the construction of increasingly elaborate domestic habitations, the consolidation of the patriarchal family, the development of the convention of marriage, and the emergence of the individual moral conscience, he traces human societal evolution from an initial state of "utter barbarism" to a "maximum of civilisation" that very much resembles the Tory agrarian ideal (75–77). From this vantage point, he argues that the English working class is sinking into a condition of barbarism not because it has been infected by the "savage" Irish but because mechanized industry's effort "to do away with the necessity for human labour" is itself a retrogressive force (322).

Gaskell grants the proposition, articulated by Ure and others, that "as the internal economy of the mills goes on to perfection, order and morality must reign within their walls" (102), but he also holds that this order is purchased at the expense of the nuclear family. Partisans of the factory system, he writes, conveniently ignore the fact that "before this consummation of what they style the 'palladium' of British industry is reached, the operatives actually engaged will be reduced to a fragment, and that that fragment will consist almost entirely of women and girls" (102). The premium he places on patriarchal authority forces him to ask, "[W]hy thus, laying the axe to the root of the social confederacy, pave the way for breaking up the bonds which hold society together, and which are the basis of national and domestic happiness and virtue?" (145). Just as Kay objects to the importation of cheap Irish labor on the grounds that the "introduction of an uncivilized race" cannot be considered economical in the larger sense (*Moral and Physical Condition* 82), so Gaskell condemns the systematic displacement of adult male labor as the misguided action of mill owners "wishing to rid themselves of a turbulent set of workmen" and to purchase labor "at a cheaper rate" (146). Like Kay, he urges mill owners to adopt a posture of enlightened self-interest and to look beyond what he elsewhere calls the narrow "commercial economy" (102) of their operations to the wider social consequences of their employment practices.

Despite this appeal, Gaskell remains pessimistic. He concurs with less ambivalent proponents of industry that soon "we shall find that *automata* have done away with the necessity for adult workmen," but he challenges their utopian interpretation of this development:

> This point reached, according to Dr. Ure, Mr. Baines, Mr. M'Culloch, Mr. Scrope, and others, the very perfection of manufacture has been attained. A vast series of automatic machines will be seen revolving in palaces, pouring out produce in endless profusion; but the question deserves being asked— Where is the adult labourer? Even now we find him toiling in damp, unwholesome cellars, perishing of want; or, if better paid, leagued with his fellows, and holding machinery at bay, with the deadly resolve of not yielding one step further. (331–32)

In precise contrast to Ure, who portrays factory labor as a kind of social contract that transforms the "wandering savage" into a "citizen" (Ure 278), Gaskell maintains that the factory system casts the bulk of workers into a virtual savage state. Although the "primitive nature" of the desperate artisan and the harried operative have been "disguised and modified by the force of external circumstances," Gaskell sees them as differing "but little in inherent qualities from the uncultivated child of nature" (77–78).

Gaskell uses this analogy between the savage and the modern worker to help sort through his confusion over whether the condition of the working classes is due primarily to "physical" or to "moral" causes. On the one hand, he contends that the situation of factory operatives is due not to general socioeconomic forces but to their surrender to their base appetites and their abdication of domestic responsibility. He is therefore drawn to both typically liberal and typically conservative approaches to the personal improvement of factory operatives. On the other hand, he also attributes the manufacturing population's purported degeneration to the social conditions produced by steam power and the factory system. He takes it as a truism that "a deterioration . . . in the moral condition of some portions of the community" necessarily follows the amassing of large populations, and on this basis he argues that the factory system, which works "to crowd workmen together," must be held responsible, to some degree, for the manufacturing population's current state (93–94).

To complicate matters further, Gaskell recognizes that steam power destroys the individual agency upon which his appeals to self-help depend: "In all, it destroys domestic labour; in all, it congregates labourers into towns, or densely peopled neighbourhoods; in all, it separates families; and in all, it lessens the demand for human strength, reducing man to a mere watcher or feeder of his mighty assistant" (7). The emphatic repetition of the subjective pronoun "it," coupled with Gaskell's use of the active voice, syntactically mirrors his characterization of steam power as an "agent" and the human worker as a "mere watcher or feeder." Drawing on a characteristic trope of anti-industrial rhetoric, Gaskell figures this loss of autonomy as a mechanization of the worker. Soon, he observes, the term "artisan" will be a "misnomer" when applied to the industrial operative. Having "lost all free agency," the operative will cease to be "a man proud of his skill and ingenuity, and conscious that he is a valuable member of society" and will become instead "as much a part of the machines around him as the wheels or cranks which communicate motion" (358).

Gaskell seeks to reconcile these divergent lines of argument by juxtaposing savageness as a social condition, in which a savage state is produced by larger social and cultural forces, with savageness as a moral condition, in which the savage body serves as the locus of undisciplined appetite and desire. This emphasis on the savage qualities of the industrialized body connects Gaskell's clinical survey of the condition of the manufacturing population with his wider reflections on the social and cultural implications of mechanized industry. Specifically, he appeals to Johann Blumenbach's influential account of the origin of racial differences to justify his contention that the physical degeneration of the manufacturing population reflects its moral and social retrogression. Blumenbach's racial classifications, the most widely accepted in the period, were based on the "monogenetic" premise that all human beings were members of a single species with a single origin. Given this view, racial differences could not be explained away as consequences of separate acts of divine creation; instead, they had to be attributed to diversifying environmental factors. Blumenbach argued that there were five separate races which had descended from a single primeval Caucasian type. Europeans continued to exemplify the features of this original type, while the other four races were considered products of two separate lines of degeneration: from the Caucasian through the Native American to the Mongolian on the one hand, and from the Caucasian through the Malayan to the Ethiopian on the other (Stocking, *Victorian Anthropology* 26).

Central to Blumenbach's theory is the notion that the physiological characteristics of different peoples, nations, or races correlate with the level of civilization they have attained. Gaskell quotes Blumenbach's *Physiology* (in John Elliotson's English translation) to this effect: "Uncivilized nations, exposed to the inclemency of the weather, supported by precarious and frequently unwholesome food, and having none of the distinguishing energies of their nature called forth, are almost invariably dark coloured and ugly, while those who enjoy the blessings of civilisation, that is, good food and covering, with mental cultivation and enjoyment, acquire, in the same proportion, the Caucasian characteristics" (177). More immediately relevant to Gaskell's analysis of the manufacturing population is the corollary to this rule, that social strata within racial groups may be differentiated by analogous behavioral and physiological markers. In America, Blumenbach observes, African domestic servants gradually assume the manners and habits of "their superiors," while the ordinary "field slave" retains "the aspect and figure of Africa." Likewise, he reports that the physiological characteristics of Pacific Islanders, whom he takes to be members of one racial family, "vary according to the degree of their cultivation" (qtd. 178).

Gaskell amplifies these theories with additional examples culled from other sources. He gives particular attention to the contrast between the "Caffres of Southern Africa," whom he describes as a "remarkably well-built and handsome race of men," and their cousins "the Bosjesman, or Bushmen," whom he calls "as ugly a race as any under the sun," because this contrast seems to confirm the monogenetic thesis that social and environmental factors are responsible for racial differences. Although both peoples appear to derive from the same racial origin, the Caffres have "made some advances in civilisation, and present as perfect a picture of patriarchal existence as can well be imagined," while the Bushmen are characterized as "leading a wandering life; frequently half-starved; then indulging ravenously, and to a most enormous extent, in eating—rivalling even the Esquimaux as to quantity; almost naked; and hunted by the colonists and their dependents." Gaskell concludes this comparison by emphasizing that the Bushmen's physical inferiority is not inherent to their race but is a reflection of their uncivilized state: "Their bodily form is but an index of their barbarism" (179–80).

Gaskell pursues these ethnological speculations at such length because they offer a quasi-scientific justification for his interpretation of the industrial working class's physical condition as an index of its level of civilization. Indeed, he regards his own study as a contribution to ethnological science, suggesting that the manufacturing population "offers an admirable field for examining how far external causes, aided by morals, can modify the physical proportions of man" (181). It is important to recognize, therefore, that Gaskell is not advocating a racially inflected class determinism. On the contrary, his entire argument presupposes the radical malleability of the body in response to "social factors": "Wherever men are condemned to toil—wherever wide distinction of caste separates them from their superiors—wherever their manners and domestic habits are coarse and improvident—their bodies uniformly become stunted, ill-shaped, wanting elegance of contour, and that development and arrangement of parts constituting beauty" (181). Gaskell uses this principle to document the manufacturing population's retrogression. In contrast to the "robust and well-made" rural laborers and domestic manufacturers of "by-gone times" (182), modern factory workers strike Gaskell as frail and sickly. Their complexions are "sallow and pallid," their faces characterized by "a peculiar flatness of feature, caused by the want of a proper quantity of adipose substance to cushion out the cheeks," their "stature low," and their "limbs slender, and playing badly and ungracefully" when they move (184).

Gaskell is particularly disturbed by the apparent blurring of physical distinctions between the sexes. Male operatives, he observes, have "but little beard, . . . and an appearance, taken as a whole, giving the world but 'little assurance of a man'" (184), while female operatives evince "a peculiar roughness of voice," which he attributes principally to "too early sexual excitement, producing a state of vocal organs closely resembling that of the male" (186). Gaskell's anxiety over the erosion of traditional gender roles in the home and factory thus registers as a preoccupation with the cross-gendering of working-class bodies themselves.

As his meditation on the physical condition of the working classes progresses, however, it increasingly focuses on the purported degeneration of female operatives, which becomes the cornerstone of his aesthetic critique of the factory system. Despite his general espousal of liberal economic principles, Gaskell holds that untempered market capitalism threatens the domestic order upon which social stability depends, and so he looks to the "moral influence of woman upon man's character," acting through "her natural and instinctive habits," as a countervailing force (189). He worries, though, that the female operative cannot fulfill this crucial function, and he regards her "awkward and ungainly *figure*" as both the cause and sign of this particular failing (186, emphasis added). Although he finds "many exquisite specimens of female loveliness" among Lancashire's middle and upper classes, he considers the typical factory girl to be "widely divergent from the line of womanly beauty" (186). She displays "no delicacy of figure, no elegance of tournure, and no retiring bashfulness," but rather a gait that is "ungraceful in itself, and still more so in its impression upon the mind, by the evidence it gives of certain alterations in form peculiarly unsexual" (186, 188–89). As this distinction between the female body's appearance "in itself" and the "evidence it gives" suggests, it is precisely its capacity to function as a "figure" for more general social conditions that gives it such prominence in Gaskell's study.

For Gaskell, "womanly beauty" is "founded on utility" (186). Just as Hume postulates that the beauty of animals arises from the way in which their forms are suited "to the particular manner of life, to which they are by nature destined" (Hume 226–27), so Gaskell holds that there "is something in the female figure strongly indicative of its aptitude for the performance of certain functions peculiar to her sex" (188). For this reason, he attributes a special emblematic significance to female secondary sex characteristics. He dwells at length, for example, on the premature development and desiccation of female operatives' breasts: "Very early in life, from ten to fourteen years, the breasts are often found large and firm, and highly sensitive, whilst at a later period—at a period indeed when they should show the greatest activity and vital energy—when in fact they have children to support from them, they are soft, flaccid, pendulous, and very unirritable" (189). Gaskell thus stigmatizes female factory labor on aesthetic grounds by suggesting that it produces alterations in the female figure that inhibit it from performing its natural sexual and reproductive functions: "both states" of the breast give "the most decisive proofs of perversion in the usual functional adaptation of parts" (189).[6]

Moreover, in accordance with his ethnological model, Gaskell recognizes clear moral analogues to these physical maladaptions. As the female operative's (sexual) "passions have been prematurely developed, her physical organization stimulated into precocious activity, her social affections injured," she has also ceased to be "the companion of man" and become instead "a mere instrument of labour, and a creature for satisfying his grosser appetites." She has, in other words, descended to "the same degraded level" women occupy "in countries which are called savage" (190). Again, images of transgressive female sexuality and degenerate female bodies hold such sway over Gaskell's imagination because they knit together his medical assessment of the manufacturing population and his ethnological diagnosis of the social effects of automatic industry.

Engels, for one, wholly accepted this account of the working class's condition. Relying on Gaskell's authority, he argues that the heat of the factory—like that of tropical climes—hastens the onset of puberty, so that there are factory girls from twelve to fourteen "who are already physically mature." At the extreme, Engels cites a report by Mr. John Robertson in the *North of England Medical and Surgical Journal* regarding an eleven-year-old girl who was not only physically mature but also pregnant (183).[7] For Engels, these sorts of perversions are self-evident indictments of industrial capitalism. Indeed, he charges society with mass "murder" for allowing industrialization to so undermine factory operatives' "bodily, intellectual and moral conditions" (108).[8]

Gaskell, in contrast, remains a reluctant critic of industry. Despite his sometimes heated rhetoric, he is unwilling to reject the factory system, or the liberal ideology that sustained it, solely on the basis of its effect on the manufacturing population. His hope, rather, is that industrialization itself will foster conditions conducive to the improvement of the working classes, just as it created the conditions that led to their decline. He is therefore heartened to find what he terms the "force of external circumstances in modifying bodily form" operating in a positive way among the industrial middle classes (194). Although many masters were originally operatives or laborers themselves, they and their families "now resemble but slightly, in their general aspect and deportment, the class from which they have risen," a change Gaskell attributes to their improved material and social circumstances: "Change of condition, better food, better clothing, better housing, constant cleanliness, mental cultivation, the force of example in the higher order of society in which they are now placed, have gradually converted them into respectable, and even handsome families. The first remove places them still more favourably, and, *ceteris paribus,* they become elegant and intelligent females, and well-formed and robust men" (195). The industrial middle classes evince none of the barbarism of the working classes, nor do they evince that blurring of genders which Gaskell finds so disturbing. This contrast, of course, precisely mirrors the ethnological accounts that Gaskell takes as his model. Like Blumenbach's African slaves or Gaskell's own Caffres and Bushmen, the industrial middle and working classes share a common racial ancestry but have developed differing physical characteristics reflective of their material circumstances and moral habits. If the decline of the manufacturing population marks mechanized industry as a retrogressive force, the improved physical condition of the industrial middle classes testifies to its potential to act as a civilizing agent. Gaskell thus locates a silver lining inside the dark cloud of industrial smoke hovering over his treatise which enables him to avoid the kind of radical interpretation Engels would later place on his findings.

Not unexpectedly, *Artisans and Machinery* ends on a note of uncertainty and ambivalence. Giving somber notice to mechanized industry's threat to the integrity of the social body, Gaskell warns that the time is "rapidly approaching, when the people, emphatically so called, and which have hitherto been considered the sinews of a nation's strength, will be even worse than useless" (361). Unwilling to hold the manufacturing population wholly responsible for its own condition, Gaskell cannot, like Kay, advance a rigorous program of self-help, social surveillance, and education. Unwilling to insist on the reciprocal obligations of the classes to one another, he cannot, like Alison, endorse a legalized system of relief as a means through which the "higher orders" may fulfill their moral duty to society. While Kay and Alison both find within their respective ideologies justifications for specific practical measures, Gaskell is left wondering, "What is to be done?" (361). Ironically, his anemic effort to respond to this Carlylean query leads him to recapitulate in the metaphorical structure of his closing paragraph the very displacement of "artisans" by "machinery" he so deeply dreads. Blending the metaphor of the social body with the mechanistic image of society as a great boiler he had earlier used to challenge Ure, Gaskell expresses his fear "that an explosion will be permitted to take place" within society, forcing it "to undergo a series of painful gradations" before it "can regain a healthy and permanent tone." The best he can muster is a vague hope that some "patriotic and sagacious spirit" will emerge to guide the nation through its recovery (362). Despite this apocalyptic imagery, Gaskell's sensationalized evocation of working-class degeneration goes out with a whimper rather than a bang. In its very indeterminacy, Gaskell's treatise exemplifies, if it does not resolve, the problematic disjuncture between social and commercial progress that troubled early Victorian efforts to delineate a coherent concept of industrial culture.

IN THEIR different ways, Alison, Kay, and Gaskell all offer a broadly Malthusian social vision in which images of savageness identify social forces deemed inimical to the "progress" of civilization. Given this theoretical framework, it is not surprising that references to savageness in social investigatory texts connote little that is noble. Typically, "savage" is a term of disparagement, directed at populations or classes perceived as threats to the stability and progress of commercial civilization. As Kay writes, "No modern Rousseau now rhapsodises on the happiness of the state of nature" (*Moral and Physical Condition* 78). Nevertheless, nature continued to be regarded as a source of moral, religious, and aesthetic truth, and consequently, the manufacturing population's separation from nature is itself lamented as a source of perversion. In this light, the unschooled "mechanic" may be viewed as worse off than the savage, who at least has the opportunity to imbibe religious and moral truths from the "book of nature." Paradoxically, although the progress of civilization is predicated upon the progressive refinement of "artificial wants," it has also, in its late commercial stage, created what Cooke Taylor calls a dangerous "artificial existence" in which operatives are separated from a primary source of religious and moral instruction. Like Kay,

Cooke Taylor imagines the retrogressive forces that are inextricable from civilization in terms of savageness and disease—he compares the barbarism growing up in the midst of the highest civilization to a gangrene that would "extend to the vitals" of society—and he prescribes moral education for the operative classes as a remedy (*Notes* 129). Artificiality, it seems, is a Janus-faced power: if it elevates human beings out of a primal state of nature, it can also lower them into unnatural states of brutality and perversion.

The full consequences of this paradox become particularly evident in the overdetermined invocations of the savage in Victorian discussions of industrial design and the decorative arts. This discourse is in many ways a transposition of the formal theories of political economy into the register of the aesthetic, where ideological contradictions and social issues can find imaginary, formal resolutions. In this context, the persistent representation of taste and beauty as commodities or forms of capital is not simply a rhetorical strategy calculated to convince manufacturers that it is in their economic interest to attend to matters of design; it is also a cognitive technique for working through the tangled relations between capital accumulation and commodity consumption. The discourse on design, like the discourses of political economy and social investigation, relies on images of the savage both to ground its theoretical propositions and to support its arguments for the necessity of interventions to correct public taste.

Just as political economy presumed an innate human drive to barter, truck, and exchange, so nineteenth-century theories of ornamental design presumed an innate capacity for aesthetic appreciation and a corresponding impulse to decorate and adorn. Repeatedly, commentators on the decorative arts appeal to the example of the savage to document human beings' innate need for ornament. For example, William Dyce, the School of Design's first director and author of an influential drawing manual, contends that the "love of ornament is a tendency of our being" and that industrial objects can therefore be assimilated to the human psyche through ornamental adornment (*Journal of Design* 1:65). Ralph Nicholson Wornum, a lecturer at the School of Design who wrote an important essay on the Great Exhibition, holds that decoration is "one of the mind's necessities" (1). Richard Redgrave, perhaps the most influential theorist in Cole's circle, describes ornament as "almost . . . a natural want" (708). The architect Owen Jones writes that "there is scarcely a people, in however early a stage of civilisation, with whom the desire for ornament is not a strong instinct" (13). Such views account for the apparent correlation between technological progress and aesthetic decline that troubled practical investigators such as Gaskell and political philosophers such as Mill. A number of contemporary commentators admit that the designs being brought forth by "civilized" European manufacturers are palpably inferior to the designs produced by "savage" or "Asiatic" peoples. The postulate of an innate love of ornament enables them to attribute this disparity to the fact that these peoples are closer to a primal state of nature and thus work by unerring "custom" (Merrifield 1).

Conversely, if the instincts of European ornamentists inevitably lead them astray, it is still possible to discover reliable guidelines for design through the systematic study of nature. Given the postulate of a universal human nature, which these commentators inherited from Enlightenment political philosophy and aesthetic theory, it takes little effort to move from the idea that beauty is a basic human need to the conclusion that there must exist universally valid principles of decoration applicable at all stages of civilization. Appeals to the savage state are thus central to design theory's defense of the single premise upon which all of its other claims to authority rest: that there exist objective laws of taste and beauty that can be discovered, codified, and applied systematically to manufacture.

This line of thought reaches its fruition in Owen Jones's *The Grammar of Ornament* (1856), a survey of historical styles of the decorative arts from the Egyptian through the modern Italian. The book opens with a chapter entitled "The Ornament of Savage Tribes," in which Jones treats various peoples native to the South Pacific, especially the Maoris of New Zealand, as surrogates for primeval "Man." He interprets their formidable skills in the decorative arts as evidence of a natural "desire for ornament" which is present in all societies and which "grows and increases with all in the ratio of their progress in civilisation" (13). However, when Jones revisits this correlation in his final chapter, "Leaves and Flowers from Nature," it takes on additional significance. His seemingly innocuous botanical speculations are in fact an intervention in contemporary debates about the possibility of creating a new architectural style, and his assessment of the current climate sounds uncannily Ruskinian. "The fatal facility of manufacturing ornament," he asserts, has "deadened the creative instinct in artists' minds" (155). What Jones is rejecting is the tendency among nineteenth-century designers simply to copy historical models instead of looking to nature for new inspiration:

> Who, then, will dare say that there is nothing left for us but to copy the five or seven-lobed flowers of the thirteenth century; the Honeysuckle of the Greeks or the Acanthus of the Romans,—that this alone can produce art? Is Nature so tied? See how various the forms, and how unvarying the principles. We feel

persuaded that there is yet a future open to us; we have but to arouse from our slumbers. (157)

In Jones's call for a new architectural style, we hear faint echoes of Malthus's notion that the natural needs of the body were the "first great awakeners of the mind" (Malthus 356). Civilized man must now be roused from a different kind of slumber. Nature exists, Jones asserts, "to awaken a natural instinct implanted in us . . . to emulate in the works of our hands, the order, the symmetry, the grace, the fitness, which the Creator has sown broadcast over the earth" (157).

Jones's entire study is based on the premise that the refinement of the innate human desire for ornament is coextensive with the progress of civilization. However, this claim collapses under the weight of the evident contrast between the beautiful designs of the savage and the forced and artificial productions of civilized societies: "The ornament of a savage tribe, being the result of a natural instinct, is necessarily always true to its purpose; whilst in much of the ornament of civilised nations, the first impulse which generated received forms being enfeebled by constant repetition, the ornament is oftentimes misapplied, and instead of first seeking the most convenient form and adding beauty, all beauty is destroyed, because all fitness, by superadding ornament to ill-contrived form" (16). By way of example, Jones contrasts a Maori paddle, of which he writes that "there is not a line upon its surface misapplied," with how he imagines the same object might be executed in nineteenth-century England (see fig. 2). In the Maori design, he observes, the center stripe and the outer border combine to give the paddle "an appearance of additional strength," but a "modern manufacturer . . . would have continued the bands or rings round the handle across the blade," thereby destroying that marvelous effect (16–17). Jones's focus on the specific sins of ill-conceived repetition and thoughtless copying implies that of all "civilised nations" he has his own particularly in mind. Immediately following this comparison, he challenges nineteenth-century Britain to emulate the savage's sure aesthetic sense: "If we would return to a more healthy condition, we must even be as little children or as savages; we must get rid of the acquired and artificial, and return to and develop natural instincts" (16). He thus rejects the negative image of the savage dominant in political economy and nineteenth-century social investigations and instead looks for aesthetic salvation in the Romantic ideal of the savage as child of nature.

Nevertheless, Jones is not advocating an aesthetic return to some primal anarchic state. The best way to "return to and develop natural instincts" is,

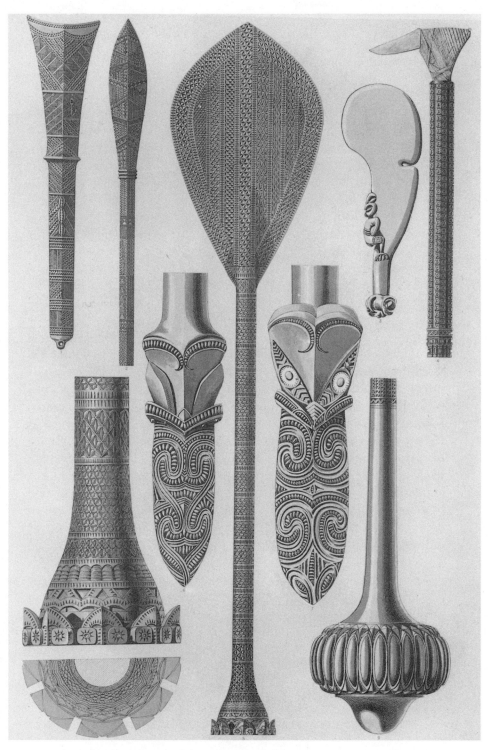

Fig. 2. "Savage Tribes No. 3," from Owen Jones, *The Grammar of Ornament,* plate 3. (Courtesy of the Yale Center for British Art, Paul Mellon Collection)

paradoxically, to master and then transcend the difficult lessons of history: "We believe that if a student in the arts . . . will only lay aside all temptation to indolence, will examine for himself the works of the past, compare them with the works of nature, bend his mind to a thorough appreciation of the principles which reign in each, he cannot fail to be himself a creator, and to individualise new forms, instead of reproducing the forms of the past" (156). Naturalness, it seems, is the most artificial state of all, since it can only be achieved through the application of a codified body of rules or principles. In other words, Jones and his associates seek to achieve a kind of "organized innocence" by distilling the "natural instinct" of the savage into science. As Wornum observes in the first of a series of lectures he delivered to the School of Design under the title "History and Principles of Ornamental Art," the South Sea Islanders who use scissors, eyeglasses, and the like as ornamental pendants do no more than "European ladies" who adorn themselves with precious stones. The crucial difference "is that we have reduced to an elaborate system what with them is but a most crude perception" (*Art-Union* 10:347).

As I discuss at length in the following chapter, a whole profession constituted itself around this need to educate the "ignorant public" in correct principles of taste. What I would like to observe at this juncture is the broad parallelism between this program and contemporaneous programs for the reform of the working classes. If such commentators as Wornum, Redgrave, Dyce, and Jones admired the instinctive sense of beauty they saw demonstrated by "savage tribes," they also used metaphors of savageness and disease to denigrate the state of modern taste and to bolster their own authority. Just as liberal studies of the manufacturing population justified the imposition of a rigorous moral discipline on the factory operative, so the discourse on design provided a rationale for disciplining the sensibilities and perceptions of the consuming public at large.

CHAPTER FOUR

"Appropriate Beauty"

THE WORK OF ORNAMENT IN THE AGE OF MECHANICAL REPRODUCTION

IN "The Nature of Gothic," Ruskin's sweeping condemnation of the division of labor culminates quite specifically in a rejection of the division of labor in ornamental design. Except for the narrow class of designs that can be "mathematically defined," he contends, "one man's thoughts can never be expressed by another" (10:200). In the lectures on design that grew out of his major writings on architecture, Ruskin develops this argument further, chastising England for its "habit of confusing art as *applied* to manufacture, with manufacture itself." He makes a basic distinction between "skill of true art," through which an "inventive workman" creates a beautiful design, and mere "skill of manufacture," through which that design "is copied and afterwards multiplied a thousandfold," and then argues that these two faculties cannot be developed simultaneously: "Try first to manufacture a Raphael; then let Raphael direct your manufacture" (15:12). Lest this aphorism create the false impression that artists can be mass-produced like pins, Ruskin later clarifies his metaphor: "[Y]ou have always to find your artist, not to make him; you can't manufacture him, any more than you can manufacture gold. You can find him, and refine him: . . . but not one grain of him can you originally produce" (16:29–30). Art education will best serve the cause of industry, Ruskin concludes, not by training students to follow formal rules but simply by identifying and developing innate artistic talent.

The ideas Ruskin here rejects arise out of an expansive Victorian discourse on design, which concerned not only the principles governing taste and the decorative arts but also the economic and social benefits of their dissemination and application to manufacture. This chapter traces the gradual evolution of this discourse from the 1830s through the Great Exhibition of 1851, as it is recorded in the pages of two early Victorian periodicals: the *Art-Journal [AJ]* or *Art-Union,* as it was called from its inception in 1839 until it was renamed in 1849, and the competing *Journal of Design and Manufactures [JD],* which ran from 1849 to 1851.[1]

The *Art-Journal* was the most prominent nineteenth-century journal of its kind. Its contents included announcements and reviews of exhibitions, notices pertaining to various artistic societies, technical and critical articles on aspects of the fine arts, and engravings of recent works, as well as miscellaneous poetry, fiction, and biographical sketches. For the first several years of its existence, it published little material on matters of ornament and design, but these subjects gradually became of greater concern. Nevertheless, the journal's conception of itself as a publication "exclusively devoted to the interests of Artists and the Arts" (*AJ* 1:iii) precluded it from recognizing design as anything more than an ancillary discipline. The *Journal of Design and Manufactures* was founded by Henry Cole, the Victorian era's most ambitious champion of art education. It was an important harbinger of the modernist technological aesthetic and (as one of the main vehicles through which Cole and his circle lobbied for control over the government Schools of Design) a valuable source of information about the early development of Britain's cultural bureaucracy.[2] In contrast to the *Art-Journal*, the *Journal of Design* aggressively sought to emancipate design from the fine arts. It rejected the entrenched opposition between art and industry that constrained its rival publication, and it argued compellingly for the status of design as a distinct domain of aesthetic expertise.

As this trajectory suggests, the discourse on design may be understood as one particularly pragmatic and instrumental permutation of what Terry Eagleton has dubbed the "ideology of the aesthetic." Like post-Enlightenment aesthetic theory generally (according to Eagleton's interpretation), it aims to reconcile the contradictions inherent in capitalism by transposing them into the register of the aesthetic.[3] From this perspective, these journals' repetitive and often diffuse ruminations on matters of beauty, taste, and commerce may be seen as contributions to a larger rhetoric through which Victorian commercial interests were working to attribute what Adrian Rifkin calls a "viable unity" and an "imaginary perfection" to industrial society (91). Although the discourse on design reached its maturation in the 1850s, it initially developed in the context of the "Condition of England" debates that ran throughout the 1830s and 1840s. Like contemporaneous defenses of the factory system and investigations into the condition of the manufacturing population, it is informed by and bolsters an incipient theory of industrial culture which works to legitimize nineteenth-century capitalism by aestheticizing manufacture and commerce.

IN 1835 Parliament convened a Select Committee on Art and the Connexion with Manufactures, chaired by the utilitarian Radical M.P. William Ewart, with the charge "to inquire into the best means of extending a knowledge of the ARTS and of the PRINCIPLES OF DESIGN among the People (especially the Manufacturing Population) of the Country" (Select Committee 586).[4] In its report, the committee offered a dual argument for art education:

> Yet to us, a peculiarly manufacturing nation, the connexion between art and manufactures is most important;—and for this merely economical reason (were there no higher motive), it equally imports us to encourage art in its loftier attributes; since it is admitted that the cultivation of the more exalted branches of design tends to advance the humblest pursuits of industry, while the connexion of art with manufacture has often developed the genius of the greatest masters in design. (568)

This presumption that "merely economical" reasons for promoting art are consistent with some "higher motive" ennobled commercial interests by allying them with the arts and provided a utilitarian justification for such state-sponsored cultural initiatives as the Schools of Design and, later, the Department of Science and Art.[5] In 1839 the painter William Etty asserted that "the BEAUTY of the Arts of Design" was a "great engine" for promoting "religion, government, moral and social order, and the consequent well-being and happiness of the human race" (*AJ* 1:182). By the late 1840s, this view had become such a commonplace that Milner Gibson, chair of the 1849 Select Committee on the School of Design, could simply find it obvious. "Upon the advantages of cultivating the taste of the people," he writes in a draft version of his committee's report, "and the moral and elevating influence of taste in legitimately attracting them from degrading objects and pursuits, it must be superfluous to dilate" (*JD* 2:33).

This perception of an intrinsic relation between art and industry was encouraged by the new vocabulary of the industrial revolution. The social and economic changes of the late eighteenth and early nineteenth centuries reciprocally influenced the terms in which industrialism and its effects were comprehended and debated (Williams, *Culture* xiii–xx). In particular, the novel differentiation between art and industry was a historical prerequisite for their subsequent reintegration within the Victorian discourse on design. In addition to reflecting and supporting the separation of mechanical or manual from intellectual or creative labor, it also enabled the discursively productive conceptual integration, or "blending," of these two now discrete concepts.[6]

Cole's address "What Is Art Culture?," delivered to the Manchester School of Art in 1877, documents this process. In this self-congratulatory, retrospective account of the blossoming of institutionalized art instruction in Britain since the Great Exhibition, Cole reiterates his lifelong conviction that art education is essential to British industrial prosperity. He frames his argument by reflecting on the evolution of the meaning of the term *art* over the preceding quarter century:

> We have to talk of "Schools of Art." Now that is an expression not older than some twenty-five years. Twenty-five years ago a "School of Art" might have been a School of Physical Art, a School of Chemical Art, or a School of Mechanical Art, &c. Milton speaks of the "arts that polish life"; that is, all arts which mean practice. Language alters and grows, and when we talk of a School of Art now, everybody understands that we mean a School of Fine Art. We used to employ the expression (which has nearly gone out of fashion) the "Fine Arts," to distinguish them from the Mechanical Arts. Now we limit the meaning of the word Art to Fine Art; that is, the art of producing beauty of all kinds. (1)

By the 1870s, this account asserts, the term "art" had settled into a determinate meaning, but at mid-century it was still in a complex transitional state. The concept was general enough to require additional adjectival specification, as in the phrases "Physical Art," "Chemical Art," and "Fine Art," but also sufficiently differentiated from concepts of manufacture to support such nontautological formulations as Cole's definition of "art manufacture": "Fine Art, or beauty applied to mechanical production" (*Fifty Years* 1:103–4).

WHAT, PRECISELY, it meant in the nineteenth-century context to "apply" art to manufacture will not be obvious to modern readers, who inevitably take their bearings on the subject from Benjamin's essay "The Work of Art in the Age of Mechanical Reproduction." Benjamin notwithstanding, early Victorian advocates of design, as represented by the contributors to the *Art-Journal* and the *Journal of Design,* did not generally regard mass production as a danger to art's "aura." On the contrary, they embraced the hope that mechanical reproduction could in fact benefit art by extending its influence. In his address to the Manchester School of Art, Cole emphatically rejected the notion that art could not be replicated without losing its status as art: "I have no objection to admit that when Art is the whole work of the one 'handicraftsman' . . . , such Art is Fine Art in its highest sense; but I still maintain that when work is repeated so well that the artist himself cannot distinguish it from his own handicraft, it is, for all the purposes for which Fine Art has ever existed in the world, worthy of being called Fine Art" (2). Cole here is recalling, at a late stage in his career, a formalist aesthetic essential to the social agenda of the early Victorian design movement. Given the premise that beauty and taste are governed by objective laws, it follows that the circumstances surrounding a work's creation have no bearing on its aesthetic properties. A perfect copy neither represents the original nor recalls the fact of its absence, but is its equivalent in all respects. This postulate of equivalency, in turn, encouraged the hope that the replication of works of art would exert an edifying influence on public taste. "I am not one of those who believe that excellence will become less excellent by being diffused, or that the sense of the true, the beautiful, the pure, will become less valuable, by being rendered more familiar," writes one frequent contributor to the *Art-Journal*. On the contrary, "the multiplication and diffusion of objects through which the taste is exercised" was thought to "facilitate comparison and quicken sensibility" and, in this way, to help secure the authority of the arts in commercial society (*AJ* 11:69).

A common criticism of the Victorian advocates of design is that they fundamentally misconstrued the proper relation between art and industry, and that therefore, rather than articulating an aesthetic appropriate to the machine age, they found themselves mired in opaque and interminable debates over such seemingly trivial matters as the propriety of carpet patterns or (to use Rifkin's emblematic instance) errors in candlesticks. But like many critical orthodoxies, this notion obscures as much as it explains. The early Victorians did tend to conflate design with decoration, but this does not mean that they were, as one critic writes, simply "confused by the belief that ornament and design were identical" (Gloag, *Victorian Taste* xv). On the contrary, the narrow identification of design and ornament follows as an analogical consequence of the generally accepted principle, inherited from Enlightenment aesthetic theory, that the relationship between beauty and utility exemplified by nature should be emulated in human productions. As William Dyce explained in an 1848 lecture to the London School of Design, the "*cosmetic* art of nature" transforms an alien universe composed of raw "pieces of mechanism" into a world of "beautiful objects," and ornament can perform an analogous mediating function for machinery and manufactures (*JD* 1:65). Far from being extraneous decoration, ornament is a primary means through which human beings apprehend their world. The hope of Victorian advocates of design was that ornament could counteract the alienation Marx saw as endemic to industrial capitalism by establishing an affinity between human beings and "mechanical contrivances" analogous to that which obtains between human beings and works of nature.

Because the Victorian design theorists were reacting against a prevailing taste for elaborate, eclectic, and excessive decoration, they approached design as a kind of limit problem. In designing an object, the aim was to reconcile form and function, or "to find the shape best suited to fulfil its uses, and at the same time to develop the utmost degree of appropriate beauty" (*AJ* 4:24). This goal reflects a crisis in what might be called the labor theory of aesthetic value, brought on by the advent of mechanical production. Once intricate decoration could no longer, in and of itself, reliably indicate economic or aesthetic value, "exquisite simplicity" (*AJ* 8:209) began to be prized (at least in principle) over gratuitous ornamentation, to the point that mechanical precision came to be seen as an ideal even for handicraft manufactures.

In this context, "fitness" emerged as a dominant aesthetic value. Although theoretical explanations of this principle can seem uncannily modern, this is deceptive. Indeed, Alf Bøe's warning that Pugin should not be taken as a "Victorian Corbusier" is applicable to Victorian design theorists generally (29). The Victorians did share certain critical terms with their modernist successors, but this common vocabulary should not be allowed to obscure real differences in aesthetic values. Sometimes the Victorians used "fitness" to mean that an object's form should be dictated by its function or, less strongly, that its decoration should not interfere with its use. On this basis, Wornum insists that we must always remember "the *fitness* of the design we are making to its intended use" (*AJ* 10:347). Equally often, however, the imperative to fitness means that decorative form should represent—rather than follow—function (Bøe 80–84). For example, commenting on some of the designs displayed at the Great Exhibition, Redgrave observes, "There seems no fitness, for instance, in surrounding the frame of a pier-glass with dead birds, game, shell-fish, nets, &c., although they may be excellent specimens of carving; nor is it clear why eagles should support a sideboard, or dogs form the arms of an elbow-chair; nor, again, why swans should make their nests under a table, at the risk of having their necks broken by everyone seated at it." Redgrave objects to these pieces not because they are not functional but because their decoration has been adopted "without motive" ("Supplementary Report," 722). The distinction between these two types of fitness is nicely illustrated by the *Art-Union*'s complaint that a certain set of buttercup-shaped wine glasses have "with singular inappropriateness . . . been used as champagne glasses"(*AJ* 6:32). Contrary to what one might expect, the reviewer objects to the glasses on mimetic rather than on functional grounds, declaring them "proper only for wines of rich *bouquet,* flowers of that shape being sweetest in scent" (*AJ* 6:32). In other words, he deems them unsuited to champagne not because their shape would allow the wine's effervescence to escape but because champagne, unlike the flower, does not have a strong fragrance.[7]

This brief explication of the principle of fitness is meant to suggest not only the sophistication of Victorian design theory but also its affinities with other strains of proindustrial discourse. Just as liberal proponents of the factory system could argue simultaneously for free trade and factory discipline, so liberal champions of design embraced the expressive possibilities opened up by technical innovation while simultaneously endeavoring to enforce a strict code of design principles. Their objections to eclectic combinations of decorative elements, their emphasis on precision of execution, and their insistence that ornament "fit" the object it adorns all follow from a fundamental regard for rational hierarchy and order. Victorian design theory may thus be construed as an attempt to reconcile capitalism's celebration of economic and creative autonomy with its concurrent insistence on discipline and control. Under this interpretation, the formal perfection of a "good design" exemplifies the organic coherence nineteenth-century political economists sought to attribute to industrial society generally.

IN THE introduction to its inaugural number, the *Art-Union* identified itself as the champion of "the profession of the Artist" and committed itself to consolidating the cultural authority of the fine arts. Its first few volumes demonstrate a wariness toward perceived threats to this authority, such as the opinions of an independent public, the proliferation of technologies of mass production, and the nation's preoccupation with commerce. The journal received word of the invention of the daguerreotype "with caution" (*AJ* 1:106), and it likewise lamented in the strongest terms the lack of patronage for the fine arts in a nation obsessed with getting and spending:

> The empire of Britain is one of the most powerful, one of the most famous, and by far the wealthiest under the sun: yet it is more parsimonious, nay, niggardly to its men of genius than any other kingdom, however humble, between east and west, which the sun of Art and Literature consents to shine on. . . . [S]he will not lend a helping hand, nor give a penny to those whose genius redeems her from the charge of being semi-barbarous; from having a taste which reaches no higher than tare and tret, and a seven per cent. sort of imagination, which even in its happiest mood is all but commercial. (*AJ* 2:123)

As it refined its ideology, however, the journal softened its antagonistic posture toward things commercial. Recognizing that automated industry and novel copying technologies had fundamentally and irreversibly altered the relationship between the fine arts and manufactures, the journal increasingly sought to describe and theorize the relationship between art and other modes of production. Rather than complaining that the drive for commercial gain had displaced the love of beauty, it contended that beauty possessed commercial and social value. Rather than decrying the lack of patronage for artists in a nation made rich through manufacture, it argued that manufacturers required artists' guidance and assistance. Rather than rejecting science and technology as inimical to the "aura" of high art, it embraced them as ways of expanding art's influence. In short, the *Art-Union* gradually came to perceive opportunities for increasing the prestige of the fine arts and the professional artist where before it had seen only threats and challenges.

This change in perspective is evident in the editorial statements opening each year's volume, which reflect the journal's efforts to cultivate a wider readership. Muting (but not abandoning) its 1839 declaration to be "exclusively devoted to the interests of Artists and the Arts" (*AJ* 1:iii), the preface to the 1842 volume asserts a "desire to promote the purposes of the *useful Arts* by showing how advantageously they may be influenced by the *Fine Arts;* and how largely our manufactures may be benefited by the aid of taste and genius" (*AJ* 4:3). In 1843 the journal solicited "the confidence of the Artists on the one hand, and the Public on the other" (*AJ* 5:5). By 1844 it was asserting its intent "to obtain such information as may be interesting, or valuable, to the STUDENT, the AMATEUR, and the CONNOISSEUR"; to be "practically useful to the MANUFACTURER and the ARTISAN"; and to bring Art's "healthful, happy, and invigorating, influences to bear upon all classes of society" (*AJ* 6:5).

Also in 1844 the journal ceased to identify itself solely as "A Monthly Journal of the Fine Arts" and officially dedicated itself to "the Arts, Decorative, and Ornamental" as well. From this point forward, it became increasingly concerned with art's relation to industry and commerce, publishing series of articles under such titles as "Art Applied to Manufactures," "The Mercantile Value of the Fine Arts," and "Applications of Science to the Fine and Useful Arts." Nevertheless, its new title page, which depicted an easel and artist's palette within a wreath of oak, graphically belied this shift of emphasis by confirming the journal's primary commitment to the fine arts, and especially to painting.

In 1848, one year before it changed its name to the *Art-Journal,* the *Art-Union* again altered its title page, dropping its explicit notice of the decorative and ornamental arts and adopting a new design by Henry Linton that visually signifies their subordinate status: the easel and palette have been replaced by a fanciful sculptural composition in which a female figure representing painting is flanked by similar figures representing sculpture and architecture (see fig. 3). This image perfectly captures the journal's attitude toward these purportedly lesser arts, which was to encourage them as a means of reinforcing the social and economic authority of high or fine art. The cultivation of taste and beauty, the journal maintained, would stimulate technological, social, and commercial progress while simultaneously working as a kind of governor to keep those forces from spinning out of control.

The opening essay of the journal's 1845 volume makes this claim in vivid fashion. Reflecting on the "probable future condition of British art," it warns against the "evil consequences" of treating the "productions of Art" as if they were "simple articles of commerce": "[W]e have left them, like hay, straw, bricks, and cotton, to find a market where they could; and, proud of mechanical power, we have used it like a brute force,—separated from invention, unconnected with design. Thus, like Frankenstein, we have been punished by the demon of our own creation" (*AJ* 7:5). Just as Mary Shelley's novel dramatizes the consequences that arise from the pursuit of science unconstrained by wisdom, so the journal treats the current state of British art as a consequence of production unconstrained by taste and design. Just as Shelley's Promethean doctor was led by his creation into the barren reaches of the Arctic, so British manufacturers have been drawn by their neglect of design into their own commercial wilderness. Taking the textile and clothing industries as its chief example, the essay offers an aesthetic explanation for Britain's colonial expansion: "Our commerce, indeed, seems to ebb from civilization, and to flow with greater force the more it streams towards savage life. In European countries it declines; with the swarth African, the Chinese, and Hindoo, it increases" (*AJ* 7:5). Crude "mechanical power" unconstrained by some higher authority is not a sign of progress and civilization but a potential source of economic and cultural degeneration. If Britain persists in producing shoddy goods for savage peoples, the essay implies, the nation will bring about its own decline. On the other hand, if art is allowed to guide commercial industry, the nation will continue on the path of progress toward social harmony and commercial prosperity.

A series of essays under the title "The Tariff," nominally concerned with Robert Peel's reduction of import and export duties in the early 1840s, demonstrates how the journal's aesthetic views complement its free-trade politics. Postulating that "political economy is much more closely connected with

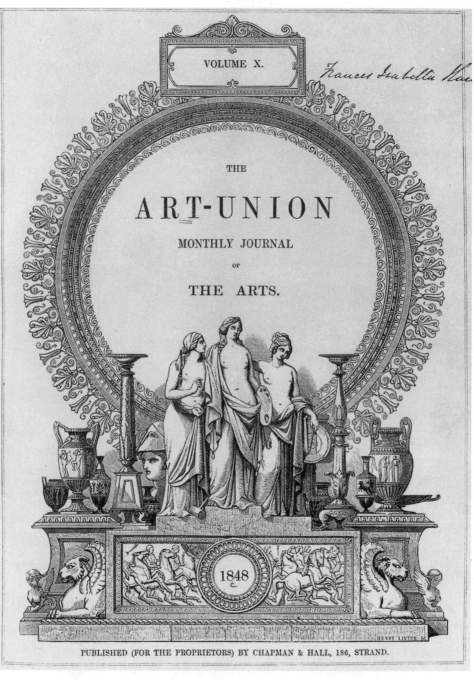

VOLUME X.

THE

ART-UNION

MONTHLY JOURNAL

OF

THE ARTS.

1848

PUBLISHED (FOR THE PROPRIETORS) BY CHAPMAN & HALL, 186, STRAND.

Fig. 3. Title page, *Art-Union,* vol. 10. (Courtesy of the Avery Architectural and Fine Arts
Library, Columbia University in the City of New York)

the progress of taste and artistic design than is generally believed" (*AJ* 8:120), the series argues that a reduction in the tariff will lead to mutually reinforcing improvements in the quality of English design, the condition of the working classes, and the competitiveness of English manufactures abroad (*AJ* 8:95–96). By effectively destroying the foreign market, protectionist tariffs provoke "a most injurious competition" at home; by raising prices, they reduce demand and court economic depression; by reducing the margin of profits, they discourage the investment of capital and technical innovation. This economic argument is readily transposable into an aesthetic register. As markets constrict, manufacturers fail "to stimulate design," and consumers come to accept "the inferiority of English patterns as an article of national faith incorporated in acts of Parliament" (*AJ* 8:96). Meanwhile, operatives pursue such "artificial means" of maintaining wages as strikes and trade unions while neglecting the "natural means" of raising wages through "the artistic improvement of the manufactured article" (*AJ* 8:96, 95).

The journal's response to the class crisis that accompanied industrialization was to rally the nation around the common goal of aesthetic improvement. In other words, it offered the aesthetic harmony of industrial design as a counterpoise to the class fragmentation of industrial society. Countering Gallic taste with Saxon pluck, it dismisses with disdain the idea of an inherent "*incapacity* of Englishmen to compete with Frenchmen" (*AJ* 8:96) and urges all segments of society to embrace unflinchingly the principle of free and open competition in the arts of design:

> Give Englishmen a fair field and no favour, and we shall look for triumphs as decisive in the arts of peace as ever were obtained in the arts of war. But there must be no folding of arms and no wringing of hands; we must not have men waiting for masters to begin improvement, and masters waiting for men; both must set to work together, because Time will wait for neither of them. We must have fewer Trades' Unions and more Art-Unions; we must have the real independence of industry in the self-dependence of industry. We must avoid the fancied evil of becoming dependent on foreigners, by grasping the real good of rendering foreigners dependent on us. (*AJ* 8:96)

The discourse on design thus supported English nationalism in two complementary ways, sharpening the distinctions between England and other nations even as it smoothed over domestic class differences in the name of "national taste" (*AJ* 8:145).

Moreover, it was presumed that the inculcation of taste would elevate standards of social behavior. As one contributor to the journal explains, taste is a "moral power," and its "cultivation" is a "powerful means of elevating the intellectual condition of humanity" (*AJ* 4:14). In keeping with the emphasis on minute nuances of sensation and feeling that typify the ideology of the aesthetic, this view authorized a rigorous attention to the design of seemingly inconsequential domestic articles. Objects of "every-day acquaintance" are presumed to be "perpetually at hand at home, and continually in our sight abroad, and therefore always active in forming the taste, whether for good or for evil" (*AJ* 2:24). "Domestic decoration" is deemed critically important "because taste is insensibly moulded and formed by the effect of familiar objects in daily use" (*AJ* 7:93). The manufacture of glass is judged an important topic because it is "those minor articles of use and ornament which produce the most direct influence on the formation of taste" (*AJ* 8:102).

Indeed, seemingly innocuous errors in aesthetic judgment were purported to have dire consequences, just as small moral lapses were deemed to place one in danger of tumbling down a slippery slope toward public drunkenness:

> We endure clumsiness, because *it is only* a brush or a razor, or a candlestick, or some other petty article of no great value in itself. But there is no more mischievous phrase than this very permissive and exceptional *it is only*. In morals, the *it is only* a petty deviation from the strict rule of rectitude soon becomes a precedent for further and wider departures. The *it is only* in vicious indulgence soon widens the exception to the utmost latitude of tippling; and the *it is only* in bad taste has a similar tendency to extend its range, until it embraces the larger share both of individual and social existence. (*AJ* 8:145)

As the right and wrong of aesthetic knowledge thus shades into the strict rule of behavior, the cultivation of taste takes on the qualities of a rigorous ascetic discipline. As the frequent understanding of decorative fitness in terms of "propriety" suggests, the *formal* coherence that follows from the exercise of aesthetic discipline has its counterpart in the *social* coherence that follows from the exercise of moral restraint. The cultivation of taste through the dissemination of well-designed manufactures links these two domains. By working to inculcate correct principles of taste, artists and the arts make their unique contribution to the current "age of improvement" (*AJ* 7:17), fostering the progress of design and taste just as mechanical innovations foster the progress of industry and commerce.

THE PUBLIC's demand for novelty or fashion, however, was deemed a serious threat to this vision. Therefore, the *Art-Journal* devoted extensive effort to curtailing this desire, first, by stigmatizing the public's untutored tastes as potentially subversive or degenerate; second, by asserting the commercial value of good design; and third, by encouraging art education. The journal condemned the blatant disregard for good design demonstrated by both manufacturers and the public as a willful rejection of civilized sensibility. As Wornum observes in one of his contributions, "untutored" modern tastes recall the crude preferences of the "savage" or "Oriental mind" (*AJ* 10:346–47). Conversely, the journal reassured manufacturers that although the market may follow the "caprice of fashion," it was a "general rule of patterns" that "though some which are bad may succeed, none which are really good can fail" (*AJ* 6:6). It thus appealed to manufacturers' self-interest by framing good design as a hedge on the uncertainty of the marketplace, even as it lauded those "enterprising gentlemen" who embraced the cause of design as a patriotic and moral duty (*AJ* 8:35).

The *Art-Journal* also supported the cultivation of taste through the direct education of the working classes. The controversies that recurred throughout the 1840s over the government Schools of Design were one manifestation of a wider concern over what Rifkin describes as "the formation of a national and popular industrial culture, oriented around the perception and consumption of commodities" (98). The debates over the role, curriculum, constituency, and efficacy of such schools reflect a growing awareness among segments of the middle as well as the working classes of the peculiar "cultural scheme of things" engendered by industrial capitalism, and of each class's need to stake out its "place within it" (Rifkin 95).

In this context, apparently trivial issues, such as whether students should be taught to draw the human figure, assumed a tremendous symbolic significance. Opponents of this practice viewed it as an encroachment on the prerogatives of the artist and felt that Schools of Design should teach only those skills which were strictly necessary to ornamental design.[8] Presumably, they did not begrudge the occasional operative a modicum of artistic ability, but they did object to a kind of instruction that blurred the boundaries between the higher and lower arts, and, by implication, between the higher and lower classes. In this dispute, the *Art-Journal* adopted the broader perspective that efforts to limit the kinds of artistic instruction offered at the schools betrayed "a very superficial and imperfect view of the nature and scope of the course of education required to produce skilled inventors" (*AJ* 4:24). Nevertheless, the journal was hardly blind to the hegemonic implications of its position. If it supported general artistic education for designers on pragmatic grounds (that is, that it would help them produce more "skilled inventors"), it also maintained that formal artistic education could exercise a powerful cultural and social agency, by catalyzing and reinforcing the edifying influence of good design.

Cooke Taylor's 1849 essay "On the Cultivation of Taste in the Operative Classes" (11:3–5), which I discussed briefly in the introduction, amplifies this claim into a comprehensive argument for the consolidation of middle-class social and cultural hegemony through the development of an "efficient" system of national technical and artistic education. Cooke Taylor sees the Continental revolutions of 1848 as revolutions of rising expectations, and he worries that the system of "National Education" being developed in England by Kay and others may have similar effects at home. His concern is that the neglect of education among the middle classes, in conjunction with misguided efforts to provide a liberal or "literary" education to the laboring population, will foster a destabilizing "upheaving of educated pauperism from beneath" and "prepare an assured way for revolutionary pressure of class upon class." The "proper business" of education, Cooke Taylor contends, is to reinforce existing social hierarchies by preparing people "to do their duty in that state of life to which it has pleased God to call them." The nation of course wants "good men, good citizens, good labourers, good operatives," but that goal does not require a working class consisting of liberal subjects "trained to *something else besides*" the skills they require to be "good contributors" to the industrial economy. This position illuminates the complementarity between the *Art-Journal*'s governing liberal ideology and its formal aesthetic principles. Individuals should fit their place within the larger class structure, just as ornament should fit the object it adorns.

In contrast to other proindustrial writers who argue that the inculcation of moral discipline among the working classes will give rise to economic benefits, Cooke Taylor argues that economic improvement will give rise to a beneficial social stability. He brushes aside the mystifying rhetoric that so frequently accompanies calls for improving the "taste" of the working classes and sets about reducing the matter of "artistic" education to "the plain intelligible form of pounds, shillings, and pence." The poor and mere laborers, he points out, have no need for an artistic education, but to artisans and operatives, it offers real advantages. In both handicraft and automated labor, Cooke Taylor observes, "Taste enters largely into that very complex quality which is usually termed mechanical skill." Taste, for Cooke Taylor, is very much like any other sort of technical expertise: it increases the value of its possessors' labor even as it enhances "the commercial prosperity of the nation."

Cooke Taylor recognizes, moreover, that the efforts of the best designers "will be in vain, so long as a perverted public taste contents itself with inferior patterns." He therefore advocates educating the middle-class public as well, as a means of setting into motion an economically beneficial cycle of supply and demand, organized around the production and consumption of goods of increased quality and value: "Appreciation produces demand, and demand leads to supply." The moral and social benefits of taste, according to Cooke Taylor, follow directly from this economic benefit. In addition to raising wages, the development of taste inculcates a "useful" pride in workmanship that leaves the artisan or operative "contented with his condition and his work" and "disinclined to disturb Law and Order."

The objective laws of economics thus converge with the objective laws of beauty to form a single, unified ideology. "Economical Science and the interests of Art, instead of being at variance," Cooke Taylor concludes, have been shown to be "identical in principle," since "whatever increased artistic beauty, added to the economic value of production." Not only does he identify the general national welfare with the development of the specifically industrial segment of Britain's economy; he also places the primary emphasis on right-minded education's economic (rather than "moral") benefits.

Nevertheless, Cooke Taylor is careful not to alienate the professional artists who constitute the journal's primary constituency, and at the end of his essay, he takes pains to reconcile his economic argument for the "cultivation of taste" with the more noble view that both "high art" and "common design" exercise a directly "beneficial influence over our moral and social relations." If he has justified "Art" on "lower grounds than should be chosen by the *Art-Journal*," he claims to have done so as a pragmatic concession to the "practical and unimaginative" spirit of the age:

> [W]e live in a generation which condemns theory, and expends more on theories than any other which the world ever saw; a generation which writes volumes against speculations, and wastes millions in them; which estimates sculpture like masonry, and bestows more on the worst of masonry than would purchase the best of sculptures; and with such a generation we must deal by pointing out that its conduct is false to its own creed, and abhorrent to its own most favoured maxims.

Like Ruskin and other Victorian "sages," Cooke Taylor treats art as a platform for pointing out the hypocrisies of commercial society, but whereas Ruskin saw this hypocrisy as inherent in industrial capitalism, Cooke Taylor attributes it to a kind of apostasy among the commercial and manufacturing interests which has led them to act at variance with their own professed economic "creed." Paradoxically, it is only the artist who has kept true to the common principles of taste and "Economical Science." The artist thus has a crucial role to play in commercial society, both by assisting manufacturers in the design and production of more beautiful—and therefore more valuable—products and by inculcating and reinforcing true economic principles through the cultivation of taste.

Such reasoning would have been highly appealing to the *Art-Journal's* audience, which had a direct interest in claiming a prominent role for the artist in the new industrial economy. Although the journal advocated the "artistic" education of artisans and operatives, it also maintained a clear distinction between the mechanical labors of the "mere workman" (*AJ* 7:17, 12:122) and the more valuable intellectual efforts of the artist. Therefore, according to Babbage's corollary to the principle of the division of labor (which holds that complex tasks ought to be decomposed into their elemental processes, each of which may then be accomplished at its minimum cost; see chap. 2), the labor of the artist ought to be conserved, since it is more expensive than the labor of less "skilled" sorts of workers. As one contributor to the *Art-Journal* observes, mechanical "improvers" must keep one principle in mind, which is "not to increase the artist's labour in order to lessen that of the mechanic" (*AJ* 12:190). Furthermore, while the mechanic retains no proprietary rights over the products of his labor, the artist suffers no such alienation. Although a manufacture may pass through myriad hands, its modeler or designer—not the manufacturer—"is, in fact, the creator of the article" (*AJ* 8:2). In its effort to distinguish the artist from the artisan, the *Art-Journal* applies to industrial manufactures the Romantic notion that there exists a special bond between creators and their creations. In so doing, it contributes as well to the reconceptualization of art in the age of mechanical reproduction as a primarily abstract and intellectual—rather than concrete and manual—pursuit.

This revised conception of art also entails a new view of the relationship between the artist and the manufacturer. As the Great Exhibition approached, the journal's repeated assertions that beauty had commercial value were mirrored by equally prominent claims that manufacturers could benefit from—and therefore should defer to—the specialized advice and expertise of the artist. Surely, one representative essay opines, "in a cause so vital" as the improvement of design, manufacturers "will not be without the aid of THE ARTIST!" (*AJ* 8:65). Another comments that "THE ARTIST" should "consider himself not only usefully, but honourably, employed, when giving purer forms to articles which THE MANUFACTURER multiplies and circulates" (*AJ* 9:393). In keeping with such views, the journal began in 1848 to publish a series called "Original Designs for Manufacturers," and it invited manufacturers to copy these designs at will. By August of that year, it was celebrating its influence over industry: "We are fast gaining our object, and receiving an abundant reward from the fact that the cooperation of good design and excellent workmanship is becoming more and more extensive and palpable, and that there is now a better understanding than ever between artists competent to design and manufacturers capable of executing" (*AJ* 10:241).

The content of such passages works to combat the anxiety, evident in their insistent tone, that artists and the arts have no real place in industrial society. By mapping the rhetoric of industrial class relations—in which "men" are figured as the "hands" and "masters" as the "heads" of industry—onto the relationship between the manufacturer and the professional artist, the journal attributes to artists an exclusive monopoly on taste and imagination and also reduces manufacturers to grand mechanics. Just as the "mechanician" merely "facilitates" the artist's designs (*AJ* 8:1), so the "manufacturer" merely "multiplies and circulates" them. The artist thus comes to mediate both the process of mechanical production and the nexus of commodity exchange. In short, the journal's response to the age of mechanical reproduction is to dress artists in capitalist garb, and to present them as manufacturers of beauty and managers of taste.

THE STRONG investment of the *Art-Journal* in the status of the professional artist, however, precluded a recognition that when artists begin to design art manufactures, they are no longer functioning as artists in any pure sense. Therefore, while the journal continued to argue for the importance of design in manufacture, it also found itself under assault from a rival publication, Henry Cole's *Journal of Design and Manufactures* (1849–52), which aimed to establish design as a distinct intellectual and aesthetic discipline. One of Cole's acknowledged talents lay in using journalism to shape public opinion. In the 1830s he wrote a number of articles for the *Athenaeum* and the *London and Westminster Review,* and in 1840 he briefly served as coeditor of the latter journal with John Hickson. He was likewise involved with the Radical newspaper *The Guide* (1837–38), organized the *Penny Circular* (1838–39) to muster support for Rowland Hill's penny post, and edited the short-lived *Historical Review* (1845) (Levine 61; Cooper 22). The *Journal of Design* was his most ambitious journalistic endeavor. Like the *Art-Journal*, it contained a remarkable range of material: speculative articles on high aesthetic theory, prescriptive discussions of the principles of design, reports on the Schools of Design and various industrial exhibitions, histories of different industries and firms, explanations of mechanical and chemical processes employed in industry, agitation for reform of the copyright laws, and commentary on the design of all sorts of manufactured products. So that its critical pronouncements "may be tested in the *very* presence of the object criticised" (*JD* 1:3), it also included numerous engravings of manufactures from beer steins to fireplace grates, as well as dozens of swatches of actual textiles and wallpapers to illustrate various patterns (see fig. 4).

The crucial difference between the two journals should be clear from their titles. The *Art-Journal* was dedicated first and foremost to advancing the authority and status of professional artists and championed design primarily as a means to this end. The *Journal of Design* championed the cause of design much more directly and aggressively. Because Cole was more bureaucrat than artist, he felt no particular loyalty to either the Royal Academy or the constituency represented by the *Art-Journal*. On the contrary, he perceived in the *Art-Journal*'s failure to take up the issue of design with sufficient vigor an opportunity to extend his own sphere of influence.[9] Yet Cole's journal has a more lasting significance too, as the first English-language publication dedicated specifically to the cause of industrial design (Levine 63). Unlike the *Art-Journal*, the *Journal of Design* did not seek to subordinate design to high art but treated it as a discrete discipline constituted around a proprietary body of specialized knowledge and skills. The journal deserves careful study for its sustained effort to trace out the various aesthetic, social, and economic implications of this position.

In contradistinction to Ruskin and his successors, Cole and his circle display an almost exclusive concern with the formal qualities of manufactured objects. Yet while the *Journal of Design*'s specific reviews and criticisms typically address themselves to formal considerations, they are themselves motivated by a more general conviction that the aesthetic qualities of manufactures have a broad commercial, social, and even moral significance. As its "political creed" makes clear, the *Journal of Design* sought to encourage good design not for its own sake but for its perceived ability to mediate the more general social and economic changes wrought by mechanical production:

> We think the restless demands of the public for constant novelty are alike mischievous to the progress of good ornamental art as they are to all commercial

MOUSSELINE DE LAINE,

Persian pattern.

BLOCK PRINTED.

By Inglis and Wakefield, Friday Street, London.

Journal of Design, No. 2.   April, 1849.

Fig. 4. "Mousseline de Laine," *Journal of Design,* vol. 1, facing p. 43.
(Courtesy of the Yale Center for British Art, Paul Mellon Fund)

interests. We think that the Schools of Design should be reformed and made business-like realities. We shall wage war against all pirates; and we hope to see the day when it will be thought as disgraceful for one manufacturer to pillage another's patterns as it is held to be if he should walk into the counting-house and rob his till. (*JD* 1:4)

Like Ruskin, Cole and his circle saw ornamental design as reflection of the organization of society. Their difference from Ruskin lies in their contrasting social ideals: if Ruskin's calls for reform are grounded in a fundamentally anticapitalist "feudal socialism," the *Journal of Design*'s practical agenda is grounded in a quasi-utopian vision of commercial society in which industrial production and the maintenance of property rights conduce to wealth, improvement, and social harmony.

Like the *Art-Journal*, the *Journal of Design* held that good taste is objective, not merely a matter of personal preference. Just as the *Art-Journal* maintained that "there *is* a right and a wrong" in art as in morals (*AJ* 11:69), so the *Journal of Design* insisted that "'Every one to their own taste,' is a proverb as true as would be the proverb, 'Every one to their morals, or their own physic, or their own mechanics!'" (*JD* 1:24). However, whereas the *Art-Journal* used such assertions to bolster the authority of the professional artist, the *Journal of Design* used them to emancipate design from art and to reconstitute it as a technical profession in its own right, along the lines of medicine or engineering. As a step in this direction, the *Journal of Design* placed tremendous emphasis on the professionalization of design education. This strategy was meant to counter the position, embraced by the *Art-Journal*, that artists were inherently qualified to serve as teachers of design.

Initially, the Schools of Design were staffed with Royal Academy–trained artists who possessed a general knowledge of the history and theory of the arts but had little sense of how this knowledge could be applied to manufactures. Moreover, many of these instructors seem to have viewed their responsibilities to the schools as secondary to their "true" callings as artists. The *Journal of Design* subtly yet incisively caricatures this attitude by printing without comment a letter signed, "A Landscape Painter, Who Has Not Been Very Successful in His Profession." This hapless artist had intended to apply to be a master at a School of Design but was discouraged from doing so by his impression that a course in ornament was required to qualify for such posts. Upon discovering that other masters had been appointed without such training, he decided to renew his application and asked the editor of the *Journal of Design* for assistance. "It seems, therefore," he writes politely, that these masters are artists who have accepted these situations as something to lean upon while pursuing their own profession. To me such a situation would be extremely convenient; and if you could afford me any information how or why these masters obtained their appointments,—whether through talent or otherwise, and what that talent was; or if you could bring me under the notice of the proper authorities through the publication of this, I should feel much obliged. (*JD* 3:28–29)

This painter has no compunction about admitting—or indeed, embracing—his incompetence. He readily admits his lack of specific training for the position for which he is applying, and he clearly believes that appointments to the schools are made on the basis of "talent" or political preference rather than on the basis of credentials or competence. Whether or not this inquiry produced its desired effect, we cannot know. Nevertheless, it illustrates the kinds of assumptions about art and design that the *Journal of Design* was seeking to dispel: that "Art" qualifies as a "profession," even when not practiced successfully, and that the teaching of design is merely a convenient "situation" for one whose real interests are elsewhere.

If the *Journal of Design* exercises restraint in responding to this particular query, it elsewhere opposes such dilettantism more vigorously, lobbying relentlessly for the professionalization of all parties associated with the Schools of Design, including masters, students, and administrators. It upbraids Parliament for the meager sum devoted to prizes in its annual appropriation to the schools, on the grounds that "the critical study of art, in regard to ornament, needs all the fostering aid and encouragement that public means can furnish, in order to extend and *elevate* this department of art *as a professional pursuit*" (*JD* 3:120). It likewise insists that the duties of school inspectors should occupy their whole time and endorses a "*laissez-nous-faire* policy" with respect to masters, so long as they remain "conscientiously alive to the responsibility of their undertaking" (*JD* 3:119). The journal even issues a direct challenge to artists to prove that they are better designers than the students in the schools (*JD* 3:160) and maintains that masters should be required to demonstrate their competence by exhibiting their own designs: "However unpalateable," its editor insists, "the truth must be reiterated again and again, that the masters of the Schools *must* qualify themselves for their specialty, and be compelled to demonstrate their ability,—or else, instead of teachers of ornamental design, they will remain, as Mr. Poynter has justly characterised them, 'mere drawing-masters'" (*JD* 3:28). Together, these contentions attribute to designers and instructors in design three major hallmarks of professional status: the possession of a particular expertise, single-minded commitment to one's occupation, and professional autonomy underwritten by an ethic of personal responsibility.

BUT WHAT of the actual *content* of this new discipline? Like medicine and engineering, design was understood to be a fundamentally practical profession, predicated upon the synthesis of multiple domains of expertise. This understanding of the profession came under attack from two directions: from those who viewed the designer as merely an inferior sort of artist, and from those who saw the designer as merely another sort of industrial worker. Further complicating the situation was the fact that this last position was espoused by two very different constituencies: manufacturers wary of funding kinds of general training that would not bring them immediate returns, and artists concerned with defending their professional turf. The *Journal of Design* approached this array of objections by attempting to integrate two potentially contradictory lines of argument. On the one hand, the journal imagined design as a kind of commodity or form of capital essential to Britain's industrial and commercial prosperity. On the other hand, it insisted that design was not merely a trade but a liberal, intellectual practice on a par with the pursuit of science and art and claimed for the new discipline a corresponding prestige.

By the late 1840s, Kay's "enlightened capitalists" had started to recognize that their "human machinery" was at least as important as their machinery of wood and metal. (Their purported awareness of this need was, in fact, the primary evidence of their "enlightenment.") In a metaphor calculated to appeal to this perspective, the *Journal of Design* describes art as a "marketable commodity, as valuable in proportion to its excellence as wood, stone, iron, or cotton" (*JD* 2:48), and argues that it is in manufacturers' interest to attend to its cultivation: "Manufacturers consider it legitimate to speculate in building new factories, in trying new materials, in patenting new processes, they should now also consider it not only legitimate, but essential, to speculate in the gift of education to their workmen, and in affording him time to obtain that, without which the produce of their manufacture can never be wrought up to the proper degree of perfection" (*JD* 2:151). This reasoning was readily extended from the factory to the entire commercial system. If the *production* of quality manufactures depends on the education of workers, the perhaps more crucial *distribution* of these goods depends on the taste of those whose task is discrimination, or aesthetic "labor" in the strictest sense. As one troubled "Observer" notes, "[T]here are two classes of persons engaged in decorative manufactures of every description, who, as a body, are infinitely behind the great bulk of the public, and these are, *those who select the patterns for execution, and those who afterwards make the wholesale choice for the retail dealer*" (*JD* 2:152). Such arguments provide a concrete, economic rationale for design education, but they also suggest that the Schools of Design should provide narrow technical training rather than more-comprehensive instruction, a position the Cole circle rejected.

To counter this implication, therefore, the two major design theorists represented in the journal, William Dyce and Richard Redgrave, conceptualize design via comparisons to art and the natural sciences. Their arguments arise from similar objections to the "copyistical" character of contemporary ornament, Redgrave lamenting its uninspired and mechanical execution, and Dyce disparaging its excessive naturalism. Redgrave argues that designers should be accorded the creative freedom of artists, but he also insists that competent designers will possess a knowledge of botany equivalent to (but not identical with) that of the natural scientist. Dyce refutes the notion that design is "a lower kind of fine art" and maintains that designers require the same sort of general education as artists. At the same time, he presents design as "a practical science" predicated upon the distillation and application of abstract principles (*JD* 1:65). The apparent inconsistencies among these views are symptoms of Dyce's and Redgrave's struggles to articulate precisely their notion of design as a hybrid discipline. In this light, their sometimes tortured equivocation may be seen as a bootstrap rhetorical tactic enabling them to define the conceptual blend "design" through a series of iterative comparisons and contrasts.

In a lecture entitled "The Importance of the Study of Botany to The Ornamentist," Redgrave argues that botany has the potential to "neutralise" the "evil condition of ornamental art"—its standardization, dull uniformity, endless repetition, and so on—brought on by its "mechanical production" (*JD* 1:178).[10] In elaborating this claim, he almost precisely anticipates Ruskin's interpretation of "accurate mouldings" and "perfect polishings" as signs of industrial "slavery," and like Ruskin, he alludes to Adam Smith's paradigmatic example of pin making in condemning the psychic effects of the division of labor: "The mechanical repetition of art tends, in its consequences, to enslave the ornamentist. Were it entirely to prevail, it would reduce him to the level of machines, working like pin-makers, one the head, another the shaft, a third the point. How different to the systems in older and better periods!" (*JD* 1:178). Redgrave's response to this condition, however, is significantly different from Ruskin's. Instead of viewing the potential mechanization of the ornamentist as an indictment of industrial capitalism, he argues more pragmatically for the elevation of design into the kind of intellectual labor valued by industrial society. To this end, he maintains that the ornamentist must acquire a knowledge of the vegetable world as detailed as that of the botanist while also remembering to approach his subject from the perspective of the artist.

Dyce likewise considers design a metadiscipline integrating the plastic arts and the natural sciences. For this reason, he holds that ornamental designers require a "more extended" preparatory education than students in other areas of the arts. "Instead of being more limited," the subjects designers must master "extend over the whole domain of the works of nature" (*JD* 1:28). The "whole domain of the works of nature," however, can hardly qualify as a professional specialty, so Dyce specifies that the salient issue for the ornamentist is not whether particular "specimens of ornament are in themselves beautiful? but whether, being so, they are adapted to particular purposes?" (*JD* 1:91).

This view both differentiates design from art (which Dyce understands to be concerned with beauty for its own sake) and lends design the character of an applied science:

> General principles have now to be considered with reference to their application in particular cases. The remains of ancient ornamental art are now to be examined, less in detail than as the constituents of whole systems or styles of decoration. Nature is now to be regarded, not merely as the source whence we are to derive general ideas of beauty in ornament, but as affording, beyond this, hints for the particular kind of decoration applicable to special cases. (*JD* 1:91)

Dyce clarifies the relationship between these two sources of guidance in a subsequent essay. Artists, he writes, should treat beauty as an "individual quality," while ornamentists should regard it as *"a quality separable from natural objects"* (*JD* 6:2). If the task of the artist is to produce representations of uniquely beautiful *things*, the task of the ornamentist is to apply nature's *principles* to new ends: "[T]he ornamentist is an imitator of nature, in a sense very analogous to that in which the man of science may be termed so, who applies her operating and governing laws and the means and hints furnished by her to the accomplishment of new ends of convenience and utility" (*JD* 6:2).[11]

This analogy between design and natural science provides a basis for distinguishing the progressive succession of bona fide historical styles from mere vacillations of fashion. Fashions emerge through simple variation, but new styles "can only be invented by the old method of imitating the cosmetic art of nature" (*JD* 6:3). Nevertheless, the study of historical styles remains crucially important to the designer's education, for the simple reason that it is impossible to recognize true novelty unless one knows what has come before. In addition, the study of past systems of ornament affords an insight into the process of invention itself. Because, in the common view of the School of Design theorists, all styles of ornament arose out of a universal human instinct for decoration, they necessarily display a Wittgensteinian family resemblance. There is no feature common to them all, but as members of a larger class, they share a general affinity with one another and can therefore be made a subject of systematic study. For both these reasons, Dyce contends that in design education the study of historical systems of ornament must become *"our starting-point"* (*JD* 6:3). Like Babbage, Baines, and other champions of the emerging technical professions, Dyce considers a familiarity with the history of one's discipline a prerequisite for making any truly original contribution.

This concern with history is central to the *Journal of Design*'s efforts to delineate an industrial culture, for at least three reasons. First, as Babbage is quick to recognize in a somewhat different context, a knowledge of the history of one's discipline is one of the hallmarks of the professional or expert (Babbage 8:186–87). While the epigraph that opens the journal's first two volumes is taken from Bacon, the epigraph of volumes 3–5 comes from Defoe's *Essay upon Projects* and emphasizes the history of technology as fully as it does technological progress: "Invention of arts, with engines and handicraft instruments for their improvement, requires a chronology as far back as the eldest son of Adam, and has to this day afforded some new discovery in every age." It is precisely an awareness of this chronology which distinguishes the serious designer from the mere dabbler or amateur. The *Journal of Design* therefore works not only to articulate "scientific" principles of design but also to recover Britain's industrial past, by describing the development of various technical processes, chronicling the evolution of Britain's industrial centers, documenting the rise of important firms, and even publishing the obituaries of "eminent manufacturers."

Second, the *Journal of Design*'s historical focus justifies its Whiggish vision of technological and economic development. Articles on such topics as the history of enameling or flax manufactures do not merely acknowledge the ingenuity and skill of preindustrial craftsmen and ratify the professionalism of contemporary designers; they also serve as occasions for the journal to celebrate the unrivaled technological abilities of the nineteenth century. As one contributor writes, "Because our manufactures are in a high state of perfection, it is not to be said that they cannot be made more perfect by the study of the products of an age when every man invented his own processes, and kept them secret when found" (*JD* 3:4). As with past styles of ornamental art, antiquated techniques should be studied but not simply copied. Just as the study of past styles can teach designers valuable guiding principles, so the recovery of forgotten technical knowledge has the potential to stimulate new innovations.

Third, the *Journal of Design* sets out to become a "most important record" of "facts of great value in commercial history" (*JD* 3:5), thus initiating the dialectical process of remembrance and surrogation that Joseph Roach argues is necessary for the perpetuation of culture generally (2–3). In its insistence that "the well-merited fame of the works of their predecessors and themselves should not pass into oblivion and be forgotten" (*JD* 3:5), the journal transforms manufacturing firms into venerable cultural institutions, worthy of the kind of reverence Macaulay shows toward England's constitutional government. This similarity should not be surprising, for like that Whig historian, the *Journal of Design* tells a story of peaceful change, of revolutionary upheaval averted, of sometimes halting but always inevitable progress toward ever higher states of perfection.

EARLY VICTORIAN advocates of industrialism almost unanimously maintained that the dissemination of scientific and technical know-how is ultimately to the benefit of all parties involved in the exchange. In the preface to his *Philosophy of Manufactures,* Andrew Ure notes that in an era of advancing knowledge, efforts to preserve technical or trade secrets only hasten obsolescence: "The few individuals who betray jealousy of intelligent inspection are usually vain persons, who, having purloined a few hints from ingenious neighbours, work upon them in secret, shut out every stranger from their mill, get consequently insulated and excluded in return, and thus, receiving no external illumination, become progressively adumbrated" (x). Seeking professional recognition for their new discipline, Cole's circle made a similar argument with respect to design, and in so doing tackled one of the basic theoretical sticking points of political economy: the need to reconcile the principle of self-interested competition with the broader value of social cohesion.

The classical political economists attempted to resolve this conundrum by bracketing their discipline as the study of the economic effects of competition per se. However, this strategy failed on two fronts. First, as Ruskin so scathingly points out in the opening of *Unto this Last,* it often seemed to purchase theoretical consistency at the high price of practical irrelevance. Second, it established unduly restrictive boundaries that were often violated in practice, as even the most theoretically minded political economists inevitably took into consideration social and psychological factors other than competition (Herbert 77).

The *Journal of Design*, in contrast, understood commercial relations not simply in terms of competition but as taking shape within a sociocultural matrix defined and maintained by the open exchange of information: "We do not admit that competition compels secrecy," it proclaims; "on the contrary, the evils of competition . . . we think would be mitigated by openness" (*JD* 1:104). In keeping with this principle, the journal consistently names the manufacturers of the products it reviews, and it vigorously defends this practice against the objections of retail merchants. It urges retailers to abandon the thin fiction that they deserve exclusive credit for their wares, since honesty and good sense demand that they acknowledge the elaborate division of labor that sustains modern industry and trade: a tradesman "might as well tell an intelligent customer that he built the shop, made the crystalline front, and did all the decorations, as tell him that the articles he sells are his own manufacture" (*JD* 1:90).

In addition, the journal actively promoted industrial exhibitions, in large measure because they appeared to embody its social values. Insisting that the opportunity to participate in such events "ought to be regarded as a privilege," it urges manufacturers of "real talent, taste, and enterprise" to lay aside their "indefinite" fears of betraying proprietary secrets and to proudly and openly display their works (*JD* 1:89).[12] Ultimately, this rhetoric is underwritten by that familiar ethic of masculine earnestness which pervades Victorian life: "No true man has any interest in deception, or in gaining the credit of another man's wit or labour" (*JD* 1:90). Just as Carlyle idealizes "Captains of Industry" and Ruskin charges that "trade [has] its heroisms as well as war" (17:39), so the *Journal of Design* cries out for "more chivalry in manufactures" (*JD* 2:199). Unlike these sages, however, the journal is less concerned with mitigating the social disruptions caused by industrial capitalism than with improving design and increasing the commercial value of British manufactures.

In a peculiar adaptation of the doctrine of the "king's two bodies," the journal treats Cole's patron Prince Albert as both the representative public head and the ideal private citizen of Britain's commercial society. To this end, the *Journal of Design* gives prominent attention to Albert's efforts to foster the union of art and industry and portrays him as one who enacts this union in his private life as well. This dual figuration becomes particularly visible in an anonymous review of a gilt centerpiece designed by the Prince (see fig. 5). While the reviewer is ambivalent about the object's merits as a piece of art manufacture, he is less equivocal about the object's social significance. Carefully distinguishing between "the Prince as prince" and "the Prince as artist," he praises "the refinement of that mind, and the true nobility of that disposition which can turn, for the amusement of its leisure hours, to the cultivation of arts, humanising not only to the proficient in them, but calculated, when universally diffused, in every way to abrogate the prejudices of every class of society" (*JD* 1:34). This celebration of Albert's efforts depends upon an almost Arnoldian concept of cultural dissemination, in which a single refined "mind" can exert a synthesizing social influence that mitigates class antagonisms.

The *Journal of Design* posits an aesthetic resolution to the conflict between competition and cooperation that troubled contemporary political economy by envisioning the reconciliation of these contrary values through art manufacture. If Carlyle and Ruskin condemn industrial capitalism by contrasting it with an idealized feudalism, Albert exemplifies a third alternative of an organic industrial society, the health of which is signified by the "graceful productions emanating from the *united* efforts of the prince, the manufacturer, the sculptor, and (last, not least) the cultivated artisan" (*JD* 1:34). Cole and company implicitly answer the "feudal socialists" by finding Carlylean and Ruskinian social ideals at work within commercial society itself.

THE *Journal of Design*'s vision of a benevolent commercial order, like the idea of culture generally, requires the disciplining of undirected and therefore potentially subversive desire. As Christopher Herbert has argued, the "culturist thinking" that emerged in the first half of the nineteenth century was not opposed to desire, nor does it require its suppression. Rather, desire and culture are bound together in a single if internally conflicted discourse (Herbert 29). Culture is not a system of restrictions on desire but the social matrix that gives desire a coherent structure (50–51). The force that threatens to unravel this matrix is not desire in general but the boundless, undirected, and restless longing that Herbert, following Durkheim, labels "anomie" (68–73). In the *Journal of Design*, anomie manifests itself in the consuming public's appetite for "novelty," which is portrayed as both a support for and a threat to Britain's commercial prosperity. In this role, the constant danger posed by a wayward "public" justifies the journal's authoritarian social and educational agenda.

Fig. 5. "Gilt Centre Piece, executed by command of Her Majesty, from a Design by his Royal Highness Prince Albert." *Journal of Design,* vol. 1, p. 33. (Courtesy of the Avery Architectural and Fine Arts Library, Columbia University in the City of New York)

While the "love of novelty" natural to most human beings is a "source of great pleasure and a considerable motive power in generating improvement," it becomes destructive when "pushed to an unearthly extreme" (*JD* 1:4). For this reason, the journal adopts a posture toward the public significantly different from that which it adopts toward the manufacturers, retailers, and designers involved in the process of production. The public is the one group consistently excluded from the *Journal of Design*'s repeated exhortations to commercial cooperation. The journal identifies design as a "source of wealth to *all* parties concerned in its production" (*JD* 1:1); it urges "the designer, the manufacturer, and the salesman" each to assume "his true position in manufacturing art," since "[a]ll interests will be promoted thereby" (*JD* 1:90); and it insists that each of these parties "has his definite and assigned position" (*JD* 1:104) in the chain of production and distribution. But the consuming "public," as a collective body, is conspicuously absent from these formulations. While the demands of the always exemplary and individual "intelligent customer" foster a coherent commercial culture, the general public's "morbid craving" and "restless appetite" for novelty encourage deception among commercial agents, aesthetic change without progress, and commercial chaos. The issue here is precisely that which confronted Smith, Malthus, and Bagehot as Herbert describes them: how to structure desire so that it can serve as an impetus for economic progress without stifling it and thereby destroying the primary engine of capitalist expansion (Herbert, chap. 2). Translated into the aesthetic register, this question becomes how to convert the public's undirected "appetite" into a "taste" predictable and robust enough to serve as the foundation of a growing commercial market (see Rifkin 99).

Like the *Art-Journal*, the *Journal of Design* claims that taste may be refined through formal instruction and repeated exposure to examples of beauty. As self-professed experts in design, the members of Cole's circle felt themselves ideally suited to meet the need for authoritative instruction in taste, and they therefore pursued an aggressive educational agenda of frequent public exhibitions of industrial manufactures, accompanied by commentary providing interpretive guidance. Nevertheless, the journal was continually frustrated by the public's unpredictable tastes and by manufacturers' willingness to pander to them: "'Novelty—give us novelty!' seems to be the cry; and good or bad, if that is obtained, the public seems satisfied." Of course, the public's seeming satisfaction is chimerical, since any novelty, once obtained, ceases to be new and thus stimulates the "ignorant public" to demand ever more "extravagant" and "*outré*" designs (*JD* 1:74). Because the efforts of designers and manufacturers to satisfy the appetite for novel designs only renders that appetite more voracious, they are unable by themselves to resist the power of anomic desire. Paradoxically echoing the rhetoric of earlier opponents of the factory system, the *Journal of Design* decries the intensification of labor endured by designers "who are unceasingly driven to this endless toil" by the machinery of fashion, and it absolves manufacturers, who "but cater for their markets," of any responsibility for the patterns they produce (*JD* 1:75). In this way, the journal clears a path for itself to step into the cultural vanguard: "The public has to be taught to appreciate the best designs.... We trust our own labours will be found, with the help of the best manufacturers also, to aid in curbing this restless appetite for novelty, which is so generally mischievous" (*JD* 1:4). Allying itself with "the best" manufacturers, the journal endeavors to tip the balance of commercial power away from the consuming public through a rational program of art education. However, since manufacturers are "compelled" to meet the demands of the market, Cole and company patriotically take upon themselves the burden of reform.

The *Journal of Design* ceased publication in 1851, and Cole opens the sixth and final volume with what amounts to a declaration of victory over the forces of bad design. Noting a "great change" in the attitudes of manufacturers since 1849, the journal's inaugural year, he asserts that it had fulfilled "the chief part of its public mission" and would therefore cease publication, although he also expresses the hope that its volumes would continue to serve in the future as "a primer on THE PRINCIPLES OF PRACTICAL ART" (*JD* 6:iii–iv). Among the journal's practical achievements, Cole lists the codification of true principles of design, the improvement of copyright and patent laws, the reform of the Schools of Design, and finally, the promotion of the Great Exhibition of 1851.

This retrospective teleology is, of course, highly artificial. In point of fact, the *Journal of Design* had been since its inception but one of Cole's many interests, and his diaries show that by 1851 he was already devoting the bulk of his attention to the planning of the exhibition rather than to his editorial duties.[13] One constant in Cole's career was his involvement with industrial exhibitions, and the *Journal of Design* certainly reflects this interest. In keeping with his conviction that exhibitions are powerful ways of improving public taste, the journal contains copious descriptive and evaluative commentary on a number of exhibitions in the 1840s and early 1850s, including various shows sponsored by the Society of Arts, the 1849 Paris Exposition of the Productions of National Industry, the 1849 Birmingham Exposition of Arts and Manufactures, the 1850 Manchester Exhibition of Manufactures, the Berlin Exhibition of 1850, and, most important, the Great Exhibition of 1851.

The *Journal of Design's* September 1849 number includes a short notice regarding Prince Albert's intention, as president of the Society of Arts, to assemble "the means of forming a great Collection of the Works of Industry of all nations" (*JD* 2:44), and from this point forward, the Great Exhibition becomes an increasingly prominent topic in the journal's pages. The journal provides extensive coverage of the myriad issues surrounding the planning and management of the exhibition (including the activities of various committees, the solicitation of subscriptions, the selection of a location and building design, the allocation of space to the various participating nations, and debates over the subsequent use of the building and surplus revenue), and after the exhibition's opening, it offers regular critical reviews of the objects on display as well as reports of day-to-day affairs. This degree of coverage was warranted not only by Cole's personal involvement in the planning of the exhibition but also by his perception of it as a realization in microcosm of the *Journal of Design's* ideal of an industrial culture, characterized by class harmony and mutually reinforcing progress in art, science, and industry. It would fall to the Great Exhibition's sanctioned interpreters—cataloguers such as John Tallis and James Ward; individuals involved in the planning of the event such as Henry Cole and Lyon Playfair; scientific and technical experts such as William Whewell, Richard Owen, and Robert Hunt; and authorities on design such as Jones, Wornum, Wyatt, and Redgrave—to establish this intellectual vision as its dominant meaning.

CHAPTER FIVE

"What You Ought to Learn"

Industrial Culture and the Exhibition of 1851

COLE's *Journal of Design*, of course, was not alone in framing the Great Exhibition of 1851 as a triumphant realization of the ideal of an industrial culture. Like the rhetoric of earlier advocates of the factory system, which was directed specifically toward subverting charges that automatic industry threatened the organic harmony of British society, the rhetoric of the exhibition's promoters is marked by recurring images of vital development and vegetable growth. One poet, mixing metaphors as he gropes for language in which to portray the Crystal Palace, imagines the iron framework of Paxton's structure both as "The bone and sinew of the edifice" and as "An iron banyan, with its thousand trunks, / And thrice a thousand branches overhead" (Edmond 1.34, 1.66–67). Another describes the building as "almost like a living World," made "to breathe and start" through the animating power of human labor (Wortley 13.2). For both poets, the exhibition represents a new synthetic order, born, in the words of the latter, of a "glad ... compact" between the formerly opposed forces of "Art" and "mighty Nature" (174.1–2). The *Art-Journal* describes the exhibition as a "seed ... of which the future is to produce the fruit" (*Crystal Palace Catalogue* vi). More elaborately, Edward Forbes, a fellow of the Royal Society and a professor of botany at King's College, London, uses an analogy between the exhibition and vegetable life to frame the event as a social model. Forbes finds much "politic meaning contained in the scientific idea of a plant," holding that the perfect division of labor it displays teaches crucial lessons that "are not dissimilar from those that constitute the true moral of the Great Exhibition" (8).

Most significant, Prince Albert, the Great Exhibition's leading public advocate, consistently discusses the event in language that has strong affinities with the idiom of culture. In an 1849 speech quoted prominently in Cole's introduction to the *Official Descriptive and Illustrated Catalogue*, he celebrates the "present era" as "a period of most wonderful transition" in history's movement toward "the realization of the unity of mankind" (3). For Albert, this "great end" is not a condition of universal uniformity, which "levels the peculiar characteristics of the different nations of the earth," but rather "the result and product of those very national varieties and antagonistic qualities." Like Coleridge, Carlyle, and Arnold, he envisions the unfolding of history as a dialectical process, culminating in a harmonious integration of differences within a single organic whole. He differs from these prophets of culture, though, in recognizing industrial capitalism as the chief agent of this transformation. Alluding to the railway, the steamship, and especially the telegraph, Albert observes that the distances separating the various parts of the world "are gradually vanishing before the achievements of modern invention." He allays any fears that this technological compression of spatial distance will also mean an eradication of enriching difference by heralding the extension of "the great principle of division of labour" into "all branches of science, industry, and art" (3–4).

From Adam Smith to Charles Babbage, commentators on manufacture consistently treat the division of labor as a means rather than an end. The analysis of tasks into elemental operations always presupposes the reintegration of these operations into more comprehensive and efficient processes. Albert similarly regards intellectual specialization as the prelude to a subsequent synthesis: "Whilst formerly the greatest mental energies strove at universal knowledge, and that knowledge was confined to the few, now they are directed to specialities, and in these again even to the minutest points; but the knowledge acquired becomes at once the property of the community at large." In this broad understanding, the division of labor is not simply a means of increasing the efficiency of manufacture; it is more fundamentally a means through which "man" may pursue his God-given purpose, which is "to discover the laws by which the Almighty governs his creation" and, through them, "to conquer Nature to his use" (4).

Albert looks to the Great Exhibition to be both "a true test and a living picture of the point of development at which the whole of mankind has arrived in this great task, and a new starting point from which all nations will be able to direct their further exertions" (4). Like Arnold, who would later contend that true culture consists "not in resting and being, but in growing and becoming, in a perpetual advance in beauty and wisdom" (130), Albert emphasizes not humanity's material achievements but its progressive self-realization. In contrast to Arnold, however, who declares the commercial and industrial middle class "self-excluded" from the ranks of the cultured by its own "incomparable self-satisfaction," Albert contends that it is through "the stimulus of competition and capital" that "man is approaching a more complete fulfilment of that great and sacred mission which he has to perform in this world" (4). Albert, in other words, assigns to capitalism and the industrial bourgeoisie precisely the role Arnold ascribes to culture, which is "to learn, in short, the will of God" and "make it *prevail*" (Arnold 93).

AFTER THE closing of the Great Exhibition in the autumn of 1851, the Society of Arts, at Albert's behest, sponsored a year-long lecture series motivated by this fundamental vision.[1] Delivered by leading men of science, industry, and art, the twenty-four lectures in the series cover an array of topics nearly as diverse as the contents of the Crystal Palace itself. Although the series was billed as a comprehensive and objective survey of the exhibition's "results," it was also a retrospective attempt to fix the exhibition's official meaning as an embodiment of the idea of an industrial culture, exemplified by the mitigation of class antagonisms and mutually reinforcing progress in art, science, and industry.

The inaugural lecture of the series, "The General Bearing of the Great Exhibition on the Progress of Art and Science," was delivered by Dr. William Whewell.[2] Although Whewell was not himself affiliated with the Society of Arts, his dual standing as a leading scientific figure and the master of Trinity College, Cambridge, ideally suited him to ratify the series's contributors as members of a broad scientific, industrial, and artistic clerisy whose appointed task would be to discern the exhibition's true meaning and convey it to the larger population. As Whewell puts it in a succinct explanation of the series's purpose: "[I]t has been determined that persons well qualified to draw from the spectacle the series of scientific morals which it offers, should present them to you here;—that critics should analyse for you some of the fine compositions with which you have become acquainted;—that men of science should explain to you what you *ought to learn* from such an exhibition of art" (1:9, emphasis added).

Whewell initially figures this task as a matter of translating the poetry of the Great Exhibition into a wholly unambiguous technical language. Acknowledging the event as a "great spectacle," he likens this process to the "criticism which comes after Poetry," which distills general truths from "picturesque and affecting" poetic language (1:4–5). This metaphor, Whewell points out, is not arbitrary but rooted in the ancient identity of "Poet" and "Maker":

> [M]an's power of making may show itself not only in the beautiful *texture* of language, the grand *machinery* of the epic, the sublime display of poetical *imagery;* but in those material works which supply the originals from which are taken the derivative terms which I have just been compelled to use: in the Textures of soft wool, or fine linen, or glossy silk, where the fancy disports itself

in wreaths of visible flowers; in the Machinery mighty as the thunderbolt to rend the oak, or light as the breath of air which carries the flower-dust to its appointed place; in the Images which express to the eye beauty and dignity, as the poet's verse does to the mind; so that it is difficult to say whether Homer or Phidias be more truly a poet. (1:5)

Through a fallacious logical inversion, Whewell presumes that if poets are makers, then makers must also be poets. Conflating words and things, he asserts that the Crystal Palace contains the works of many "Makers" in the poetic sense, that it is filled with the products of artisans and manufacturers who have "stamped upon matter, and the combinations of matter" a "significance and efficacy" that marks their creations as "articulate utterances of the human mind" (1:5–6).

Like Babbage, who uses almost identical phrases in *The Economy of Machinery and Manufactures* and *The Ninth Bridgewater Treatise*, Whewell views manufactures as material signs of conscious intention and design. His great philosophical project, which receives its most thorough exposition in his monumental *Philosophy of Science* (1840), may be characterized as effort to reconcile an essentially Aristotelian metaphysics with a commitment to the active role of the human mind in the creation of scientific knowledge. In his Society of Arts lecture, he treats industry from a similar perspective. His characterization of manufactured objects as examples of poetic making allows him to capture their evocative power, yet it also implies that, like poems, they have only a contingent existence, that they are fundamentally *expressions* of their creators' minds. Just as a poetic utterance cannot exist without a speaker, Whewell's analogy implies, so a manufacture cannot exist apart from its maker. Whewell's characterization of manufactures as poems, therefore, should disqualify them as appropriate subjects for scientific investigation, since, as expressions of creative minds, they cannot exemplify any law or order intrinsic to themselves.

When Whewell explicitly states his guiding analogy between the "criticism" of poetry and the "criticism" of manufactures, this latent difficulty comes to the fore:

As the Critic of literary art endeavours to discern the laws of man's nature by which he can produce that which is beautiful and powerful, operating through the medium of language, so the Critic of such art as we have had here presented to us—of *material* art, as we may term it—endeavours to discern the laws of material nature; to learn how man can act by these, operating through the medium of matter, and thus produce beauty, and utility, and power. (1:6)

Whewell's facile "so" glosses over a crucial dissimilarity. As Whewell presents it, the criticism of literature aims to further our understanding of the human creative faculty, or "the laws of *man's nature* by which he can produce that which is beautiful and powerful." To remain consistent, he would have to hold that the critical study of manufactures likewise aims to illuminate this faculty. Instead, he maintains something quite different, that its purpose is to reveal physical laws—the "laws of material nature"—and only secondarily "how man can act by these."

By bracketing the human element in this way, Whewell frames the study of manufactures, in contradistinction to the study of literature, as a proper science. According to his Aristotelian ontology, the "medium of matter" exists apart from the mind and is governed by objective laws, which it is the business of "science" to discover. Therefore, although manufactures resemble poems in some respects, they also remain irreducibly material, and this essential materiality makes them—unlike works of literature—a proper subject for scientific investigation: "To discover the laws of operative power in literary works, though it claims no small respect under the name of Criticism, is not commonly considered the work of a science. But to discover the laws of operative power in material productions, *whether formed by man or brought into being by Nature herself,* is the work of a science, and it is indeed what we more especially term Science" (1:7, emphasis added). Whewell disqualifies literary criticism as a science because it is not directed toward the discovery of a body of objective laws, intrinsic to its field of study. Conversely, he sets the study of manufactures on a scientific basis by subordinating their status as inventions (which is the basis of their affinity to poetry) to their raw materiality (which aligns them with other elements of "Nature"), paradoxically effacing the initial source of his interest in the exhibition—the remarkable applications of inventive power demonstrated in its various "treasures." Whewell thus exchanges the joys of spectacle for a more abstract, scientific understanding of the event's significance. He ceases to portray the exhibition as a "great and grand Drama" (1:4), capable of provoking and sustaining multiple readings and interpretations, and begins to celebrate it instead as a unique opportunity for acquiring objective, scientific knowledge.

In this context, the solitary observer—inexorably anchored to a particular location in space and time and, therefore, to a particular and necessarily partial point of view—becomes an emblem of the cognitive limitations it is the business of collective science to overcome. Whewell, who himself embraced omniscience as an attainable ideal (Yeo 56–61), explains these limitations through the example of an imaginary "intelligent spectator" who endeavors to acquire an understanding of "the whole progress of human art and industry up to the last moment" by traveling from land to land. Even if this ambitious peripatetic could complete his survey, his knowledge would still be "defective" in one respect: he would never be able to achieve a "*simultaneous* view of the condition of the whole globe as to the material arts" because the necessity of moving from place to place would render obsolete large portions of the knowledge he possesses at any given time. The best that this traveler could achieve would be a composite picture patched together from impressions gathered at different times and places and recollected with greater or lesser accuracy (1:10–11).

Two decades earlier, Carlyle offered a similar reflection in his essay "On History." Definitive historical explication was impossible, he argued, for at least two reasons. First, even the most sensitive observer cannot capture events in their entirety, because he has access only to the sequence of his own impressions: "[H]is observation . . . must be *successive,* while the things done were often *simultaneous*" (27:88). Second, the historian's linguistic medium is similarly limited: "Narrative is *linear,* Action is *solid*" (27:89). For Carlyle, these limitations are insurmountable. They are, in fact, what makes writing history an art rather than a science.

Whewell, however, does not consider the essentially serial nature of experience and language inescapable constraints. The "great achievement" of the exhibition was that it allowed the practical limitations of solitary observation to be transcended through a kind of collaborative intellectual "vision," characterized not by sequentiality but by simultaneity. Like other contemporary technologies such as the railway and the telegraph, the exhibition seemed to collapse space and time: "By annihilating the space which separates different nations," Whewell states, "we produce a spectacle in which is also annihilated the time which separates one stage of a nation's progress from another" (1:14). Whewell struggles to express the novel quality of this "spectacle" because he remains committed to representing understanding through the metaphor of vision. Just as lightning makes distant objects visible for a single instant, he offers, so the exhibition illuminates the "infancy of nations, their youth, their middle age, and their maturity" in "their simultaneous aspect" (1:13). Or, like a vast photographic montage, it presents "instantaneously a permanent picture" of the whole "surface of the globe, with all its workshops and markets" (1:14). Neither of these metaphors, however, wholly captures the sense of spatiotemporal compression that characterizes Whewell's experience of the exhibition, the first making it seem too fleeting, the second too static. Recognizing their inadequacy, Whewell resorts to the even more fanciful and elaborate image of a spectator traveling "but a very little faster than light itself" and thus becoming a "bodily and contemporaneous eye-witness" to "all the events which have passed since man has existed upon the earth" (1:14).

The Great Exhibition, Whewell asserts, made this "scientific dream" of omniscience a "visible reality," not simply because it included representative examples of products of "nations in every stage of the progress of art" (1:15) but also because these products were arranged according to a judiciously devised system of classification that effectively reconciled the competing demands of objective taxonomy and practical utility. If the exhibition was comprehensive, it also, in its very eclecticism and excess, threatened to evade authoritative interpretation. While some commentators evinced a strong faith in the exhibition's ultimate coherence—as one poet wrote, "All seems confusion rich, yet reigns, bright Order in the array!" (Wortley 176.4)—others took a more skeptical view, emphasizing its potential to erupt into conceptual chaos. In his satirical cartoon "The House That Paxton Built," for example, George Augustus Sala depicts the Crystal Palace's "multifarious" contents overflowing the "exquisite *classification* and *regularity* of arrangement" by which they were supposed to be ordered and governed (8; see fig. 6).

Whewell, for his part, hoped that the exhibition's classificatory system would develop into "a permanent and generally accepted classification of all the materials, instruments, and productions of human art and industry" and thus provide the basis for a detailed technical vocabulary capable of plucking referents out of the world with mechanical precision: "It is not only necessary that they [workmen] should call a brick a brick, and a wire a wire, and a nail a nail, and a tube a tube, and a wheel a wheel; but it is desirable, also, that wires, and nails, and tubes, and wheels, should each be classified and named, so that a wire number 3, or a tube section 1, or a six-inch wheel, should have a fixed and definite signification" (1:25, 26). Such a vocabulary, Whewell holds, would both minimize the confusion arising from linguistic "diversity and ambiguity" and facilitate manufacture and repair by enforcing a standardization of parts: "[W]ires, and tubes, and wheels, should be constructed so as to correspond to such significations; and even, except for special purposes, no others than such" (1:26).

In this claim that a precise technical vocabulary would possess a performative capacity to control speciation in the industrial universe, Whewell suggests that the exhibition, in its animating conception, mirrors at a philosophical level the disciplinary impulse of industrial capitalism. In Whewell's idealized world of fixed names and settled meanings, there is, as William Cooke

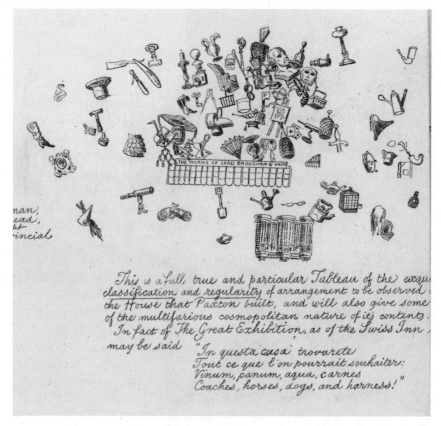

Fig. 6. "Tableau of the exquisite *classification* and *regularity* of arrangement to be observed"
at the Great Exhibition, George Augustus Sala, *The House That Paxton Built*, p. 8.
(Courtesy of the Yale Center for British Art, Paul Mellon Collection)

Taylor said a decade earlier of the perfect factory, "a place for everything,
and everything in its place" (*Notes* 123). Moreover, just as individual factory
operatives are judged incapable of assessing the consequences of violating
"the rules of automatic labour" (Ure 279) because they have only a partial
knowledge of the productive systems of which they are a part, so individual
spectators are not in a position to question the collective assessments of expert
commentators. By taking the limitations of embodied vision as a metaphor
for the intellectual limitations on individual understanding, the exhibition's
sanctioned interpreters could implicitly affirm the superiority of their collective "vision." The Society of Arts thus assumes an interpretive authority
precisely analogous to the authority of the master of an automated mill. Just

as the master tells operatives what they ought to do, so expert commentators will tell lay spectators what they ought to learn and know.

But if the trajectory of Whewell's argument leads to an implicit analogy between the lay spectator and the industrial operative, the esteemed master of Trinity College softens this association by likening the exhibition to a great university, encompassing all the world's workshops, factories, and technical schools. In an almost Newmanesque fashion, he asserts that the crucial function of the university is not the advancement of knowledge for its own sake but the perpetuation and maintenance of a general liberal culture: out of the processes of intercourse and exchange it is the purpose of the university to foster, "there is generated a community of view, a mutual respect, and a general sympathy" which sustains a healthy "national, social, and individual life" (1:33). In the future, he predicts, the "Great University of 1851" will be recognized for having fostered a similar community of "sympathy," "regard," and "good-will" among the world's manufacturers and artisans (1:34). The legacy of the Great Exhibition, Whewell thus suggests, lies less in its particular contributions to the advancement of scientific and technical knowledge than in its broader contributions to a specifically industrial culture.

SUBSEQUENT LECTURES in the Society of Arts's series amplify and develop the implications of Whewell's conclusion, presenting science, industry, and trade as pacifying influences capable of mitigating antagonisms among social classes, economic sectors, and even nations. S. H. Blackwell, for example, opens his account of the iron-making resources of the United Kingdom by identifying the Crystal Palace as a symbol of the way in which iron has brought all branches of manufacture together "in one great bond of unity" (2:147*). Jacob Bell, in a largely technical survey of chemical and pharmaceutical processes and products, describes the exhibition as "a means of promoting peace and harmony by the encouragement of commercial and friendly intercourse throughout the world" (1:153). John Wilson, in a lecture on agricultural products and machinery, argues that the spectacle of agricultural machinery both fostered "friendly relations" between "master" and "man" and prompted the "manufacturer of *cotton*" and the "manufacturer of *corn*" to recognize "their identity of interests" (2:39–40). He predicts that the laborer will come to admire "his iron substitute," and that the farmer will gradually perceive "that every flight of the shuttle must be followed by a blow of the sickle, and that every revolution of the mill-wheel must tend to drive his ploughs deeper into the soil" (2:39–40). While proponents of the factory system writing in the 1830s typically portrayed industry as a kind of cultivation, Wilson here presents cultivation as a kind of industry. Moreover, while his observation recapitulates almost precisely Cooke Taylor's contention of a decade earlier that "the soil has literally been ploughed by the spindle and sowed by the shuttle and the loom" (*Notes* 54), Wilson's tone is markedly less combative. Cooke Taylor argues and insists; Wilson simply asserts and assumes. Both of these rhetorical adjustments—Wilson's inversion of the older metaphor of industry as cultivation and his confident softening of Cooke Taylor's strident tone—indicate the degree to which industry had indeed been naturalized over the course of the two decades preceding the exhibition.

In certain contexts, this argument takes on a racial inflection, with England's industrial preeminence being construed as evidence of Anglo-Saxon superiority, even as the trajectory of history is seen as being toward the ultimate unity of all humankind. To offer a single case in point, S. H. Blackwell praises the "wise and beneficent arrangement" through which diverse mineral resources have been entrusted to a "strong and vigorous Anglo-Saxon race" capable of bringing them into productive use, but he also regards the mid-nineteenth century's paradigmatic technologies as emblems of industry's synthesizing power:

> The steam-engine, the railroad, and the electric telegraph, the characteristic features of the present day, are indeed preparing a quiet revolution for the world; breaking down class interests and substituting universal interests in their place, they are fast uniting in one bond of unity the entire human race, and are leading rapidly, to use the words of His Royal Highness Prince Albert, "to the accomplishment of that end to which, indeed, all history points,—the realisation of the unity of mankind." (2:182)

Such statements were no mere platitudes. On the contrary, they were anticipations of the culmination of a dialectical process through which industrial civilization, characterized by dynamic technological innovation and unrestrained commercial competition, would be transformed into a synthetic and harmonious industrial culture.

In the final lecture of the series, delivered appropriately enough by Henry Cole, the single individual most responsible for planning the Great Exhibition, the event is immortalized as both the culmination of two millennia of English history and the harbinger of a dawning age of international commercial harmony. Cole reconciles these potentially conflicting nationalistic and cosmopolitan views by appealing to the unique constitution of the English race. Unlike earlier proindustrial writers such as Baines, Ure, Cooke Taylor,

and Kay (and unlike many of his fellow lecturers as well), Cole does not attribute his nation's commercial and industrial prosperity to a distinct racial
or national character. Rather, he holds that it is the English people's essential
hybridity that makes them the rightful representatives of all the world's
peoples. England was not the first nation to hold an industrial exhibition, he
observes, but it was the first to sponsor such an event on an international
scale. Although it was in France that the idea of an "International Exhibition" first developed as "a philosophical theory," it was in England that the
idea "became a practical reality" (2:423). For Cole, it was only fitting that
"the most cosmopolitan nation in the whole world" should have hosted "the
first cosmopolitan Exhibition of Industry": "What more natural than that
the first Exhibition of the Works of Industry of *all* Nations should take place
among a people which beyond every other in the world is composed of *all*
nations? If we were to examine the various races which have been concerned
in the production of this very audience, we should find the blood of Saxons,
Celts, Germans, Dutchmen, Frenchmen, Hindoos, and probably even Negroes,
flowing among it" (2:420). In Cole's opinion, the English should be regarded
as a favored race not because of their Anglo-Saxon ancestry but because they
are a synthesis of all the world's peoples. Seen from this perspective, England's
industrial achievements become the world's achievements, England's prosperity the world's prosperity.

Cole uses the same dual logic to defend the free-trade views he had championed throughout the 1840s. "Free Trade" or "unrestricted competition," he
argues, enabled the practical realization of the exhibition, which, in turn,
ushered in a new era of international cooperation (2:420–21). The exhibition marked the beginning of a new epoch because "for the *first* time in the
world's history," an international "Parliament of Art, Science, and Commerce"
had assumed its rightful place at the forefront of the world's affairs (2:427–28).
Since commercial interests are essentially rational, Cole contends, potential
conflicts among nations are subject to resolution "without appeal to the
sword." Just as his *Journal of Design* had urged manufacturers and retailers
to greater "openness" in their commercial dealings, so Cole here anticipates
that "the old-fashioned, narrow suspicions and secrecy of diplomacy" will
be superseded by "public confidence and public discussion" (2:429). He thus
identifies the exhibition as the harbinger of a postnational capitalism in
which commercial ties trump political rivalries among nation-states.

This view leads Cole to dismiss the worry of many of his peers that England had been surpassed in art by France and in science by Germany. If
these nations are advancing more rapidly than England in art and science,

he observes, England is still preeminent in manufacture. This distribution of strengths within an "advancing unity of nations," Cole suggests, should not be a cause of alarm but a source of "unmixed satisfaction," since it amounts to "only a proper division of labour between friends" (2:442). Just as the hybridity of the English people means that England's successes belong to the world, so the specialization of organs within the body of nations means that the world's successes also belong to England.

OTHER CONTRIBUTORS to the Society of Arts's lecture series were notably less sanguine. In particular, they were disturbed by the apparent disjuncture between England's scientific, technological, and commercial advancement on the one hand, and its aesthetic retardation or retrogression on the other. Before 1851 a number of commentators had noted that the handicraft productions of nonindustrialized societies (typically identified as "oriental" or "savage") were often aesthetically superior to their modern English counterparts. By bringing together actual examples of traditional handicrafts and modern manufactures, the Great Exhibition elevated this judgment to the level of conventional wisdom. Some commentators attempted to minimize the significance of this contrast by attributing the beautiful works of purportedly uncivilized peoples to instinct, custom, or tradition, rather than to conscious design.[3] Conversely, they suggested that the aesthetic quality of manufactures would improve as the principles of taste and beauty were discovered, codified, and applied to industry. In this way, they found within the purported source of England's aesthetic troubles—its exclusive concern with scientific and technical knowledge—the germ of their solution.

A related response to the nagging ugliness of English manufactures was to emphasize the sophistication of the mode of production over the aesthetic quality of the product. Lyon Playfair, for example, takes it as a general principle that "that civilized states differ from barbarous nations in their manner of employing natural forces as aids to production" (1:159). This criterion renders it inconsequential that European manufacturers displayed nothing at the exhibition that could rival, say, the carpets and shawls of India or the elegantly modeled pottery of Tunisia. He grants that "the less civilized states" may have matched or surpassed the European nations in those branches of manufacture that rely primarily on "human labour and the perception of beauty as their principal elements," but he also holds that the "striking progress of European manufactures" becomes immediately apparent when such factors as economy of production and the application of scientific principles are taken into account (1:160). Playfair is able to treat India and

Tunisia as less civilized nations because he defines civilization exclusively in terms of technological capacity. "The position of nations in the scale of civilization," he states categorically, "depends upon their greater or less acquaintance with, and employment of, natural forces" (1:160).

While this measure secures the place of Western nations, and particularly England, at the pinnacle of civilization, it does so by bracketing aesthetic considerations as irrelevant, a strategy entirely at odds with the exhibition's expressed agenda. Throughout the nineteenth century, social critics in the tradition of Southey, Ruskin, and Arnold condemned industrial capitalism as a willing sacrifice of higher moral, intellectual, and aesthetic values to mere material acquisition. From at least the 1830s forward, proponents of industrialization had taken pains to resist this charge by portraying industrial manufacture as itself a contribution to aesthetic culture, and one of the main purposes of the Great Exhibition was to reinforce and consolidate this position. Its organizers deemed the inclusion of sculpture essential to this aim, not because, as Babbage charges, they could not imagine a purely industrial exhibition (10:29), but rather because the presence of high art ratified the exhibition's status as a specifically *cultural* event.

In this charged context, the aesthetic value of English manufactures—the quality of their "design"—was taken as a crucial indicator of the degree to which England had attained a full industrial culture, rather than merely an industrial civilization. Given these stakes, those speakers troubled by the state of English design could not, like Whewell and Playfair, simply emphasize England's scientific and technological accomplishments. On the contrary, they had to confront the disturbing possibility that England's technological progress had actually *caused* its aesthetic regression. If this were the case, and the situation could not be corrected, it would be impossible to make the case for an industrial culture, since industrial capitalism would be fundamentally incompatible with high aesthetic development. The Great Exhibition thus confronted its aesthetically minded interpreters with two critical tasks: first, they had to account for the disjuncture between the technical proficiency of English manufacturers and the aesthetic inferiority of their works, and second, they had to articulate a new aesthetic appropriate to the conditions of industrial manufacture.

M. Digby Wyatt and Owen Jones, the two professional architects who contributed lectures to the Society of Arts's series, made this dual project their explicit concern.[4] Wyatt takes the unfavorable contrast between English design and the more successful efforts of "savage" nations as a bracing wake-up call:

The debilitating effects of nearly a century's incessant copying without discrimination, appropriating without compunction, and falsifying without blushing, still bind our powers in a vicious circle, from which we have hardly yet strength to burst the spell. Some extraordinary stimulant could alone awaken all our energies, and that stimulant came,—it may not, perhaps, be impious to esteem providentially,—in the form of the great and glorious Exhibition. It was but natural that we should be startled when we found that in consistency of design in industrial art, those we had been too apt to regard as almost savages were infinitely our superiors. (2:229–30)

Jones takes a similar lesson from the evident contrast between England's achievements in science and industry and its neglect of art: "[F]rom leading the van in the march of progress," he tells his audience, "we must fall into the rear, and suffer to pass before us nations whose efforts we have hitherto but imperfectly appreciated" (2:255). This disparity must be remedied, he warns, lest "England, in the midst of her material greatness, become a byword and a reproach amongst nations" (2:300). Unlike Whewell and Playfair, Wyatt and Jones rejected the comfortable notion that progress in science and technology would inevitably lead to progress in the arts. Indeed, they deemed aesthetic improvement at least as important as the expansion of industry and trade, because they looked to design as both a stimulus to and a ratification of the reciprocal connection between art and industry.

Jones in particular considered the neglect of design unconscionable in an era characterized by a dedication to improvement in virtually every area of material life: "cheap literature" carries scientific knowledge to all classes, the blessing of free trade brings "food and raiment to all," the "railway movement quadruples the power of locomotion," the "sanitary movement" endeavors not merely to extend the duration of life but to make it "a blessing rather than a curse" (2:297–98). In this catalogue of improvements, Jones gives special notice to the possibility that urban sewage could be turned to productive use as agricultural fertilizer: "The movement in favour of the drainage and irrigation of the soil now dawning, promises to so far increase the productiveness of the country, by pouring on it the waste of towns, that what are now the luxuries only of the few will, hereafter, be daily supplied to the many" (2:297–98).

Jones's surprising enthusiasm for sanitation brings into focus the ideological affinity between the design movement and other types of liberal reform. The prospect of using sewage as manure is most closely associated with the public health advocate Edwin Chadwick, who continued to pursue the idea despite ample evidence that it could actually pose a threat to health in rural areas (Flinn 59–60). Chadwick's preoccupation with this kind of scheme derived more from its symbolic value than from its practical utility. As a number of scholars have argued, the drive to integrate bodies and machines into coherent, unified systems is one of the defining features of a modernist ideology that took efficiency as its highest value.[5]

This impulse, I would argue, is evident much earlier in the nineteenth century, in debates over the factory question, studies of the manufacturing population, reflections on the phenomenological and physiological effects of new technologies such as the telegraph and the railroad, and especially in the concern over sanitation and public health. Critics of industrial capitalism typically stigmatized "the machine" as a threat to the integrity of human bodies, while its defenders portrayed steam power as the laborer's salvation. On a broader scale, automatic manufacture and the "great towns" to which it gave rise were alternately decried as catalysts of moral degradation and political unrest and defended as new sources of wealth that enriched both manufacturing and agricultural interests. The public health movement straddled this divide between criticism and celebration. On the one hand, it was motivated in large part by the examples of the industrial towns, which visibly suffered from overcrowding, poor drainage and ventilation, insufficient water supplies, and inadequate sewage disposal. On the other hand, its main advocates were largely sympathetic to manufacturing interests, so they were wary of specifically identifying industrialism as the chief source of these conditions. Rather, they preferred to direct their attentions to the sanitary conditions in both rural and urban districts. The use of urban sewage as an agricultural manure would require bureaucratic oversight and would therefore reinforce contemporaneous arguments for centralized, efficient governance. More important, it would incorporate town and country into a productive, organic cycle and would thus represent on the broadest possible scale the essential contributions of both to the proper functioning of the social body.

The Victorian design movement was predicated upon a similar cyclic economy in which an outpouring of sound aesthetic principles from London was supposed to encourage the improvement of taste among the populace. This association is suggested by the structure of Jones's own lecture, for immediately after lauding the sanitary movement, he urges society to dedicate itself with equal vigor to the "noble task" of disseminating what he calls "art-knowledge." Like the sanitary movement, the design movement was characterized by a strong impulse toward bureaucratic centralization. An appreciation for art and beauty can be encouraged in any number of ways, but Jones argues specifically for a system of provincial museums and drawing schools, which he envisioned as satellites of the London School of Design. The "cultivation of the eye" through an organized system of art education would not only encourage the production of good designs; it would also unite manufacturers and consumers in a fertile cycle precisely analogous to that which Chadwick envisions joining city and country. Like Chadwick's plans for sanitary reform, Jones's cry that "[e]very town should have its art museum, every village its drawing-school" (2:298) reflects a quintessentially liberal desire to realize the national social body in concrete, institutional form.

WHILE THE state of art manufacture as revealed by the Great Exhibition was a topic of widespread discussion, the specific matter of reconciling the principles of design with the principles of liberal capitalism was a special preoccupation of those commentators affiliated with Cole and the London School of Design. Members of this circle had been arguing for more than a decade that because the improvement of design was essential to the commercial success of British manufactures, both the state and individual manufacturers should support their efforts to improve public taste and to train professional designers. More abstractly, their discourse was an attempt to articulate aesthetic laws in harmony with the purportedly objective laws of capitalism. The Great Exhibition afforded exemplary opportunities for the retrospective assessment of Britain's progress in design (measured variously against the handicrafts of "savage" or "barbarous" nations, the purportedly superior art manufactures of the French, or Britain's own earlier productions), as well as for the systematic explication of principles of design in relation to the technical and commercial requirements of automatic manufacture.

In particular, commentators such as M. Digby Wyatt, Ralph Nicholson Wornum, and Richard Redgrave—all of whom were either involved in planning the exhibition or affiliated with the London School of Design— concentrated on three main issues, each of which had been discussed at length during the 1840s but which took on a new import after 1851. First, viewing the exhibition as what Wornum calls a "lesson in taste," they urged manufacturers to abandon their apparently relentless quest for "novelty" and instead follow "correct" principles of design. Second, they continued to advocate the institutionalization of art education in Britain, on the grounds that British manufacturers required the services of trained designers if they hoped to remain competitive. Third and most important, they endeavored to situate design within the new commercial and social contexts produced by the advancement of industry since the beginning of the century. Simultaneously threatened and exhilarated by these new conditions, Wyatt, Wornum, and Redgrave each treated design not only as the application to manufacture of a codified set of objective aesthetic principles but also as a vehicle for recalibrating the economic and social relations automatic industry had done so much to derange. Consequently, they are as concerned with the commercial and productive contexts in which manufactures are embedded as they are with the formal aesthetic qualities of the objects themselves.

I have already noted Wyatt's contention, expressed in his Society of Arts lecture, that England was suffering the "debilitating effects" of its neglect of design. The most serious of these effects, for Wyatt, was not the proliferation of ugly or awkward designs but the way in which this neglect had entangled English manufacturers in a "vicious circle" of copying, appropriation, and fraud. This issue continues to be a concern in Wyatt's *Industrial Arts of the Nineteenth Century*, a lavishly illustrated study of the "choicest specimens" of sculpture and art manufacture displayed at the Great Exhibition. While his commentaries on examples of sculpture focus solely on their aesthetic merit, his discussions of manufactures attend in addition to the techniques through which they were made and to the social relations governing their production and reception. In his introduction, Wyatt gives special notice to the new economic conditions that had developed since the end of the Napoleonic Wars and to the novel difficulties these conditions posed for the industrial arts. The past thirty-six years, he asserts, have witnessed the introduction of "elements of change" which might have been "calculated to derange the whole previous system of fabrication and demand":

> Sympathising, on the one hand, with the highest excellence both of art and manufacture, modern English production has, on the other, effected a concurrent and unprecedented reduction in price. An amount of thought and ingenuity equal to the origination of many of the monster engineering works which form the pride, the boast, and the glory of the present day, has been bestowed upon an attempt to reduce the cost of a common cotton print the fraction of a farthing per yard. (vii)

In *Past and Present*, Carlyle takes it as the "saddest news" that England's "National Existence" should "depend on selling manufactured cotton at a farthing an ell cheaper than any other People" (10:82–83). Wyatt, in contrast, regards the meticulous attention to such economies as its own kind of quiet heroism. Moreover, he suggests that if reductions in price are less spectacular than the mammoth bridges and tunnels of the great engineers, their effects may be more lasting and profound.

Wyatt's obvious admiration for automatic industry, however, is tempered by his fear that the novel democratization of consumption it enables would increasingly exert a retarding effect on the progress of English design. Wyatt addresses this anxiety by interpreting the respective successes of India and France as symbols of England's deficits. India represents the contingent connection between aesthetic and technological progress, while France represents the dangers of neglecting design education. For Wyatt, the beauty of some of India's contributions to the exhibition gave the lie to the comfortable presumption that aesthetic superiority inevitably accompanies technological advancement. Commenting on "the extraordinary discrepancy between the rudeness of the Indian looms and the refined beauty and delicacy of the fabrics produced by them," he draws attention to what he takes to be England's peculiar failure: its technological advancement seems to have led to its aesthetic retrogression (Wyatt, at plate 24).

Wyatt holds that this situation can be rectified through art education, and in this area he takes France as his model. Quoting James Ward, he notes that France "has studiously cultivated the art of design, and advanced its professors to the rank of gentlemen," while in England design "has been degraded to a mechanical employment, and remunerated at weekly wages." The real issue is whether design is a manual or intellectual form of labor. At stake for Wyatt is less the tastefulness of English manufactures than the social and professional status of the discipline of design itself. What he proposes, implicitly, is the reconstitution of the "circle" of industrial production and consumption around the coordinating center of design. Only the pursuit of "better educational principles in matters of art-manufacture," he states, will "promote that recognition and expression of beautiful forms which can alone lead to excellence of production" (plate 26).

This crucial theme receives especially incisive treatment in two critical assessments of the art manufactures displayed at the Great Exhibition: Wornum's well-known essay "The Exhibition as a Lesson in Taste," which appeared in the *Art-Journal*'s *Illustrated Catalogue*, and Redgrave's "Supplementary Report on Design," which appeared in 1852 as an appendix to the *Reports by the Juries*. Although these texts were occasional pieces, they were both subsequently published separately, Wornum's essay as part of the introduction to his *Analysis of Ornament*, a collection of lectures he had prepared for the government Schools of Design between 1848 and 1850, and Redgrave's report as an independent pamphlet. Wornum's essay has been praised for its balanced and sensitive critical judgments and, more recently, condemned as an exercise in aesthetic hegemony and social control (Gloag, Introduction vi; Rifkin

92). My interest in the piece lies in its integration of three specific theses: first, that beauty is "an essential element in commercial prosperity"; second, that good design depends upon the acquisition and application of specialized knowledge and expertise; and third, that the inculcation of taste plays a crucial disciplinary function in modern industrial society (Wornum 1–2).

Redgrave's report is less well known, but it is perhaps the most cogent early statement of what might be called the official South Kensington position on design. Like Wornum, Redgrave perceived the Great Exhibition as a unique opportunity to assess the present state of industrial design, but he differs somewhat from Wornum in his specific concerns. While Wornum offers an abstract defense of the commercial value of taste, Redgrave explains in detail the principles of ornamental design and argues for the central role of the designer in modern manufacture. In so doing, he gives voice to a sophisticated theory of the cultural dynamics of industrial production, taking into account not only the formal qualities of manufactured objects but also the technological, commercial, and aesthetic systems that enable their production. Redgrave's report thus complements Wornum's essay by tracing out the specific implications of Wornum's contention that taste is the ultimate form of capital.

WORNUM'S CLAIMS for the commercial and social value of taste emerge most clearly when his essay is read in its original context, as the last of a series of studies published in the *Illustrated Catalogue*. A theme that reverberates through each of these essays is that genuine progress in art, science, and industry requires the disciplining and restraint of individual ingenuity and taste. Robert Hunt, the Keeper of Mining Records and a frequent contributor to the *Art-Journal*, argues in "The Science of the Exhibition" that industrial advancement depends upon scientific training, that "inventive genius . . . must be restrained by a philosophical education to become of value to its possessor, or available for the benefit of his race" (1). In her essay "The Harmony of Colours, As Exemplified in the Exhibition," one Mrs. Merrifield asserts that the use of color "is governed by fixed laws, in the same manner as the other branches of natural philosophy," and like Hunt, she subordinates untutored individual preference to discipline and training. A "good eye," she writes, may "greatly assist" in the selection and combination of colors, "but nine times out of ten the *good eye* will be found to mean the *educated eye*" (1). The reward of such self-mastery (whether of the individual or of the "race") is a reciprocal power over the material world. Edward Forbes argues that it "is an instinct of man's nature to subdue the vegetable kingdom to his service" and characterizes the advancement of civilization as the progressive consolidation of this mastery through technique (1–2), while Lewis D. B. Gordon, Regius Professor of Mechanics at the University of Glasgow, describes industrial machinery as technique's material embodiment.

Wornum's claims for taste are of a piece with these arguments. Identifying aesthetic principles as "fixed natural laws" and ornament as "one of the mind's necessities," he elaborates an aesthetic economy that unites beauty and utility under the single rubric of commercial fitness. Like Malthus, Smith, and the political economists who succeeded them, Wornum associates civilization and culture with the proliferation and refinement of desire: "Universal efforts show a universal want," he writes, "and beauty of effect and decoration are no more a luxury in a civilised state of society than warmth or clothing are a luxury to any state." Given this understanding, the premise that England exemplifies the highest state of civilization yet attained (surely uncontroversial among his audience) logically requires the conclusion that ornament has tremendous commercial value. Wornum explains that "in a less cultivated state we are quite satisfied with the gratification of our merely physical wants; but in an advanced state, the more extensive wants of the mind demand still more pressingly to be satisfied. Hence ornament is now as material an interest in a commercial community as the raw materials of manufacture themselves." As the wants of the mind assume priority over the needs of the body, the focus of commercial competition shifts from utility or "mechanical fitness" to beauty or "elegance." Nations unwilling to acknowledge this fact, Wornum warns, "must send their wares to the ruder markets of the world and resign the great marts of commerce to those of superior taste who deserve a higher reward" (1).

This argument is predicated upon a sense of the inexhaustibility of the aesthetic similar to that which underlies the claims of such post-Ruskinian figures as William Morris and Oscar Wilde regarding the role of art in a socialist society. In contrast to these later figures, however, Wornum looks to the aesthetic not as an alternative to capitalism but as a potentially unlimited source of commercial value.[6] He regards taste and beauty as economic resources, subject to the same dialectic of accumulation and expenditure as other varieties of capital.

In defending this position, Wornum must reconcile capitalism's relentless drive for innovation and often traumatic change—its characteristic pattern of "creative destruction"—with a contrary impulse toward organic stability intrinsic to the idea of culture. More specifically, he must accommodate his inherent ambivalence toward erratic or random aesthetic variation within a

Whiggish ideal of steady and perpetual advancement. Like the other con-tributors to the *Art-Journal*'s *Illustrated Catalogue,* he insists that ingenuity and invention must be disciplined by systematic knowledge, or science: "Efforts at variety," he writes, "unless founded on the sincerest study of what has already been done, . . . are at most but assumed novelties" whose sole recommendation is their spurious originality. It would be a fortunate de-signer, Wornum comments ironically, "who alights upon a valuable system of forms or combinations which have escaped all the eager searchers after beauty of the last 3000 years" (11).

This skepticism follows from Wornum's conviction that the principles of ornament, as currently constituted, make up a closed system of knowledge, or what might be called a "grammar." Only nine styles of ornament, he declares, have influenced European civilization: "three ancient, the Egyptian, the Greek, and the Roman; three middle-age, the Byzantine, the Saracenic, and the Gothic; and three modern, the Renaissance, the Cinquecento, and the Louis Quatorze" (2). Wornum's system is complete; the addition of any new style would disrupt its cubic symmetry. This does not mean, however, that innovation must stagnate. Wornum takes it as an article of faith that beauty is "in itself inexhaustible" (11) and argues that individual elements of the nine historical styles may be joined in innumerable combinations. In this regard, the process of ornamental design, as Wornum conceives of it, paral-lels the process of "contriving machinery" as described by Babbage in *The Economy of Machinery and Manufactures.* Both Babbage and Wornum con-sider invention to be largely a matter of conjoining existing elements, and they both recognize that while this power is not uncommon, what Babbage calls "beautiful combinations" are exceptionally rare (8:182). They are virtu-ally impossible to arrive at by mere trial and error, and in ornament as in mechanics, the result of such ill-informed labor is typically a tired recapitu-lation of past forms. This is precisely what Wornum finds at the Great Exhi-bition. There was "nothing new" to be found among the myriad displays of art manufacture, he laments, "not a scheme, not a detail that has not been treated over and over again in ages that are gone" (5).

Anticipating Arnold's verdict that the nineteenth century was an age of "concentration" rather than "expansion," Wornum contends that the task of the present time is to preserve past styles of ornament as aesthetic resources. "The time has perhaps now gone by, at least in Europe," Wornum writes with more than a hint of Arnold's sense of belatedness, "for the develop-ment of any particular or national style, and for this reason it is necessary to distinguish the various tastes that have prevailed throughout past ages, and preserve them as distinct expressions" (22). Wornum's real fear is that his century's wholesale mining of the past will produce not novelty but, paradoxically, a stultifying monotony:

> [B]y using indiscriminately all materials, we should lose all expression, and the very essence of ornament, the conveying of a distinct aesthetic expression, be utterly destroyed. For if all objects in a room were of the same shape and details, however beautiful these details might be, the mind would soon be utterly disgusted. This is, however, exactly what must happen on a large scale; if all our decoration is to degenerate into a uniform mixture of all elements, nothing will be beautiful, for nothing will present a new or varied image to the mind. (22)

Wornum appeals to what Ruskin would soon call the "changefulness" of good ornament as a potential counterforce to such homogenization, but he offers his observation not as a critique of industrial capitalism but as a helpful suggestion to manufacturers seeking to improve their competitive edge.

Although recent criticism has tended to view Wornum's essay as an argument for the hegemonic function of taste, he in fact devotes the bulk of his attention to formal criticism and to the comparative analysis of historical styles of ornament. He nevertheless ends the essay with a bald assertion of the social benefits of design. Advancing a specifically aesthetic version of what earlier advocates of the factory system had called "enlightened" capitalism, Wornum contends that the improvement of design is in the interest of both manufacturers and society at large. The whole purpose of his analysis, he states in his closing sentence, has been to aid manufacturers in "the cultivation of pure and rational individualities of design, which will not only add to their own material prosperity, but will also largely contribute towards the general elevation of the social standard" (22). Wornum's meaning is clear enough. For society as for the decorative arts, his ideal is a highly stratified, rational order. Just as modern ornament must be allowed neither to mimic past styles nor "to degenerate into a uniform mixture of all elements," so, he implies, modern society must not be allowed to degenerate into a great homogenous mass. The good design, in which discrete ornamental elements are arranged into a coherent and hierarchical order, thus becomes a model for the good society, in which the various classes or orders contribute to a harmonious and organic whole. Bourdieu reminds us of what Wornum in his own century had already perceived: that the discipline of taste is an ideal mechanism for creating and sustaining differential social distinctions amenable to industrial capitalism.

LIKE WORNUM'S essay, Redgrave's "Supplementary Report" identifies as major concerns the public's apparently insatiable desire for novelty, on the one hand, and manufacturers' apparent lack of interest in the proper principles of design, on the other. Redgrave therefore rejects the prevailing preference for elaborate, naturalistic ornament and emphasizes instead the value of functionality and "simplicity," a word that recurs repeatedly in the report. He is unusual, however, in treating the public's demand for novelty as a symptom rather than a cause of the current crisis in design. In his view, the development of new plastic materials (such as gutta-percha) and new manufacturing techniques (such as pressure stamping and electroplating) meant that the visible attributes of a given article could no longer testify to its authenticity or merit. He laments the degree of attention given to what he considers clearly inferior designs and worries that, in the absence of appropriate interpretive regulation, the Great Exhibition will corrupt rather than improve the public taste:

> But without some critical guidance, some judicial canons, or some careful separation of the meretricious from the beautiful, it is to be feared that the public taste will rather be vitiated than improved by an examination of the Exhibition, as it will readily be allowed that the mass of ornament applied to the works therein exhibited is of the former character, and from that very cause more likely to impose on the uninformed taste of the multitude than the simpler qualities of real excellence to impress us with a just sense of their worth. (708)

For Redgrave, the public's inability to discern the "real excellence" and "character" of displayed objects is an indication of a crisis of representation in manufacture precisely analogous to that which accompanied the increase in class mobility in mid-century British society at large. Simply put, judgments regarding the class and quality of objects, as of people, are necessarily provisional, since they are predicated upon rapid and cursory estimations of apparent "worth." Just as Wornum views the good design as a static image of the ideal society, so Redgrave regards the exhibition as a model of the dynamic circulation of people and things within the larger social body. In this context, the implied association between corrupt design and prostitution is not to be overlooked. Just as liberal reformers sought to guard public health by restricting the movements and contacts of "fallen" women, so the School of Design theorists hoped to protect public taste by forestalling the corrupting influence of "meretricious" manufactures. In public taste as in public health, faith in expert guidance was a hallmark of liberal reform.

Redgrave's analysis of this crisis in taste, however, is more Ruskinian than reformist. Uncannily anticipating the argument of "The Nature of Gothic," he identifies two factors responsible for the deplorable state of modern industrial design: consumers' restless desire for novel fashions and the division of labor in industrial manufacture. In this respect, the "India Department" of the Great Exhibition is Redgrave's Venice. Just as Ruskin found in Venetian Gothic an alternative to the aesthetic poverty of the industrial present, so Redgrave's examination of the textiles exhibited by the East India Company provokes a nostalgic longing for a lost era of handicraft labor, when the roles of artist, designer, ornamentist, and craftsman were united in a single person. Mapping an eastern present onto a western past, Redgrave contrasts the "beautiful results" of traditional Indian design with the "solecisms," "strange incongruities," and "gross absurdities" put forth by modern manufacturers:

> [T]o this day Indian ornament is composed of the same forms as it was in the earliest known works: the principles that governed ornamental practice in those works seem still to be a tradition with the artist and the workman, and still to produce the same beautiful results, as is abundantly seen in the fabrics and tissues of the Indian department of the Great Exhibition. Now, however, our efforts are of an entirely different nature, and the hunger after novelty is quite insatiable; heaven and earth are racked for novel inventions, and happy is the man who lights upon something, however *outré*, that shall strike the vulgar mind, and obtain the "run of the season." (710)

Modern fashion, Redgrave suggests, demands a kind of aesthetic imperialism involving the relentless appropriation of traditional forms in the pursuit of "novel inventions."

Redgrave considers this whole process to be ultimately self-defeating, for at least two reasons. First, the forms and principles of a traditional ornamental style, like the lexicon and syntax of a language, allow for an endless series of meaningful expressions. Wrenched out of context, however, those same forms and principles produce the ornamental equivalent of noise. (Given this emphasis on the importance of meaningful intention in design, it is not surprising that he is especially scornful of patterns that result purely from "the caprice of accident," such as the "diorama pattern" in cottons, which arose from the accidental folding of the fabric on the printing cylinder.) Second, the conditions of modern manufacture inhibit the kind of creative expression of thought in labor upon which true invention would seem to depend. As Redgrave explains:

The ornament of past ages was chiefly the offspring of handicraft labour, that of the present age is of the engine and the machine. This great difference in the mode of production causes a like difference in the results. In old times the artist was at once designer, ornamentist, and craftsman, and to him was indifferent the use of the pencil or the brush, of the hammer, the chisel, or the punch: his hand and his mind wrought together, not only in the design, but in every stage of its completion, and thus there entered a portion of that mind into every minute detail, and into every stage of finish, and many a beautiful after-thought was embodied by the hand of the "cunning artificer," many a grace added to the work by his mastery and skill. (710)

Just as Ruskin lauds the "changefulness" and "naturalism" of Gothic ornament, so Redgrave celebrates those bygone days in which the worker labored "not to produce a rigid sameness, but as Nature works," expressing in every "changing grace" and "differing beauty" the "feeling of his overflowing mind." The modern resort to stamps and presses, molds and dies—"the ornamental agents of our days"—forestalls such expressiveness, substituting in its stead a "sickening monotony" and a "tired sameness" foreign to nature and peculiar to the "artificial works of man." Laboring under such conditions, the worker cannot help but become "only the servant of the machine" (710).

But if Redgrave's diagnosis of the conditions afflicting modern design parallels Ruskin's, his remedy is markedly different. While Ruskin decries the division of labor and urges his readers to engage in a morally responsible consumerism, Redgrave accepts the dynamics of capitalism and seeks to articulate principles of design responsive to the demands of mechanical production. In contrast to Ruskin, Redgrave treats the low aesthetic quality of modern manufactures not as a sign of nineteenth-century industrial society's moral bankruptcy but as an unfortunate side effect of the elimination of certain practical constraints inherent to handicraft production. With handmade objects, the intricacy and quantity of ornamentation are reliable indicators of the pains taken in its production and, hence, of its expected commercial value. Mechanical production, however, allows these signs of laborious craftsmanship to be faked at negligible cost, encouraging the production of "meretricious" goods that debase real beauty even as they adopt its forms in an effort to incite the desires of the consuming public. The extraordinary gaudiness of mid-nineteenth-century design, Redgrave concludes, arises largely "from the facilities which machinery gives to the manufacturer, enabling him to produce the florid and overloaded as cheaply as the simple forms, and thus to satisfy the larger market for the multitude, who desire quantity rather than quality, and value a thing the more, the more it is ornamented" (711).

Redgrave accepts mechanical production as a fact of modern life, but that does not mean he also accepts the debased condition of contemporary ornament. Two decades earlier, Babbage noted that manufacturers, in their quest for productive efficiency, are willing to take "almost unlimited pains" in the development of the original model, mold, die, or stamp from which multiple copies will be produced (8:49). Now, in the wake of the Great Exhibition, Redgrave wonders why manufacturers do not give similar attention to design: "The state of modern manufacture, whereby ornament is multiplied without limit from a given model, by the machine or the mould, ought at least to awaken in the manufacturer a sense of the importance of the first design. One would think that what was to be produced by thousands and tens of thousands should at least be a work of beauty, and no pains be spared to insure its excellence" (711). Redgrave claims to be puzzled by the apparent willingness of manufacturers to "throw away great expense" on designs that are "hardly worth paying for," especially since the cost of good designs is infinitesimally small—"a mere atom"—when distributed over myriad copies. Of course, he knows full well why manufacturers give so little heed to design: they simply do not see that it pays.

Redgrave therefore insists that the commercial value of manufactures stems ultimately from their beauty. Like Wornum, he justifies this claim on ethnographic grounds, taking the presence of ornament in all human societies as evidence of its specific value in modern commercial society: "The desire evinced by the rudest as well as the most civilized nations for the decoration of their buildings, utensils, and clothing, almost raises ornament into a natural want, and must render its proper application of the utmost consequence to the manufacturer, since upon it the value of his manufactures in the various markets of the world greatly depends" (708). Decoration may be a "natural want," but contrary to the Romantic orthodoxy represented by such emblematic figures as Ruskin's medieval stone carver or Dickens's Sissy Jupe, this does not mean that untutored taste possesses any particular authority. For Redgrave as for Wornum, the cultivation of taste in accordance with recognized "judicial canons" is one aspect of the civilizing process, of the refinement of raw desire that elevates humanity above the savage state. Similarly, Redgrave insists that competence in design depends upon "knowledge, skill, and taste" best acquired through formal training and apprenticeship. On this basis, he differentiates designers from common "workmen," decrying their "niggardly" wages as well as the penchant of manufacturers to arbitrarily alter their efforts (711). Designers, Redgrave suggests, are artists in the medium of the commodity, and manufacturers would benefit from compensating them accordingly and deferring to their special expertise.

While Redgrave acknowledges that all societies from the "rudest" to the "most civilized" practice some form of decoration, he presents design as a quintessentially modern discipline, born of the increasing reliance on automatic machinery and the progressive division of labor in industrial manufacture. Modern industry, he notes, demands the separation of the creative and executive functions formerly united in the person of the craftsman or artisan. The nineteenth century's particular error was not the transformation of workers into machines, as Ruskin and countless lesser critics of the factory system contended. Rather, it was a failure to account for the creative functions formerly performed by the handicraft artisan within the myriad discrete processes involved in manufacture. Whereas Ruskin proposes the reintegration of the executive and creative aspects of manufacture, arguing that "the workman ought often to be thinking, and the thinker often to be working" (10:201), Redgrave holds that manufacturers ought to recognize the necessary and special contributions of the designer.

Because design is a hybrid occupation, Redgrave takes pains to distinguish it from mere mechanical labor, on the one hand, and from true "art," on the other. Because the work of the designer is strictly creative, it must be given material form by "art-workmen," whose task it is to "carry out" the designer's ideas. Redgrave expresses a dim view of the competence of these art-workmen, contending that "they are mostly men of slow minds, who enter little into the spirit of the artist's labours, and who work without feeling as without fire" (711).[7] Whatever the historical validity of this opinion, it is obviously colored by Redgrave's overarching need to distance the designer from actual executive labor. The skilled art-workman is the most obvious parallel to the bygone handicraft artist eulogized at the beginning of his essay. Redgrave therefore strives to minimize this resemblance by severely curtailing the art-workman's creative autonomy and rejecting any suggestion that the art-workman may be considered the designer's collaborator.

This strict separation of creative from manual labor becomes particularly evident in Redgrave's suggestion that the Schools of Design should offer different sorts of training to these "two classes" of workers (748). Although most students of design came from the working classes, Redgrave maintains that they should be educated almost as gentlemen, fitted out with "general principles of design" and trusted to speedily acquire the "amount of *special* knowledge" necessary to accomplish any specific task to which they may turn their attention (748). If the designer in this regard is like the artist—

whose imagination also ought not be burdened with excessive technical concerns—then the art-workman, whom Redgrave calls a "mere copyist" (711), should work like a machine, with perfect efficiency and precision. "That the art-workman should know *all* the processes of the manufacture he is engaged upon is absolutely necessary," writes Redgrave, because this knowledge will enable him "thoroughly to appreciate and perfectly to carry out the work of the designer" (748). While Ruskin would later object that such demand for perfection transforms men into machines, Redgrave remains indifferent to this distinction. From his perspective, both human workers and automatic machines may be grouped together as general executive agents; the designer requires only "such an insight into the processes of *the workman or the machine* as will enable him to fit his design to the difficulties of production" (748, emphasis added). Skilled handwork, which Redgrave had earlier opposed to the rote manipulations of "the engine and the machine" (710), now becomes itself mindless and mechanical. With this conflation, Redgrave wills himself into a state of historical amnesia, dispelling the very memories of the ancient artist-craftsman that had initially troubled his vision of the industrial future.

Having distinguished design from executive labor, Redgrave sets out to clarify the difference between art, which he defines as the "imitation" of natural elements, and ornament, which he defines as a distillation of what is "most characteristic" in nature (736). He is so insistent about this distinction because he views the confusion between art and ornament as a primary factor in the perpetuation of an obsolete labor theory of aesthetic value and as an impediment to the emergence of a new system of value based on excellence in design. He devotes special attention to works in precious metals because they constitute a kind of limiting case in which "more than in any other the labours of the artist and the ornamentist seem to concur, and are often so intermixed that it is difficult to designate their several provinces" (736). In effect, Redgrave hopes that by resolving the distinction between art and ornament in this particular instance, he can articulate a general theory of design applicable to all classes of manufacture.

Good designs, Redgrave maintains, should be governed by the principle of fitness, which demands, first, that ornament never interfere with an object's utility, and second, that it not convey meanings inconsistent with an object's intended function (see chap. 4). He is also scathingly critical of the *"naturalism"* so prevalent in mid-Victorian metalwork, which in addition to encouraging a "great waste of skill and labour" in the production of absurdly elaborate sculptural compositions, also renders many objects unfit for practical use:

Thus it is impossible to justify large and florid groups of dead game, of fish, of fishing utensils, or the like imitative treatments, as the knobs of dish-covers, or the hands of tureens; however beautiful of design or excellently chased, they are not convenient for use; nor can the hand be safely brought in contact with the metallic toes of a pheasant, the tentaculae of a lobster, or the twigs of a fish-basket, any more than stags with their branched antlers can well be laid hold of to remove a venison dish. (739)

Redgrave chides manufacturers for their willingness to cater to wealthy patrons who demand such displays of what he ironically calls *"art"* (737) and argues that such passive pandering to public taste is in fact detrimental to manufacturers' economic interests. The public prefers highly ornate, naturalistic ornament not only because great amounts of labor appear to have been expended on it but also because it uses a great deal of metal. The metalwork displayed at the Great Exhibition, Redgrave comments, almost seems as if its value were meant "to be estimated in *tons*," rather than in terms of the beauty of its design (737).

In Redgrave's interpretation, however, the Victorians' penchant for elaborate ornamentation is not a manifestation of their tremendous self-importance, as later critics such as Nikolaus Pevsner would have it. Rather, it is a symptom of their anxiety over their inability to make reliable assessments of value. (The "mere weight of metal" [737] is a crude but at least objective measure.) Redgrave's belief in the objectivity of taste allows him to dismiss this concern. A greater emphasis on "art," he offers, in the older and more expansive meaning of that term, would "give a more real and permanent value" to art manufactures and would "at the same time separate the precious metals from the plated substitutes which ape their richness" (737).

Redgrave thus attributes to design the same function Babbage attributes to price: that of verifying the true nature and composition of manufactures (see chap. 2). Unlike its price, however, an article's design is intrinsic to its nature. It is, as Redgrave suggests at the outset of his essay, precisely analogous to the "character" of a human being. For this reason, Redgrave's approach to the problem of verification is in at least one way superior to Babbage's. While it is possible to display manufactures without their prices, it is impossible to display them without revealing their design. Consequently, the person of taste will always be able to assess the value of a given article, even in the absence of extrinsic indicators such as price. In a commercial world in which prices can float dramatically, real hierarchies of value must be based on qualities intrinsic to objects themselves.

Once such a hierarchy is in place, the kinds of works Redgrave had earlier denigrated as "meretricious" shams or "plated substitutes" can be admitted, as it were, into the respectable society of manufactures. If a "false view of art tends to assimilate the costly with the cheap," Redgrave writes, a true view will exercise a countervailing influence (740). If genuine works in gold and silver set a true standard of design, plated works or works in cheaper metals can perform legitimate work as what Asa Briggs calls "emissaries" of taste (11–51). In the late 1840s, the *Journal of Design,* to which Redgrave was a principal contributor, insisted that inexpensive things must be beautiful, because they were the things most capable of influencing public taste: "It is the worst of all mistakes to imagine that because a thing is cheap the artistic finish of its design is unimportant, since it is in exactly the ratio of its probable dissemination among the public that the influence on popular taste must be effected" (*JD* 1:54). Redgrave, in his "Supplementary Report," elaborates on this notion, observing that while "the rarer efforts in the richer material will always set the taste in the imitative productions," the "art applied to gold or silver in its turn descends to plated wares and manufactures in the baser metals" (740). Redgrave's principles of design, like his careful effort to separate the "two classes" of designers and art-workmen, thus express a yearning for a stable hierarchical order in which canons of taste trickle down from rich "classes" of goods to cheap.

CHAPTER SIX

"Only a Machine Before"

MANLINESS AND MECHANISM IN
RUSKIN AND MORRIS

IN THE preceding chapters, I have charted the emergence during the second quarter of the nineteenth century of a new proindustrial rhetoric predicated upon the representation of automatic manufacture as a contribution to aesthetic culture. By way of conclusion, I now turn to examine the ways in which two prominent critics of nineteenth-century industrialism—John Ruskin and William Morris—resist this appropriation by seeking in abstract ideals of cultured manliness a new "invisible hand," capable of replacing the desire to barter, truck, and exchange as society's motive force.

In the debates over the factory question during the 1830s and 1840s, masculine free agency served as a coordinating value. Opponents of factory legislation objected even to restricting the hours of labor for women and minors on the grounds that it would inevitably impinge upon the economic freedom of adult male workers. Proponents of factory legislation, conversely, imagined labor as a form of property requiring protection and, on this basis, argued that the regulation of labor would in fact safeguard the independence of working-class men (Gray 31). In the line of social criticism that runs from Carlyle through Ruskin to Morris, this concern with the liberty of working men merges with the more abstract idea that culture's ability to operate as a counterpoise to material "civilization" depends upon the prior existence of autonomous selves, capable of rendering independent ethical and aesthetic judgments. As Coleridge writes: "[C]ivilization is itself but a mixed good, if not far more a corrupting influence, the hectic of disease, not the bloom of health, and a nation so distinguished more fitly to be called a varnished than a polished people; where this civilization is not grounded in *cultivation,* in the harmonious developement of those qualities and faculties that characterise our *humanity.* We must be men in order to be citizens" (42–43). The association between culture and manliness implicit here in Coleridge becomes explicit in Carlyle, who provocatively offers his highly conflicted masculine ideal as the solution to the social crises of the 1840s.

As Herbert Sussman has shown, in such texts as *Sartor Resartus,* "The Hero as Man of Letters," and *Past and Present,* Carlyle sets forth "a foundation myth of manliness for industrial society" (*Victorian Masculinities* 51, 16). He imagines manliness—as opposed to mere maleness—as a dynamic equilibrium maintained through a rigorous self-discipline that protects against both the emasculating dissipation and the unproductive eruption of male seminal power. Carlylean manliness, in other words, is not an essence but an ongoing process of psychic restraint through which chaotic drives and desires can be channeled into meaningful work (24–34). This idea manifests itself in Carlyle's works through myriad images of what Sussman calls the "hydraulic body," whose hard exterior surface shapes and regulates the inchoate and potentially destructive energies within (19).

Carlyle's model is, of course, fraught with contradiction. He celebrates the Wordsworthian overflow of masculine creative power even as he imagines this power as polluted and unclean (*Victorian Masculinities* 20–21). But despite its intrinsic pathology, it exerted a strong influence throughout the nineteenth century. As James Eli Adams observes, the convergence of athleticism and aestheticism in the Victorian ideal of the gentleman testifies to Carlyle's abiding relevance, since Kingsley, Pater, and Ruskin all adopt the Carlylean strategy of invoking "the impulses of the virile body in opposition to a self-baffling 'speculation'" (*Dandies* 153). More broadly, Adams shows that a diverse host of male Victorian authors, including Tennyson, Thomas Arnold, Newman, Dickens, and Wilde in addition to Carlyle, Kingsley, Ruskin, and Pater, consistently present their own intellectual labors as exercises in ascetic self-discipline (*Dandies* 2). Sussman adds Browning, Rossetti, Swinburne, and several others.

Strikingly absent from this pantheon is William Morris, whom Sussman mentions only tangentially and Adams not at all. Sussman and Adams are concerned primarily with the psychosexual dynamics of Victorian manhood, as well as with the role of ascetic self-discipline in the self-fashioning of Victorian male writers and artists. From this perspective, their omission of Morris, who seems to celebrate the unfettered pursuit of healthy desire rather than restraint or reserve, is understandable. Morris, though, does participate in the cultural dynamics Sussman and Adams trace, if not primarily by embracing an overt program of masculine restraint, then by following Carlyle and Ruskin in their attempts to envision an alternative to industrial society, predicated not upon individual self-interest but upon vitalistic and communal manliness.

As Sussman recognizes, Carlyle's model of the "hydraulic body" shares a schematic affinity with nineteenth-century industry's paradigmatic technology.

Like the steam engine, Carlyle's "technology of the self" functions to transform violent internal energy into controlled and useful power (*Victorian Masculinities* 34), and this resemblance enables it to perform a similar function in society at large. In *Past and Present*, Carlyle recasts the "Condition of England" question as a "Condition of Manliness" question, imagining a redeemed industrial society, analogous to the all-male community of St. Edmundsbury, built on masculine rather than mechanical power (*Victorian Masculinities* 51). For Carlyle, the cure mimics the poison, transforming piratical Plugsons into chivalric captains of industry.

Ruskin revises Carlyle's "hydraulic body" to reflect his greater emphasis on expression and feeling, envisioning animal and human bodies not as hard surfaces controlling internal fluid energies but rather as organic forms shaped by subordinate interior anatomies. If, as Ruskin argues in "The Nature of Gothic," the demand for precise execution in the carving of architectural ornament mechanizes the worker, it still does not eradicate workers' unique identities: each "man" is transformed into a discrete "machine" (1:192). Industrial labor, in contrast, dissolves the identities of workers by integrating their bodies into the apparatus of the factory: "[T]o make the flesh and skin which, after the worm's work on it, is to see God, into leathern thongs to yoke machinery with,—this is to be slave-masters indeed" (10:193). In this highly stylized image of bodily mutilation, Ruskin represents industrial labor's threat to masculine creative autonomy as an assault on the very integrity of the laboring body. Against this background, he advances a new ethics of production and consumption, organized around the making of "men" rather than the circulation of things.[1] Nevertheless, he refuses to recognize any connection between the "rude" creative efforts of manual workers and the refinement of feeling he regards as the essential quality of a gentleman. This reluctance to reconcile his competing, class-bound ideals of expressive and receptive manliness inevitably dilutes the radical potential of his proposal.

Morris develops this Ruskinian opposition between manliness and mechanism into a comprehensive critique of commercial civilization. In his socialist lectures and essays, he identifies a masculine desire for pleasure in art, labor, and the various aspects of "animal life" not only as an impetus for revolution but as socialism's animating force. "Manliness" functions as a transcendent ideal that both marks a point of rupture within capitalist ideology and enables Morris to imagine a future that does not (like that of Edward Bellamy's *Looking Backward*) simply reproduce existing social categories. The genre of utopian romance, however, presents opportunities and challenges that more expository genres do not. While *News from Nowhere* develops Morris's vision of life under socialism with a depth and immediacy unmatched in his lectures and essays, it also reveals, as these other writings do not, the fissures within the cultural ideal that supports that vision.

THE GENERAL model of the body that informs the argument of "The Nature of Gothic" emerges out of the theory of "Vital Beauty" that Ruskin develops in *Modern Painters* II.[2] Just as a body's internal anatomical structures both give shape to and are contained by its external form, so, Ruskin holds, narrowly utilitarian considerations ought always to be subordinated to higher aesthetic values. Elaborating on this idea, he declares it "a beautiful ordinance of the Creator" that animals' anatomical "mechanisms are concealed from sight, though open to investigation," so that "in all which is outwardly manifested, we seem to see His presence rather than His workmanship" (4:155). Although Ruskin does not expressly forbid the investigation of such mechanisms, he warns against the temptation to misapprehend "neatness of mechanical contrivance" for true organic "beauty" (4:154). In *The Seven Lamps of Architecture* and *The Stones of Venice*, he applies this principle to human productions, celebrating a "Living Architecture" that displays "the structure of organic form" (8:204). Just as the body's form is supported by yet bounds its internal anatomy, so good architecture acknowledges the practical "necessities" of construction yet impresses buildings with ornamental "characters" that transcend considerations of utility (8:28). The railroad, which serves as a synecdoche for all mass technologies, inverts this ideal hierarchy. In *Modern Painters* II, Ruskin asserts that the slightest wound to an animal's frame "is regarded with intense horror, merely from the sense of pain it conveys" (4:154). Against this background, he portrays the railroad as a expansive network of "iron veins" and "throbbing arteries" traversing "the frame of our country" (8:246). He thus signifies his profound aversion to the excessive "materialism" of his age by representing the industrialized landscape itself as a vast, flayed body.[3]

In "The Nature of Gothic," this abstract and allegorical challenge to industrial capitalism becomes startlingly particular and concrete. Although some interpreters have been troubled by the chapter's apparent digressiveness, Ruskin's incisive critique of industry is less a departure from aesthetic criticism than an effort to apply his theories to a pressing social problem.[4] Like Southey in his *Colloquies,* Ruskin condemns the conditions of industrial labor through images of mechanization, slavery, and bodily mutilation. But while Southey treats the authority of such images as self-evident, Ruskin, writing twenty years later, is acutely aware that their edge has been blunted by two decades of repetition. He therefore works to extend their resonance beyond the issue-specific debates of the 1830s and 1840s by resituating them within his broader moral and aesthetic argument.

"The Nature of Gothic" includes a number of references that link it specifically to the cause of factory reform. Ruskin's objection that human beings cannot be made to perform repetitive mechanical tasks for "ten hours a day" without becoming machines themselves clearly recalls the protracted political struggle for a standard workday that ran from the 1830s into the 1850s. One need only remember the failure of John Fielden's 1847 Ten Hours Act to realize the timeliness of Ruskin's allusion.[5] Likewise, Ruskin's repeated recourse to the trope of slavery shows him slipping into the language of Richard Oastler's Factory Movement almost in spite of himself. In his discussion of "Servile ornament," Ruskin argues that because the Assyrians and Egyptians enforced a rigid discipline among their workers, and because the Greeks withheld from theirs any subject they could not execute with perfection, the worker was in both cases "a slave" (10:189). The "accurate mouldings" and "perfect polishings" (10:193) of the middle-class Victorian interior should therefore suggest an analogy between the English worker and the Greek, since in both cases it is the demand for precise execution that enforces conditions of servitude. Ruskin, however, does not make this obvious connection but opts instead for a comparison with more contemporary relevance: "Alas! if read rightly, these perfectnesses are signs of a slavery in our England a thousand times more bitter and more degrading than that of the scourged African, or helot Greek" (10:193). The syntactically marginal mention of the "helot Greek" only emphasizes the unexpected quality of the principal comparison.

Although this reference to the African slave seems out of place in Ruskin's discussion of architectural ornament, the figure was of central importance to the short-time rhetoric of 1830s and 1840s, in which the sufferings of the "white" or "factory" slave, registered on the body in terms of malnourishment and deformity, are portrayed as being even worse than the sufferings of the black plantation slave, who, the argument ran, at least possessed physical health and strength. Metaphors of factory slavery tapped into an abiding English aversion to political bondage, and they played upon a justifiable working-class suspicion of the abolitionist cause, which often found its main local proponents among the very body of liberal mill owners the Factory Movement was struggling against (Gray 39–40). In addition, they worked to illuminate an apparent hypocrisy in nineteenth-century liberalism, which attributed to workers a formal economic freedom without allowing them to exercise this freedom in practice. Charges of factory slavery also implied that the intrinsic right of the "freeborn Englishman" to contract for his hours and wages had been perverted by the factory system into a de facto instrument of bondage. It should be remembered that the ten-hours agitation of the 1830s and 1840s aimed (at least overtly) at limiting only the hours of the child or infant laborer and that ensuing legislative measures placed no restrictions on the right of adult male workers to negotiate the terms of their employment. However, as opponents of factory regulation repeatedly observed, efforts to restrict the labor of women and children were in fact strategically designed to limit the hours of adult male operatives as well. Although images of factory slavery were used primarily to condemn the excessive exploitation of women and children, they could readily be expanded to include adult male workers, when rhetorically efficacious.[6]

Richard Oastler's letter on "Yorkshire slavery," which contrasts the "emaciated frames" of factory children with the "strong and healthy" bodies of black slaves, exemplifies these rhetorical dynamics. In the eyes of this self-proclaimed "old-fashioned Ultra-Tory" (qtd. in Driver 428), the facade of personal liberty makes the situation of Yorkshire's operatives worse than that of plantation slaves. The wage system, based on a "free" market for labor, guarantees a steady supply of workers and thus enables employers to show a wanton disregard for workers' physical health. Ruskin, who would style himself a "Tory of the old school" (27:167), similarly associates industrial labor with images of mutilation and slavery, but unlike Oastler, he develops this association into a contrast between the conditions of the modern worker and the feudal serf. There was more freedom in medieval England, he contends, than there can be while the nation's laboring "multitudes" are "sent like fuel to feed the factory smoke" (10:193). The feudal comparison is more in keeping with the broader context of Ruskin's chapter, but his passing reference to the "scourged African" is still essential, because it establishes an explicit link between the anti-industrial rhetoric of the 1830s and 1840s and his broader effort to elevate the Gothic style into a social ideal.

Moreover, by specifically situating his attack on the conditions of modern labor within a discussion of Gothic "savageness," Ruskin obliquely challenges the basic presumption upon which the whole discourse of industrial culture was predicated: that industrial and aesthetic progress are not only compatible but in fact mutually sustaining. In pitting the savageness of Gothic against the "engine-turned precision" of modern manufactures, Ruskin is of course appealing to the familiar Romantic figure of the "noble savage." Just as Rousseau portrays civilization as a fall from a happy savage state, so Ruskin,

in insisting that savageness "may be considered, in some sort, a noble character" (10:188), associates Gothic with powers of imagination that have been
sacrificed in the rush for mechanical precision. Ruskin, however, hardly
espouses the egalitarian values typically associated with Romantic idealiza-
tions of the savage state. He advocates obedience to social hierarchies as
much as he does personal expression, and he embraces the savageness of
Gothic not as an aesthetic value in its own right but as a pragmatic concession
to human limitations. He celebrates the "rudeness" of Gothic ornament
only "where it was impossible to get design or thought without it" and objects
to "refinement of execution" only when it comes at the expense of thought
and invention (10:198–99).

In this context, the medieval stone carver, whose own "savageness" and
"rudeness" mirrors that of his productions, is the antithesis of the modern
worker, whose expressive freedom has been surrendered to demands for
standardization and efficiency. Ruskin amplifies this contrast by identifying
an implicitly masculine autonomy as the essence of the worker's humanity:
"Men were not intended to work with the accuracy of tools, to be precise
and perfect in all their actions. If you will have that precision out of them,
and make their fingers measure degrees like cog-wheels, and their arms
strike curves like compasses, you must unhumanize them" (10:192). This
statement would have resonated strongly with those familiar with the discourse of political economy or the extensive contemporary literature on the
condition of the working classes. In the work of Smith, Malthus, and their
nineteenth-century successors, an idealized and artificial concept of the
"savage state" works to ground theoretical speculations about the economic
relations that obtain in commercial "civilization." Similarly, in liberal investigations of the manufacturing population, images of savageness were used
to represent specific segments of the working classes rendered obsolete
through advances in automatic manufacture, facilitating the identification
of classes of others against whom the concept of an industrial culture could
be delineated. By contending that the demand for precision "unhumanizes"
workers, Ruskin identifies the increasing regimentation and automation of
labor as a brutalizing force that thrusts laboring men into a kind of savage
state, even as its transforms them into cogs and tools.

In the tradition of Enlightenment conjectural history out of which the
discourse of political economy arose, the march toward civilization com-
mences when savage or "infant man" is roused from his primal torpidity and
begins to develop his higher desires and faculties. Ruskin attributes to creative
manual labor just such a civilizing agency. When we encourage the worker

to take the first "tottering steps of thought," he tells his middle-class audience, we begin to cultivate the "tardy imagination" and "torpid capacity of emotion" that lie within "the nature of every man" (10:191). The pressures faced by the nineteenth-century industrial worker were not uniquely modern—they were experienced by the Assyrian, the Egyptian, and the Greek as well—but Ruskin believed they were being felt with an unprecedented intensity. The reason, he suggests, is that the advent of mechanized, industrial production magnifies the retrogressive forces inherent in the very division of labor on which civilization is based.

Writing in the wake of the political revolutions of 1848 abroad and the struggles associated with England's industrial growth at home, Ruskin argues that modern labor conditions make workers "less than men" by fostering yearnings for the false freedom of the savage state. Whereas the medieval worker possessed a positive "freedom of thought" in labor that compensated for his subjection to an absolute political authority, the nineteenth-century operative is denied such independence by the rigid discipline of the factory and is therefore driven to seek a wholly negative political liberty. "It is verily this degradation of the operative into a machine," Ruskin writes, "which, more than any other evil of the times, is leading the mass of the nations everywhere into vain, incoherent, destructive struggling for a freedom of which they cannot explain the nature to themselves" (10:194). Consequently, a "precipice" has been thrown up between the "upper and lower grounds in the field of humanity," with a "pestilential air at the bottom of it" (10:194). Like proponents of the factory system such as William Cooke Taylor and liberal social investigators such as James Kay-Shuttleworth, Ruskin figures middle-class fears of class alienation and political instability through images of degeneration and disease. He does so, however, in order to illuminate what he takes to be the fundamental incoherence of the position such writers represent. Paradoxically, Ruskin maintains, the cultivation of aesthetic "savageness" stimulates precisely the "*thoughtful* part" (10:191) of human beings that the refinement of desire, and therefore the progress of civilization, requires. The demand for an excessive "refinement of execution" (10:199), conversely, deadens workers' intellects and sensibilities and thus contributes to precisely the kind of retrogression it endeavors to deny.

As if to confirm Ruskin's sense of the incompatibility of industrial and aesthetic development, liberal advocates of industrial design such as Redgrave, Dyce, Jones, and Wornum struggled with the discomfiting recognition that the handicraft productions of nonindustrialized cultures often surpassed western manufactures in refinement and beauty. In their writings, ideas of

savageness come to localize anxieties over the apparent bifurcation of technological and aesthetic progress, even as they are used to explain away the
aesthetic quality of "primitive" and non-Western arts. The often striking
beauty of such productions, a typical version of the argument ran, is merely a
manifestation of an innate and universal aesthetic faculty, which can operate without interference among savage peoples because they live in a virtual
state of nature. If this aesthetic faculty has been blunted by industrial civilization, it can be rejuvenated and refined through the discovery, codification,
and promulgation of objective aesthetic laws. In this way, the very ugliness of
nineteenth-century manufactures warrants the development of a scientific
aesthetics applicable to industrial production.

Such a scientific aesthetics was one element of the extensive discourse on
design that ran from the 1830s well into the second half of the nineteenth
century. In the 1830s and 1840s, as we have seen, such periodicals as the *Art-
Journal* and *Journal of Design and Manufactures* dedicated themselves to the
proposition that Britain's future commercial prosperity depended upon the
application of "correct" rules of taste and beauty to manufacture. This discourse took institutional form first in the government Schools of Design
and subsequently in the Department of Science and Art (originally the
Department of Practical Art), which was established in the wake of the
Great Exhibition to promote art education throughout the nation. Under
Cole's direction, the department flourished, expanding, as he put it shortly
before his retirement in 1873, from "twenty limp Schools of Design into one
hundred and twenty flourishing Schools of Art in all parts of the United
Kingdom" (qtd. in Bonython 9). Ruskin, for his part, grew increasingly critical
of the regimented system of art instruction practiced in these institutions,
going so far as to assert that Cole had "corrupted the system of art-teaching
all over England into a state of abortion and falsehood from which it will
take twenty years to recover" (29:154).[7] The causticity of this remark reflects
more than Ruskin's personal distaste for systematized art instruction. It is
also a register of just how threatening the idea of industrial culture was to
the line of social criticism he represents.

Indeed, the concerns that motivate Ruskin's attack on Cole are already
evident in "The Nature of Gothic," where he draws an explicit connection
between the division of labor in manufacture and modern principles of
design. Except for the narrow range of designs that can be "mathematically
defined," Ruskin contends, "one man's thoughts can never be expressed by
another" (10:200). There is a subtle yet crucial difference between the "touch of
the man who is inventing" and that of "the man who is obeying directions."

Ruskin illustrates this point through a contrast between old Venetian and modern English glass. He celebrates the former because in its manufacture, invention and execution occurred simultaneously, in the mind and at the hands of a single maker. He condemns the latter, with its exquisite clarity and accurate cutting, as the emblem of an oppressive system that limits opportunities for humanizing labor by separating design and execution.

The attention Ruskin's chapter gives to the making of all manner of things, from moldings to glass beads, should not obscure its primary concern with the making of men: "And the great cry that rises from all our manufacturing cities, louder than their furnace blast, is all in very deed for this,—that we manufacture everything there except men; we blanch cotton, and strengthen steel, and refine sugar, and shape pottery; but to brighten, to strengthen, to refine, or to form a single living spirit, never enters into our estimate of advantages" (10:196). This criticism anticipates Ruskin's wholesale excoriation of the division of labor for being, in actuality, a division of men. Alluding to Adam Smith's paradigmatic example of pin making, he charges that we call the "great civilized invention of the division of labour" by a "false name." "It is not, truly speaking, the labour that is divided; but the men:—Divided into mere segments of men—broken into small fragments and crumbs of life; so that all the little piece of intelligence that is left in a man is not enough to make a pin, or a nail, but exhausts itself in making the point of a pin or the head of a nail" (10:196). Rather than actively making men, nineteenth-century industrial society happily sacrifices them to the cause of efficient material production. The division of labor, in other words, is not simply an efficient method for distributing work. It also systematically forestalls the creative autonomy essential to the expression of what Ruskin calls in *The Seven Lamps of Architecture* the "true life" of man (8:191).

In Ruskin's view, this sorry state of affairs demands a fundamental revolution in consciousness: "It can be met only by a right understanding, on the part of all classes, of what kinds of labour are good for men, raising them, and making them happy; by a determined sacrifice of such convenience, or beauty, or cheapness as is to be got only by the degradation of the workman; and by equally determined demand for the products and results of healthy and ennobling labour" (10:196). Ruskin endeavors to reconcile this radical gesture toward an alternative economics with his conservative valorization of stable social hierarchies by elevating the class-specific norm of the "gentleman" into a universal ideal. By challenging the rigid separation of mental and manual labor, he also challenges the validity of corresponding social distinctions between the working-class operative and the middle-class gentleman.

Even as he rejects these class-bound norms, however, he also takes the gentleman "in the best sense" as a general masculine ideal: "[W]e want one man to be always thinking, and another to be always working, and we call one a gentleman, and the other an operative; whereas the workman ought often to be thinking, and the thinker often to be working, and both should be gentlemen, in the best sense" (10:201). The chiastic structure of his proclamation emphasizes that Ruskin's first pair of terms ("gentleman" and "operative") is not in fact synonymous with his second ("thinker" and "workman"), despite their interchangeability in conventional usage. The former pair makes a distinction of class, the latter a distinction of occupation. In Ruskin's view, those whose labor is primarily intellectual do not on that basis alone warrant the status of gentlemen; they are more properly classed as thinkers. Likewise, those whose labor is primarily manual should not be objectified as operatives; rather, they are more properly understood as workmen. Indeed, in Ruskin's ideal society, operatives in the strict sense—that is, factory hands whose task is merely to attend machinery—would not exist. Having made these clarifications, Ruskin is free to treat the "gentleman" as a universal ideal to which both the "thinker" and the "workman" may aspire.

In "The Nature of Gothic," Ruskin invokes but never explicitly defines this masculine ideal. However, in his later chapter "Of Vulgarity" in *Modern Painters* V (1860) and his essay "Of Kings Treasuries" in *Sesame and Lilies* (1865), he explains that gentlemen differ from ordinary men in their superior capacity for sensation and feeling. "A gentleman's first characteristic," Ruskin offers, "is that fineness of structure in the body, which renders it capable of the most delicate sensation; and of structure in the mind which renders it capable of the most delicate sympathies" (7:345). He then characterizes the moral sense as a kind of sublimation of these capacities, holding that "a true gentleman . . . simply feels rightly on all occasions" (7:349). Such claims are in keeping with the Victorians' propensity for treating physical health as a marker of, or metaphor for, moral or spiritual vitality. As Bruce Haley has shown, the Victorians' veneration of the "healthy body" gave rise to a corresponding ideal of the "healthy man," embracing such concepts as Carlylean heroism and Kingsleyan muscular Christianity (Haley 19–22). Ruskin, however, does not identify manliness with physical vigor or robust "character," as do Kingsley and Thomas Hughes. Rather, he defines it in terms of twin capacities for sensation and sympathy, calling the latter the "'touch-faculty,' of body and soul" (18:80). This "touch-faculty," in turn, serves as the foundation for a standard of social judgment that avoids both the brittle rigidity of moral dogmatism and the indeterminacy of moral relativism.[8]

Ruskin's concept of the gentleman is so useful in the context of "The Nature of Gothic" because it facilitates his attempt to affirm traditional social hierarchies based on such essential qualities as "fineness of nature" and "breeding" (7:345) while simultaneously condemning the stratification of society on the basis of profession or occupation. Yet in retrospect, it also reveals the limitations of his critique. Just as Kingsley's muscular Christian must reconcile the vigorous celebration of the "animal spirits" with the antithetical demands of a rigorous ascetic self-renunciation (Adams, *Dandies* 107–12), so Ruskin's gentleman is torn between conflicting requirements for self-expression and restraint. The very intensity of his feelings requires that he contain them beneath a facade of "apparent reserve" (7:347), which mediates between his personal emotions and his public persona. This conflict in Ruskin's masculine ideal mirrors the contradictory egalitarian and aristocratic impulses in his social philosophy. We might reasonably infer that the "touch of the man who is inventing" celebrated in "The Nature of Gothic" is the active manifestation of the gentlemanly "touch-faculty" that gives rise to moral conscience, but Ruskin himself never makes this connection explicitly. Indeed, he resists this natural conclusion by characterizing the sensibilities of the workman as crude and primitive, the very opposite of the cultured refinement of the gentleman.

Ultimately, he balks at admitting the laboring masses into his aristocracy of feeling. Like Marx, Ruskin recognizes the revolutionary potential arising out of the conditions of factory labor, and like Morris, he attributes this impulse to a crisis of desire: the working classes do not know what they should want. But in contrast to these more radical thinkers, Ruskin endeavors to defuse this potential by substituting aesthetic autonomy for political liberty. This refusal to follow through on the radical implications of his own arguments is why socially committed commentators such as William Morris, E. P. Thompson, and Raymond Williams find Ruskin at once so compelling and so frustrating. While "The Nature of Gothic" is highly effective as negative criticism, Ruskin's proposal that all should become gentlemen "in the best sense" (10:201) is vitiated by its reliance on an inherently ambiguous masculine ideal.

MORRIS EMBRACED the lessons of "The Nature of Gothic" enthusiastically, and he repeatedly praised the chapter in the most effusive terms. By purging the chapter of its religious overtones, he finds in it several of his own central themes, "that art is the expression of man's pleasure in labour; that it is possible for man to rejoice in his work, for, strange as it may seem to us to-day, there have been times when he did rejoice in it; and lastly, that unless man's work once again becomes a pleasure to him, . . . all but the worthless must toil in pain, and therefore live in pain" (M. Morris 1:292). Morris, who in his socialist writings repeatedly fuses Ruskinian moral and aesthetic critique with astute Marxist economic and historical analysis, expresses clear reservations about the class-specific nature of Ruskin's masculine ideal. In a passage that can be read as a gloss on Ruskin, the *Newcastle Chronicle* reports Morris as asserting his hope that the working man "might have a life of refinement and education and all those things which made what some people called a gentleman, but what he called a man" (qtd. in Thompson, *William Morris* 444). Nevertheless, like Ruskin, he repeatedly uses vitalistic "manliness" as a cipher for the redeemed human nature that will emerge under socialism. Also like Ruskin, he leaves his ideal a tantalizingly vague (and therefore rhetorically effective) abstraction that signifies social and aesthetic values without requiring their explicit specification or definition.

Recounting the transition from the eighteenth-century workshop system, which sought efficiency through the division of manual labor, to the nineteenth-century factory system, which sought to eliminate the need for manual labor through automation, Morris observes that "having turned the man into a machine, the next stage for commerce to aim at was to contrive machines which would widely dispense with human labour" (*Works* 23:68). He likewise describes the factory system as one in which "the machine-like workmen of the workshop period are supplanted by actual machines, of which the operatives (as they are now called) are but a portion" (*Works* 23:178). These passages adjust Ruskin's opposition between "man" and "machine" to reflect Morris's more nuanced understanding of industrial history. In an age of mechanical reproduction, Ruskin's vigorous objections to the division of labor are markedly anachronistic. Andrew Ure noted as early as 1835 that automated industry relied not on the division of labor but on its "equalization" (Ure 21), an observation Marx uses to differentiate between the era of "manufacture" and the era of the "automatic factory" (*Capital* 544–45). Morris, as one of the very few British social critics to acknowledge this distinction consistently, thus lends an additional historical specificity to the polemically powerful tropes he finds in "The Nature of Gothic."

Like Carlyle and Ruskin, Morris rejects the tenet of classical liberalism that the social consequences of industrial capitalism are simply by-products of "natural" economic law. He repeatedly criticizes capitalism as a system predicated upon the stimulation of artificial desires for luxuries and makeshift goods and sustained through an artificial coercive authority. In his lecture "The Society of the Future," Morris calls in Kingsleyan fashion for an end to "artificial systems made to save men manly trouble and responsibility" and demands instead "a free and unfettered animal life for man" (M. Morris 2:457). This demand entails a rejection of both asceticism, which requires the suppression of natural bodily desires, and luxury, which Morris takes to mean not the satisfaction of bodily desire but its perversion. In this vein, he launches into a scathing caricature of the middle-class gentleman:

> What brings about luxury but a sickly discontent with the simple joys of the lovely earth? What is it but a warping of the natural beauty of things into a perverse ugliness to satisfy the jaded appetite of a man who is ceasing to be a man—a man who will not work, and cannot rest? . . . Luxury rather builds clubs in Pall Mall, and upholsters them as though for delicate invalid ladies, for the behoof of big whiskered men, that they may lounge there amidst such preposterous effeminacy that the very plushed-breeched flunkies that wait upon the loungers are better men than they are. (M. Morris 2:458)

Capitalism, Morris suggests, is not the embodiment of manly competition, as some of its apologists would have it. Rather, it is an "effete system of production" (M. Morris 2:453) that forces the working-class operative into a brutalizing mechanical servitude and the middle-class gentleman into an enervating, decadent idleness.

Morris surpasses both Carlyle and Ruskin, though, in explicitly recognizing capitalist monopoly as a condition of "artificial restrictions" on labor and production that can be maintained only through the complicity of those it oppresses: "[I]f the whole class of workers could be convinced on one day or in one year of the necessity of abolishing monopoly, it would pass away like the clouds of night" (*Works* 23:252). Yet capitalism has effects that are not so ephemeral as the system itself. Marx, in "The Communist Manifesto," suggests that its "distinctive feature" is its distillation of the complex class structures of previous epochs into "two great hostile classes directly facing each other: Bourgeoisie and Proletariat" (222). Ruskin, in "The Nature of Gothic," observes that the once merely conventional or legal "wall" separating the "noble" from the "poor" had become, by the nineteenth century, "a veritable difference in level of standing" (10:194). In a synthesis of these insights, Morris contends that capitalism creates a "real" distinction between men by substituting for the universal rudeness of the Middle Ages the refinement of the rich and the degradation of the poor:

> The difference between lord and commoner, noble and burgher, was purely arbitrary; but how does it fare now with the distinction between class and class? Is it not the sad fact that the difference is no longer arbitrary but real?

Down to a certain class, that of the educated gentleman, as he is called, there
is indeed equality of manners and bearing, and if the commoners still choose
to humble themselves and play the flunkey, that is their own affair; but below
that class there is, as it were, the stroke of the knife, and gentlemen and non-
gentlemen divide the world. (*Works* 23:153)

Or as he puts it in another lecture:

Once all society was rude, there was little real difference between the gentleman and the non-gentleman, and you had to dress them differently from one
another in order to distinguish them. But now a well-to-do man is a refined and
cultivated being, enjoying to the full his share of the conquest over Nature
which the modern world has achieved, while the poor man is rude and degraded,
and has no share in the wealth conquered by modern science from Nature.
(*Works* 23:125)

By distinguishing "gentlemen" from "non-gentlemen" on the basis of manners, bearing, and refinement, Morris identifies culture rather than property
as the true source of class distinctions. The "real test of the contrast" between
the classes, he writes, lies "in the taste for reading and the habit of it, and the
capacity for the enjoyment of refined thought and the expression of it, which
the more expensive class really has . . . and which unhappily the working or
un-expensive class lacks" (*Works* 23:240).

This approbation of gentlemanly refinement and cultivation is not inconsistent with Morris's condemnation of the capitalist class structure. On
the contrary, it enables him to resolve what E. P. Thompson describes as the
"hardy perennial" among the various issues Morris had to confront upon his
conversion to socialism: "the relation of the individual man of the middle-
class, with goodwill and lofty motives, to the historical concept of the class
war" (*William Morris* 322–23). Ruskin argues that the refined manners of
true gentlemen are but the external manifestations of innate moral and aesthetic impulses conducive to social change. Morris calls on middle-class men
to actualize this potential through concrete political action. After describing
the plight of the working class in an 1884 lecture to the Secular Society of
Leicester, he asks his audience: "And how can we of the middle classes, we
the capitalists, and our hangers-on, help them? By renouncing our class, and
on all occasions when antagonism rises up between the classes casting in
our lot with the victims" (*Works* 23:213). In its specific context, this charge is
a call to join the socialist Democratic Federation, to which Morris belonged
before starting his own Socialist League later in the year. Yet it also affirms
Morris's conviction that aesthetic culture, embodied however imperfectly in

Victorian middle-class men, could provide the impetus for moving society beyond laissez-faire capitalism.

In the refined tastes and capacities of the gentleman, Morris recognizes (albeit through a glass darkly) a prefiguration of the healthy desire for beauty and pleasure that will underwrite the socialist future. Like a great many nineteenth-century writers, he also identifies the capacity for the appreciation of beauty as a masculine faculty: "[W]e lack beauty in our lives, or, in other words, man-like pleasure" ("Worker's Share" 142). Industrial life, however, threatens this faculty and the "manhood" with which it is associated: "The advance of the industrial army ... compels us to *get used* to our degradation at the expense of losing our manhood, and producing children doomed to live less like men than ourselves. Men living amidst such ugliness cannot conceive of beauty, and, therefore, cannot express it" ("Worker's Share" 141). Morris holds that any true revolution (as opposed to distracting ameliorative reforms) must proceed from the working class, but he also worries that the horizons of this class have become so restricted that it cannot imagine a truly fulfilling alternative to its current state. Consequently, he looks to those individuals of the higher classes who have renounced their class affiliation to reform and expand working-class desire. In this way, Morris discovers in his privileged socioeconomic position a mandate for his utopian socialism. As he says in his lecture "The Society of the Future," "I have always belonged to the well-to-do classes, and was born into luxury, so that necessarily I ask much more of the future than many of you do" (M. Morris 2:455). His self-appointed task, as a socialist and a gentleman, is to teach those less fortunate than himself to desire as expansively as he desires and, in this way, to sow the seeds of discontent and hope that will lead to revolution. To this end, he must articulate a compelling vision of life under socialism without resorting to literal predictions about the future. While he demurs from offering specific forecasts, he captures the general character of the coming socialist epoch by transposing Marx's dialectical model of historical progress into romance (Spear 232–33).

In his influential account of this genre, Northrop Frye emphasizes not only romance's "extraordinarily persistent nostalgia" but also its "curiously paradoxical role" in society. Romance, he offers, is principally a literary mode through which a dominant class may express its values and ideals, but it also contains "a genuinely 'proletarian' element ... which is never satisfied with its various incarnations" (Frye 186). Romance can serve this dual function because of its unique capacity for expressing wishes and desires, even as it insists on their perpetual mutability and deferral. The essential feature of this analysis, as Fredric Jameson recognizes, is Frye's insistence that romance aims not at escape but at transfiguration (Jameson 110). It is precisely for this reason that Frye characterizes romance as "the search of the libido or desiring self for a fulfilment that will deliver it from the anxieties of reality but will still contain that reality" (193). Jameson, however, objects to this fuzzy invocation of "reality" and maintains that Frye misconstrues romance's mystification of historically determined structures of power as a nascent critical potential (Jameson 110–19).

Without denying the validity of this critique, Jeffrey Spear intervenes to keep Morris from being swept up in Jameson's wholesale rejection of romance as a genre linked to "an archaic mentality and political reaction" (Spear 231). Quoting Morris's own understanding of romance as a "power for making the past part of the present" (M. Morris 1:148), Spear argues that Morris's Marxism "makes him, as it were, nostalgic for the future" (Spear 229, 231). Morris, I take Spear to mean, is drawn to romance not because he possesses an "archaic mentality" but because he requires a means of contemplating in a provisional and imaginative way the transformations of desire prerequisite to the socialist future. Morris acknowledges that "it would be futile to map out the details of life in a condition of things so different from that in which we have been born and bred" (M. Morris 2:130), but he also recognizes his responsibility—at once moral, aesthetic, and political—to imagine what this future might feel like, so as to facilitate its realization.

In his lecture "How We Live and How We Might Live," Morris presents "the history of man" in precisely this way, as a quest romance turning on a pivotal confrontation between a heroic, masculinized humanity and an oppressive, feminized "Nature": "Observe, in the early days of the history of man he was the slave of his most immediate necessities; Nature was mighty and he was feeble, and he had to wage constant war with her for his daily food and such shelter as he could get. . . . Time passed, and little by little, step by step, he grew stronger, till now after all these ages he has almost completely conquered Nature" (*Works* 23:14). In its paradigmatic form, as Frye explains, the quest romance proceeds through three stages: the (typically masculine) hero undertakes a preliminary journey, he struggles with and bests a (typically feminine) enemy, and he undergoes a final transformation or exaltation (Frye 187). "Nature," as represented here by Morris, is not the benign maternal presence it is for Wordsworth or the source of moral and aesthetic rejuvenation it is for Ruskin. Rather, it—or, perhaps better, she—is the sadistically amoral force that so horrified Tennyson and Mill: a Nature "red in tooth and claw" ("In Memoriam" 56.15) who subjects "men" to torturous deaths of "ingenious cruelty" with "the most supercilious disregard both of mercy and of justice" (Mill, *Works* 10:385).[9]

In subduing this hostile feminine power, however, Morris's hero reveals a more subtle foe within himself: the instinctual presumption of scarcity that is the foundational principle of capitalist economics. "It would almost seem," Morris muses, "as if some phantom of the ceaseless pursuit of food which was once the master of the savage was still hunting the civilized man; who toils in a dream, as it were, haunted by mere dim unreal hopes, born of vague recollections of the days gone by" (*Works* 23:15). This false consciousness, which sustains the volatile union of desire and denial characteristic of capitalism, is for James Eli Adams exemplified by the heroes of Kingsley's novels, who "typically experience an unusually violent oscillation of desire and restraint" (*Dandies* 110). Just as Kingsley urges the true man to be "bold against himself"—to achieve a self-mastery equivalent to his mastery of external circumstances—so Morris asserts that although man "has indeed conquered Nature and has her forces under his control to do what he will with, he still has himself to conquer" (*Works* 23:14). Yet while the psychology of the Kingsleyan hero mirrors the contrary pressures within capitalist ideology, Morris calls on man to renounce the illusion of necessity itself: "Out of that dream he must wake, and face things as they really are" (*Works* 23:15). Having mastered Nature in her manifestation as necessity, humanity is poised to construct a utopian society in cooperation with Nature in her manifestation as beauty.

THE HISTORICAL inevitability of revolution, Morris writes, "cannot fail to rouse our imaginations into picturing for ourselves that life at once happy and manly which we *know* social revolution will put within reach of all men" (M. Morris 2:130–31). While capitalism pushes men into effeminate luxury or mechanical servitude, socialism will sustain and be sustained by a healthy, pervasive manliness. In his lecture "Useful Work *versus* Useless Toil," Morris contends that in the socialist future, the more onerous sorts of work will be performed by volunteers, "who would surely be forthcoming, unless men in a state of freedom should lose the sparks of manliness which they possessed as slaves" (*Works* 23:118). Likewise, in "How We Live and How We Might Live," he asserts that he would "think very little of the manhood of a stout and healthy man who did not feel a pleasure in doing rough work" (*Works* 23:21). In such passages, "manliness" (or "manhood") serves as both a source of and a metaphor for the cooperative impulse that Morris hopes will replace competitive self-interest as society's organizing value.

News from Nowhere is, of course, Morris's most sustained effort to imagine the quality of life under such conditions. At least in part, this "utopian romance" is a response to Edward Bellamy's *Looking Backward,* which envisions an efficiently regimented industrial society under the control of a centralized state bureaucracy. Bellamy's main fault, in Morris's eyes, is that his "unhistoric and unartistic" modern temper prevents him from desiring anything more than the absorption of all people into a homogeneous middle class (M. Morris 2:502). In *News from Nowhere,* Morris uses the genre of romance to model a truly revolutionary imagination that does not merely replicate contemporary social categories. By facilitating the imaginative apprehension of the past in relation to the present, romance allows him to contextualize current social structures, render them subject to analysis, and propose real but nonliteral alternatives.

As he does in his lectures and essays, Morris represents life after the socialist revolution in terms of an idealized, organic masculinity. In his account of the "Change," old Hammond portrays the struggles that led to the fall of capitalism as a clash of nineteenth-century masculine types: "the two combatants, the workman and the gentleman, between them"—Guest jumps in to complete the sentence—"Between them . . . they destroyed commercialism!" (*Works* 16:131). The fragmented masculinities characteristic of the nineteenth century destroy the system that created them, thereby allowing the new society to emerge. The governing "spirit" of this new age, Hammond tells Guest, is an "intense and overweening love of the very skin and surface of the earth on which man dwells, such as a lover has in the fair flesh of the woman he loves" (16:132). Within this speculative history, male heterosexual desire thus becomes a principal emblem for the natural, productive impulse that supplants the artificially conflicted structures of desire and restraint endemic to capitalism.

Significantly, the women as well as the men of Morris's imaginary future are imbued with this masculine spirit. Guest recognizes it in Dick's "passionate love of the earth" (16:207), but it also infuses Ellen, the enchanting "fairy godmother" (16:181) who throws her charm over the latter part of Guest, Dick, and Clara's journey up the Thames. Indeed, Ellen's exclamation at the climax of this journey—"O me! O me! How I love the earth, and the seasons, and weather, and all things that deal with it, and all that grows out of it . . . !" (16:202)—echoes both the language and the metaphoric structure of Hammond's characterization of the "spirit of the new days." If, as Morris insists and virtually all his interpreters recognize, *News from Nowhere* is not a literal depiction of life under socialism but a figurative representation meant to communicate the general character of the new age, then this same awareness should be extended as well to the metaphoric vocabulary in which Morris couches his theoretical pronouncements. Such formulations as Hammond's assertion that "we live amidst beauty without any fear of becoming effeminate" (16:72) should not be interpreted, as one critic would have it, primarily as derogations of femininity.[10] Just as Arnold and Ruskin offer their respective notions of the "best self" and the gentleman "in the best sense" as ideals that transcend social class, so Morris through the example of Ellen identifies his masculine spirit as a universal ideal that transcends gender.

Nevertheless, in a text that depicts a society characterized by the dissolution of "classes" of all kinds—the distinctions between town and country, work and leisure, artwork and commodity, and nature and civilization, as well as between social classes, all have disappeared—Morris's treatment of gender roles remains conspicuous for the degree to which he portrays them as "natural" (Boos and Boos 25). The men in his utopia perform most of the strenuous physical labor and no domestic chores, while the women gravitate toward such occupations as raising children and housekeeping. Moreover, the women are continually subjected to an ubiquitous male "gaze." Early on, Guest stares unabashedly at the beautiful women he meets at the Hammersmith guest house. "As they were the first of the sex I had seen on this eventful morning," he comments, "I naturally looked at them very attentively, and found them at least as good as the gardens, the architecture, and the male men" (16:14). Lest this brazenness be excused as the product of Guest's crude Victorian consciousness, Morris shows his exemplary man of the future to be similarly voyeuristic. When Dick enlists a "maiden" to hold his and Guest's horses while they enter a tobacco shop, the two men almost lasciviously remark on her physical beauty:

> "What a beautiful creature!" said I to Dick as we entered.
> "What, old Greylocks?" said he, with a sly grin.
> "No, no," said I; "Goldylocks,—the lady."
> "Well so she is," said he. (16:35)

Although Morris's women notice the physical attractions of the men—Clara is described as watching Dick and "admiring his manly beauty and heartily good-natured face, and thinking . . . of nothing else" (16:144)—they do not regard the opposite sex with the same sort of evaluative detachment. Even Ellen has internalized her role as sexual object, telling Guest in one conversation, "I work hard when I like it, because I like it, and think it does me good, and knits up my muscles, and *makes me prettier to look at*, and healthier and happier" (16:158, emphasis added). The asymmetry of this sexual gaze hints at a destructive potential latent within Morris's masculine ideal.

Critics have long recognized that masculine desire, in its specifically sexual dimension, seems to threaten the stability of Morris's utopia. As Florence and William Boos observe, Morris "makes clear his view that male egoism and impulses toward revenge, not female disloyalty or maternal irresponsibility, create the greatest threats to domestic social harmony" (23). *News from Nowhere* may be Morris's "anti-novel," in that it challenges what he sees as the novel's preoccupation with individual personalities and disregard for broader historical movements (Brantlinger, "News" 41), but its sexual economy is still novelistic. In nineteenth-century fiction, as Eve Sedgewick shows, masculine desire is often articulated within the context of an "erotic triangle" in which the bonds between the two male rivals are as potent as those between either of the men and the woman who is the object of their desire (21). The potential for such conflict is at least implicit in Dick's wishful comment to Guest regarding the benevolent distribution of beautiful women in Nowherian society: "'Tis a good job there are so many of them that every Jack may have his Jill: else I fear that we should get fighting for them" (16:35). Dick imagines a utopian sexual economy predicated upon the same sort of abundance as the Nowherian material economy. In both cases, (feminine) supply far exceeds (masculine) demand.[11] Immediately, though, he qualifies his observation, noting that "love is not a very reasonable thing, and perversity and self-will are commoner than some of our moralists think" (16:35). Dick's reflections lead him to recall a recent "mishap" that his friend Walter Allen later describes in detail. As Allen recounts the tale, a man driven by "love-madness" attacked his rival with an axe and was killed in the ensuing struggle. The rival, Allen fears, will have to go abroad to keep the "evil and feverish element round about him" (16:166) from infecting the larger community. Morris offers this parody of the Victorian sensation plot as both an example of the rational handling of homosocial conflict in the utopian future and a warning about the destructive power of masculine desire unsubordinated to a communal consciousness. If capitalist society was haunted by the "phantom" of material need, Morris's society of the future is similarly haunted by the specter of a perverse "self-will" incongruent with actual social relations.

In the latter half of the text, Ellen emerges as the focal point of Morris's exploration of the productive and destructive permutations of masculine desire. She represents the best elements of her society, yet she also aggravates the forces that threaten to destroy it. On the one hand, she unites a passionate love for the earth with a mature appreciation for the lessons of history and thus represents the best hope for the future. On the other hand, she has a profoundly destabilizing influence on the men she encounters. She mentions "dealing with two or three young men who have taken a special liking to me, and all of whom I cannot please at once" (16:184) and confides to Guest that she has "often troubled men's minds disastrously" (16:188). Musing on his affection for Ellen, Guest notes such effects within himself: "As for me I felt young again, and strange hopes of my youth were mingling with the pleasure of the present; almost destroying it, and quickening it into something like pain" (16:187). Guest's inability to consummate his relationship with Ellen at the end of *News from Nowhere* signifies the ephemeral nature of his, and Morris's, vision. Ellen tells him as he recedes into the nineteenth century, "you belong so entirely to the unhappiness of the past that our happiness even would weary you" (16:210). In keeping with the genre of romance, satisfaction in *News from Nowhere* is always promised but perpetually deferred. Yet desire is also endlessly mutable, and Guest's memories remain to inspire all who would quest after "the new day of fellowship, and rest, and happiness." His personal longing for Ellen and the world she represents does not dissolve. Rather, it reemerges as a potent faith in the possibility of structural change that Morris calls "a vision rather than a dream" (16:211).

THIS AMBIVALENT ending testifies to Morris's literary mastery. *News from Nowhere* is, if nothing else, a brilliantly constructed self-consuming artifact. The apparent ease with which he first conjures and then dispels his utopian vision not only reinforces the aesthetic posture toward life that permeates his "epoch of rest" but also quite effectively insulates his text from unsympathetic or even merely excessively pragmatic criticism. As Morris himself notes, a utopia is best read not as a literal prediction but "as the expression of the temperament of its author" (M. Morris 2:502).

However compelling, there is a certain caginess to such posturing, and it is at least possible that Morris so intently explores the contours of desire not because he is truly disturbed by its disruptive potential but rather because it affords him an occasion to dramatize the socializing power of a cultured manliness. If Morris identifies masculine egoism and sexual passion as the "greatest threats" to his utopia, he also finds within his masculine ideal a mechanism for countering these destructive forces. Since conflicts and emotional suffering are inevitable, old Hammond observes, "we shake off these griefs in a way which perhaps the sentimentalists of other times would think contemptible and unheroic, but which we think necessary and manlike"

(16:58). Just as Carlyle insists that men must harden themselves into heroes, and Ruskin argues that the gentleman must hide his feelings of sympathy behind a facade of "reserve," so Morris suggests that male sexual passion may be controlled by subjecting it to the governance of a "manlike" ethic of personal restraint. Morris is not, finally, worried that unconstrained masculine desire will fracture the "social harmony," for in every case its potentially subversive power is disciplined, deflected, or contained. His true worry, at which he hints only obliquely, is that what Langdon Winner terms "autonomous technology" threatens the presumption of human autonomy essential to his utopian vision.

This view diverges somewhat from prevailing critical opinion, and I do not wish to be misunderstood as resurrecting the dead notion that Morris was an enemy of the machine in any crude sense. Scholars have long recognized that Morris objects not to machinery as such but quite specifically to its inappropriate application under capitalism to increase profits or eliminate the need for skilled labor.[12] Moreover, he does offer a speculative account of the fate of the machine under socialism, hypothesizing that after an initial spate of mechanical invention, reliance on machinery will gradually decline. In "How We Live and How We Might Live," he expresses the "hope that the very elaboration of machinery in a society whose purpose is not the multiplication of labour . . . will lead to the simplification of life, and so once more to the limitation of machinery" (23:24–25). In *News from Nowhere*, a second "old antiquary" by the name of Henry Morsom describes precisely this process (16:178). By the time of the civil war, Morsom tells Guest, improvements in machinery had all but eliminated the need for work, creating a Carlylean "Sphinx-riddle" for the future: not "What do you mean to do with us?" (Carlyle 10:17), but more simply and profoundly, what do you mean to do?

The answer, which Morris finds prefigured in the relative refinement of the middle classes, lies in the dissolution of the artificial boundary between work and leisure Morris sees as characteristic of capitalism. Gradually, Morsom reports, the "feeling against a mechanical life" that had developed among the leisured classes before the "Great Change" spread throughout society. Under the influence of this new "feeling," which has at least a remote antecedent in the sensibilities of Ruskin's idealized gentleman, "machine after machine was quietly dropped under the excuse that the machines could not produce works of art" (16:179).

In this account, the conundrum created by the proliferation of the machine immediately after the revolution exposes the inadequacy of the values of a "Mechanical Age," while the machine's subsequent decline symbolizes the utopian possibilities inherent in a "manly" love of beauty and "work pleasure." Such a scenario, of course, presupposes that human beings will maintain full control over the machines they create. "You see, Guest," Walter Allen explains, "this is not an age of inventions. The last epoch did all that for us, and we are now content to use such of its inventions as we find handy, and leaving those alone which we don't want" (16:169–70). The inhabitants of Morris's utopia are radically free to choose the "inventions" they will use, unconstrained by either the legacy of past decisions or the need for ancillary supporting systems.

But as Morris's Edwardian successors recognized, such speculations can be pushed only so far. H. G. Wells, for one, was exasperated by Morris's propensity to regard advanced technologies as simple tools. Over thirty years ago, Herbert Sussman aptly characterized *A Modern Utopia* as an expression of Wells's "humanistic faith in the machine." The book's fundamental argument, Sussman asserts, is "that technology can make possible the rich inner life that earlier Victorian writers thought attainable only by insulating the mind from technology" (*Victorians and the Machine* 170). Wells's deeper insight, though, was that the realization of this potential requires vigilant attention to the ramifications of technological decisions. In *The Time Machine*, which has long been recognized as a satire of certain elements of *News from Nowhere*, the social classes Morris synecdochically represents by the "workman" and the "gentleman" are not subsumed by a pervasive utopian "manliness" but instead evolve into separate and equally degenerate species. The surface world of the docile and effeminate Eloi clearly parodies Morris's vision of the future as an "epoch of rest," but less obviously, the subterranean world of the animalistic and technically proficient Morlocks also satirizes Morris's blithe inattention to the potential of technological systems to escape conscious control. In the future of *The Time Machine*, as in Morris's Nowhere, machines have been "quietly dropped," but to starkly different effect. In *A Modern Utopia*, Wells, like Morris, imagines a utopian society guided by the values of aesthetic culture, but in contrast to Morris, he holds that this ideal "State" must be kept up to a "minimum standard of efficiency" through the benevolent management of a caste of disinterested and ascetic "voluntary nobility," who are the Morlocks' conceptual opposites. These "samurai," drawn from what Wells calls the "Poietic" and "Kinetic" (265) classes, perform precisely the leavening and regulatory function Arnold assigns to "men of culture," whom he lauds as "the true apostles of equality" (113). Moreover, like Arnold's collective "best self," the samurai do not merely serve the State but are in fact coextensive with it: "Ah!," exclaims Wells's speaker, in a moment of insight, "it is quite clear in my mind, that these *samurai* form the real body of the State" (277).

A Modern Utopia, in other words, anticipates the very reconciliation of technology and culture that Arnold is at pains to deny, but it also insists that this reconciliation must be purchased through a disciplined vigilance that comes from the denial rather than the development of the self. As Winner and others have perceived, the commonsense presumption of mastery that has long structured responses to the machine has become, since the beginning of the nineteenth century, increasingly untenable. It is becoming more and more doubtful that human beings understand the things they have made, that these things are under firm control, or that the benefit or harm of these things depends only on the use to which human beings put them (Winner 25–27). The ever-increasing gap between human beings' experience of and reliance on complex technologies and their ability to understand them produces a parallel and dangerous erosion of personal and political agency (Winner 296).

In this light, the "force-barges" Guest witnesses on the Thames suggest the inadequacy of Morris's notion that technologies may be taken up or dropped at will, even as they exemplify this precise ideal. These barges are frequently recruited to demonstrate the harmonious integration of "appropriate" or "alternative" technologies into Morris's future society.[13] Yet in their vague and magical perfection—they demand no infrastructural support, produce no waste or exhaust, and require no cadre of technical experts to oversee their operation—they also hint at a reluctance on his part to approach the issue of autonomous technology too closely, lest such an examination damage the ideal of manliness on which his utopia is based. Walter Allen's tale of homosocial conflict and murder, we should remember, comes almost immediately after Guest spies the force-barges, and while Guest is fascinated by the sensational episode Allen describes, he shies away from inquiring too closely into the workings of these mysterious vehicles: "I took good care not to ask any questions about them, as I knew well enough both that I should never be able to understand how they worked, and that in attempting to do so I should betray myself" (16:162). It almost seems as if Morris's flirtation with advanced technology precipitates Allen's cautionary tale of sexualized violence, and from a certain perspective it does, since Morris uses it to deflect attention away from Guest's ambivalent and inadequate response to the force-barges. Allen's story, this is to say, disguises rather than reveals the true source of Morris's anxiety for the future, which is less the threat of rivalry between men than the latent capacity of advanced machines to usurp the metaphorically masculine human autonomy that underpins his entire socialist project.

RAYMOND WILLIAMS opens the second part of *Culture and Society*, in which he argues passionately for the continuing relevance of the discourse on culture, by singling out William Morris for particular approbation: "The pivotal figure of the tradition which has been examined," he writes, "and which we shall see continued and extended to our own day, is William Morris" (161). All other late Victorian and Edwardian writers, including Pater, Wilde, Gissing, and Shaw, pale before Morris's luminous presence. Neither a "period of masters" nor the "period of our contemporaries," the years between 1880 and 1914 are for Williams "a kind of interregnum," to which he gives brief notice only to preserve the coherence of his critical narrative. This low opinion arises from his disappointment that the writers of this period largely recapitulated in diluted form the ideas of the past and so made only incremental contributions to the tradition he traces. But it also, I believe, reflects his stronger sense that these writers, in softening the strong distinction between "industry" and "culture" so crucial to nineteenth-century social criticism, betrayed the ethical legacy bequeathed to them by the line of "great Victorian rebels" Morris represents. From the perspective of this study, however, this softening marks not the abandonment of the nineteenth-century tradition but an attempt to salvage it.

To this end, such "period figures" as George Bernard Shaw, Arnold Bennett, and H. G. Wells sought to subsume the old opposition between culture and industry—or in the terms of the current chapter, between manliness and mechanism—into a new and synthetic ideal of "efficiency." Tellingly, the word *efficiency* underwent at the end of the nineteenth century a process of abstraction similar to that which the word *culture* underwent at the end of the eighteenth. As Williams reminds us, before the middle of the eighteenth century, *culture* took its primary meaning from agriculture and animal husbandry, where it referred to the tending of crops and livestock. In this early period, the term was typically used concretely, to refer to the "culture *of* something," but over the course of the nineteenth century the term came to signify the process of development in itself: "*culture* as such." With this emergence as an independent, abstract noun, the term entered into its complex modern history (*Culture and Society* xvi).[14] In the same fashion, the words *efficient* and *efficiency* were used, until the latter decades of the nineteenth century, primarily to distinguish immediate from proximate or final causality, with the adjectival form predominating. By the end of the century, the nominal form had come into more general usage, and its meaning had expanded dramatically. Through its technical applications in such fields as thermodynamics and statistics, efficiency became associated with optimization, and it was employed in this modern sense to describe not only machines and business enterprises but also bodies, societies, and even works of art. The efficiency movement at the turn of the century was not an outright rejection of the Victorian discourse of culture but an attempt to dispense with the obsolete binaries it perpetuated. The Edwardians recognized the limitations of the Victorian tradition and sought to transcend them by explicitly embracing "efficiency" as a social and aesthetic ideal. In doing so, however, they succeeded less in resolving the contradictions inherent to the discourse of culture than in transposing its tensions and ambiguities into another register.[15]

To take a single representative example, Shaw imagines his work as an exercise in "personal efficiency" that verges on Paterian aestheticism: "My passion, like that of all artists," he wrote to the playwright Henry Arthur Jones in 1894, "is for efficiency, which means intensity of life and breadth and variety of experience" (*Letters* 1:463).[16] Shaw uses the term efficiency here to mean something very like that habit of inward thought and feeling his nineteenth-century precursors called "culture."

In his plays, however, he complicates this equation by calling into question the ideal of autonomous manliness that Pater's aesthetic "critic" (like Carlyle's "Hero," Kingsley's "Christian," Ruskin's "gentleman," and Morris's "man") exemplifies. In *Man and Superman,* Shaw employs pairs of contrasting masculine types—Octavius "Tavy" Robinson and Roebuck Ramsden represent obsolete Victorian sensibilities, while Jack Tanner and his chauffeur Henry Straker represent two versions of the modern "New Man"—to dramatize the ultimate incompatibility of masculine self-creation and the impersonal evolutionary ends of the "Life Force." In *Major Barbara,* he elaborates on the Devil's paradoxical claim that "the inner need" of the Life Force is "for a more efficient engine of destruction" (*Plays* 3:621). In his preface as well as in the play itself, Shaw uses deft allusions to Carlyle, Dickens, Ruskin, and Morris to argue for a new ideal of industrial masculinity organized around the value of systemic efficiency, rather than around the value of individual mastery that underwrites such Victorian masculine types as the gentleman and the captain of industry. Throughout, Andrew Undershaft self-consciously differentiates himself from the antiquated masculine norms represented by his son and his daughter's suitors, telling his family, "I am not a gentleman; and

I was never educated" (1:358). Yet neither is he a typical Victorian captain of industry. In contrast to Gaskell's mill owner John Thornton, Dickens's parody of the self-made man Josiah Bounderby, or Carlyle's Plugson of Undershot, to whom his own name alludes, Undershaft understands that the massive authority he wields in society—"*I* am the government of your country" (1:416)—is accompanied by a paradoxical absence of personal power within his own factory. He readily acknowledges that the establishment is "kept in order" not through the moral authority of a single master but through an efficient, incremental discipline: "Practically, every man of them keeps the man just below him in his place" (1:419).

While *Major Barbara* seems to affirm Undershaft's sense that he is, as Shaw puts it in the play's preface, "only the instrument of a Will or Life Force which uses him for purposes wider than his own" (1:312), his nearly contemporaneous play *John Bull's Other Island* reveals the narrowness of this view. Like Henry Straker and Andrew Undershaft, the English engineer Thomas Broadbent is a representation of the efficient "New Man," but he is subjected to an ironizing light Shaw spares those other characters. The play's final scene exposes the poverty of Broadbent's belief that "there are only two qualities in the world: efficiency and inefficiency" (2:604) by juxtaposing it with the defrocked priest Father Keegan's emphasis on final "salvation and damnation" (2:610). Through this exchange, Shaw dramatizes a "truth" he had earlier expressed in a 1901 letter to Beatrice Webb: "that efficiency is obviously not a final term & cannot be held up as an end" (*Letters* 2:235). Despite his effort to extricate himself from the nineteenth-century discourse of culture by locating within industrial society itself a viable social and aesthetic ideal, Shaw nevertheless finds himself thrown upon the shore of Arnold's "distant northern sea."

NOTES

INTRODUCTION

1. John Holloway, in his early defense of the literariness of Victorian sage writing, portrays the Victorian sage writers (exemplified most strongly by Carlyle) as attempting to adopt an "oracular pose" in an age of doubt (chap. 1). Building on this fundamental insight, George Landow argues that sage writing derives directly from eighteenth- and nineteenth-century attitudes toward the Old Testament and succinctly enumerates the main features of the genre: an oscillation between satire and visionary earnestness; an alternation between aggressive and conciliatory postures toward the audience; a tendency toward analogical rather than logical structures of argument; an emphasis on grotesque images and episodes drawn from contemporary life; a predilection for idiosyncratic or satirical definitions of terms; and a basic reliance on appeals to authorial credibility (*Elegant Jeremiahs* 28–29).

2. See Herbert; Pecora; Stocking, *Race, Culture, and Evolution*.

3. This is not to suggest that Lloyd and Thomas wholly embrace Hunter's Foucauldian argument. In fact, they take serious issue with Hunter on both empirical and theoretical grounds, objecting to what they view as his willingness to ignore historical evidence unamenable to his argument, and to what they see as his inadequate model of the process through which ideas and ideologies exert their social effects (19).

4. In *The Machinery Question and the Making of Political Economy*, Maxine Berg self-consciously treats the "machine" as an "issue" rather than a material thing and sets out to trace the ways in which "the great debate over machinery" in the first half of the nineteenth century fundamentally structured the emerging discipline of political economy (3). In *Languages of Class*, Gareth Stedman Jones describes the term *class* as a "congested point of intersection between many competing, overlapping, or simply differing forms of discourse" (2) and, in the central essay of that volume, advances a specifically "linguistic interpretation" of Chartism grounded in the analysis of "what Chartists actually said or wrote, the terms in which they addressed each other or their opponents" (2, 94–95). Patrick Joyce, in *Visions of the People,* treats "the formation of social identities" as "something accomplished in and by language" (16). Robert Gray, in *The Factory Question and Industrial England,* characterizes the second quarter of the nineteenth century as a period "of some cultural uncertainty, when discursive hierarchies were unsettled and open to challenge," and takes as his specific subject "the variable and contested meanings of the factory question, and the construction of these meanings in specific contexts, in both time and space" (9–11). For a survey of the "linguistic turn" in British social history, see Kent.

1. "One Co-operative Body"

1. In September of 1830, the prominent Bradford spinner John Wood described to a then ignorant Richard Oastler the cruelties children suffered in the mills: the thirteen-hour days, the harsh and arbitrary discipline, the injuries caused by unsafe machinery and physical exhaustion, the near total neglect of their religious and moral educations. As Oastler would report years later in his periodical *The Home,* he interpreted this intelligence as nothing less than a divine mandate to combat the factory system and promised Wood he would work to eliminate "the cruelties which are regularly practised in our mills." "I knew that that vow was recorded in Heaven," he writes. "I have kept it, . . . the grace of God having upholden me; I have been faithful." The following day, Oastler wrote the inaugural document of the Factory Movement, his first letter on "Yorkshire slavery" (Alfred 1:96–98). See also Driver 36–38.

2. Gray likewise singles out these three texts for special notice (132–38).

3. For a discussion of conventions of technical illustration, see Purbrick.

4. See Berg 20–31.

5. On the genre of industrial tourism, see Gray 134–38; and Schaffer.

6. See Adas 173–77.

7. Cooke Taylor wishes to forestall all forms of legislative interference in the manufacturing districts. For this reason, he consistently maintains that the crises of the 1840s were economic rather than political. For example, he insists that the Preston strikes of 1842 were not an "insurrection" to be "suppressed," but simply a "social commotion" to be "tranquillised" by opening foreign markets and thereby easing pressure on wages (329–31).

8. Marx writes: "These two descriptions are far from being identical. In one, the combined collective worker appears as the dominant subject [*übergreifendes Subjekt*], and the mechanical automaton as the object; in the other, the automaton itself is the subject, and the workers are merely conscious organs, co-ordinated with the unconscious organs of the automaton, and together with the latter subordinated to the central moving force" (*Capital* 544–45).

9. For a discussion of the connection between Scottish physiology and Scottish social theory, see Lawrence 23–28.

10. See Poovey 7–8 for the waning of the metaphor of the body politic and its replacement by the image of the social body. See also chap. 3 of this study.

11. See Thompson, "Time, Work-Discipline."

12. Marx writes of this passage that Ure "prefers to present the central machine from which the motion comes as not only an automaton but an autocrat" (*Capital* 545).

13. See chap. 3 for a more detailed discussion of Kay's views on the various factors affecting the condition of the working classes.

14. See Gray 53–55, and Driver 13–24, for discussions of Oastler's Methodism and its influence on his polemic and oratory.

15. Cooke Taylor's likely source is de la Sagra's 1831 *Historia economico-politica y estadistica de la isla de Cuba.*

2. "Beautiful Combinations"

1. See Schaffer 219–24.

2. See, for example, Romano, who surveys Babbage's contributions to economic theory and concludes that while he should be remembered principally for his contributions to science, he also "exhibited considerable skill" as a political economist (405).

3. See Hyman 31, 34–37, 51, 88, 120, 227.

4. Babbage's interest in signification has gone largely unnoticed in the scholarship, even though it is the unifying feature of his many diverse pursuits. Ashworth's article on the importance of the discipline of algebraic analysis to Babbage and Herschel's philosophy of mind is one exception to this generalization. However, in his discussions of Babbage's theory of signification, Ashworth largely restricts himself to Babbage's mathematical work and has little to say about his broader interest in signifying systems of all sorts.

5. See also Ashworth 636.

6. The *Memoirs* were written jointly by Herschel and Babbage. Hyman attributes the early drafts of the preface to Babbage (25–26 n).

7. While I accept the general validity of Miller's, Schaffer's, and Ashworth's arguments, I find their claims that Babbage was attempting to produce intelligent or thinking machines to be overstated. Babbage certainly uses analogies to human mental faculties to describe the operations performed by his engines. However, he demurs from any idea that his engines could in fact remember or foresee, writing that the "mechanical means" through which they performed their calculations "bears some *slight analogy* to the operation of the faculty of memory" (11:46, emphasis added).

8. See Sussman, *Victorians and the Machine* 29–31.

9. For a comparison of Ure's and Babbage's different conceptions of the factory, see Berg 179–202.

10. For assessments of the Babbage Principle and its significance in the history of economic theory, see Braverman 79–83; and Romano 390–93.

11. Ashworth argues that Babbage and Herschel believed that Britain's future prosperity depended upon the cultivation of "expert industrial analysts" (644) and that they saw themselves as "the philosophical equivalents" of such figures as Strutt, Wedgwood, Boulton, and Watt (629, 638).

12. For a discussion of induction and early nineteenth-century scientific method, see Jonathan Smith 11–44.

13. For Babbage's involvement with the BAAS, see Morrell and Thackray; and Hyman, esp. 143–64.

14. Ashworth notes that Paley's *Evidences of Christianity* (1794) was standard reading when Babbage was at Cambridge (642).

15. Babbage based his campaign for government support of the Difference Engine on its ability to calculate reliable navigational tables and in this way help prevent expensive and tragic losses of life and property at sea (Hyman 49). In *The Economy,* he identified the cost of verifying the quality of commodities as a significant component of price (8:95–96). In 1836 he sat on a committee appointed by the Bank of England to inquire into methods of preventing the forgery of bank notes (11:316). He also amassed a large collection of ciphers and coded messages, many clipped from the pages of newspapers and journals. See BL Add. MSS 37205.

16. The disturbing implications of Babbage's speculations were not lost on his contemporaries. Dickens attacked the idea in one of his speeches (Hyman 40); several readers were sufficiently intrigued as to request demonstrations of the calculating engine; and when one American professor used Babbage's theory to illuminate a passage from Chaucer, his audience was spooked into a fear of talking (BL Add. MSS 37195, fol. 568). For the relationship between Babbage's and Bentham's views on testimony and writing, see Welsh, "Writing and Copying."

17. For a discussion of this episode, see Hyman 216.

18. Jeffrey Auerbach astutely interprets the debate over the display of prices at the Great Exhibition as a specific symptom of the more general conflict between the older labor theory and the emerging exchange theory of value (118–21).

19. Thomas Richards suggests that price tags would have interfered with "the kind of phenomenological immediacy" the Great Exhibition aimed to foster (38). Larry Lutchmansingh observes that the "overriding logic of capital development" required industrial exhibitions "as a necessary instrument of free trade and imperial expansion, while occluding the immediate and local features of exhibited manufactures and conjuring out of sight the actual operations of productive labor" (208). Andrew Miller, commenting specifically on Babbage's objection that the absence of prices reduced the exhibition's usefulness, holds that the event's organizers "appeared to have banished commerce from its halls" only to install in its stead "new practical and conceptual orders" of objects grounded upon "relational categories of gender, nationality, labor, and taste" (64).

20. For a detailed treatment of Victorian design theory, see chap. 4.

3. "A Debilitated Race"

1. Himmelfarb argues that Malthus's real purpose was to refute Smith's optimistic economic theory, not the Romantic utopianism of Godwin and Condorcet, which she asserts was already discredited by the end of the eighteenth century (101–13). For Malthus as a "vindicator of the rights of the body," see Gallagher, "The Body."

2. The details of Gaskell's life are less clear than those of Alison's or Kay's. Gray notes that he was related by marriage to Elizabeth and William Gaskell (85 n). For Gaskell's medical education, see Flinn 22–23. For his "liberal Tory" politics, see Berg 64.

3. For a comprehensive account of the intertwined discourses on disease and race in which these treatises participate, see O'Connor, chap. 1.

4. Drawing attention to the way in which the absence of poor relief can both hide and exacerbate the suffering of the poor, Alison observes drily that there are no paupers in Ireland.

5. Gaskell calls the "commercial part" of Ure's analysis of the stocking trade "strictly true," and he acknowledges Ure's account of new automated spinning and weaving techniques as "quite correct in its mechanical details" (341, 331). Likewise, in the new preface Gaskell wrote for *Artisans and Machinery,* he quotes with approval a lengthy passage from Ure's *Philosophy of Manufactures* cataloging the alarming social consequences of the factory system, and in the text itself he alters many of his own descriptions of factories and industrial working conditions to bring them into line with Ure's.

6. This strain of Gaskell's argument is even more pronounced in the earlier version of his study, *The Manufacturing Population of England* (1833), which includes a number

of specific observations regarding the effect of factory conditions on girls' sexual development which do not appear in the later *Artisans and Machinery.*

7. As Engels's editors W. O. Henderson and W. H. Chaloner note, this report, which was taken from Gaskell's study *The Manufacturing Population in England,* was in fact erroneous. Robertson's article reports several cases of menstruation at age eleven, but no cases of pregnancy (Engels 183, editors' note).

8. Henderson and Chaloner severely criticize Engels for taking Gaskell's account of eighteenth-century social conditions as the foundation for his theory of the origin of the proletariat (xi–xii). Eric Hobsbawm responds with a vindication of Engels, calling into question Henderson and Chaloner's ideological investments as well as the quality of their scholarship (105–19).

4. "Appropriate Beauty"

1. In accordance with convention, I refer to the *Art-Union* and *Art-Journal* collectively simply as the *Art-Journal.* When commenting on specific issues, however, I use the chronologically accurate titles.

2. See, for example, Pevsner 141–54. For a dissenting view, see Giedion, who denies that the journal had any lasting influence (348–60).

3. In his expansive and eclectic "anonymous history" of mechanization, Giedion presents the discourse on design as a failed response to the Victorians' misguided efforts to satisfy their innately human need for adornment through the unrestrained mechanical production of ornament (344–60). More recently, Jules Lubbock has identified the Victorian controversy over design as "the strangest episode so far" in Britain's centuries-long preoccupation with the public ramifications of private taste (248), and Patrick Brantlinger has understood it as an early instance of what have since become "endlessly recycled decline-and-fall narratives" about the triumph of mass over high culture ("Household Taste" 83).

4. For a detailed account of the workings of this select committee, see Bell, chap. 4.

5. The Department of Practical Art was founded in 1852, with Cole as its general superintendent. When it became the Department of Science and Art in 1853, he was made responsible for "Art" and Lyon Playfair for "Science." In 1859 Cole became the department's sole director. For the standard history of the government Schools of Design, see Bell. For a broader account of the institutionalization of art instruction in nineteenth-century Britain, see Minihan, esp. her chap. 4.

6. My analysis of nineteenth-century design theory is informed by the theory of conceptual integration or "blending" developed by the cognitive linguists Gilles Fauconnier and Mark Turner. An attractive feature of conceptual integration theory is its ability to accommodate gaps, tensions, and fissures within conceptual structures without denying those structures' cognitive utility. For this reason, the theory can be extremely useful in analyzing the emergence of historical discourses based on the integration and reconciliation of diverse concepts, such as "art" and "manufacture." For a general exposition of this theory, see Turner 57–84. For a more detailed technical account, see Fauconnier and Turner.

7. This example may seem trivial, but its more prominent reappearance two years later, in an article entitled "The Mercantile Value of the Fine Arts," indicates its emblematic significance (*AJ* 8:103).

8. For Dyce's dispute with Haydon over the drawing of the human figure, see Bell

85–86. For the byzantine politics surrounding the issue with respect to the curriculum of the branch schools, see Bell 111–18.

9. More than one scholar has dismissed the *Journal of Design* as simply a vehicle through which Cole promulgated his various political schemes. See Levine 63; and Cooper 43.

10. For an account of "art botany" and the science of design, see Brett.

11. See also Brett 104–5.

12. Among these anxieties, the *Journal of Design* names the following: a "fear of their competitors, an indefinite dread of the offended dignity of the retail dealer, or a still more indefinite notion that the foreigner, French, German, or American, may possibly gain a hint or two as to new modes of production" (*JD* 1:89).

13. For Cole's involvement with the planning of the Great Exhibition, see Cooper 51–73; and Auerbach 9–88.

5. "What You Ought to Learn"

1. This series was subsequently published in two volumes under the title *Lectures on the Results of the Great Exhibition of 1851*. Individual lectures are cited in the text by volume and page number.

2. Richard Yeo, in his account of Whewell as the mid-nineteenth century's preeminent commentator on science's authority and cultural status, calls this lecture "one of his most extraordinary performances" (224).

3. Whewell makes such an observation in his Society of Arts lecture (1:7), as does Mrs. Merrifield in her essay on colors in the *Art-Journal*'s *Illustrated Catalogue* (1).

4. Ironically enough, one of the most perceptive reflections on this issue in the series is to be found in the unlikely context of a technical discussion of Portland cement. Rather than exploiting cement's "peculiar properties" (2:357), Professor D. T. Anstead notes, manufacturers were merely using it as a cheap substitute for stone, forgetting "that what is beautiful in one material, or for one purpose, becomes preposterous and offensive when executed in another substance ill-adapted for it, or for a purpose altogether distinct from the right one" (2:369). Wyatt and Jones, in contrast, focus their attention specifically on the decorative arts.

5. For arguments in this vein, see Seltzer; and Armstrong, esp. his chaps. 2 and 3, which address the modernist preoccupations with bodily waste and prostheses, respectively.

6. See, for example, old Hammond's characterization of art as "work-pleasure" in Morris's *News from Nowhere* (16:92, 134), and Wilde's argument in "The Soul of Man under Socialism" that people will devote their attention to "Art" once they have relegated all work to machinery (267–70).

7. Redgrave occasionally uses the term *artist* to mean designer or ornamentist, especially when the distinction between art and ornament is not at issue.

6. "Only a Machine Before"

1. For a discussion of "making men" in early twentieth-century America, see Seltzer 149–72.

2. For the standard account of Ruskin's theory of "Vital Beauty," see Landow, *Aesthetic and Critical Theories* 146–79.

3. For a fuller discussion of Ruskin's bodily imagery, see Bizup, "Architecture, Railroads."

4. "The Nature of Gothic" has created for Ruskin scholarship its own version of the persistent if false conundrum that has been dubbed the "Adam Smith problem." Just as the study of Smith has been defined largely by an effort to reconcile *The Theory of Moral Sentiments* with *The Wealth of Nations,* so has much interpretation of Ruskin hinged on the relation between his criticism of art and his criticism of society. Raymond Williams's observation that Ruskin's art and social criticism "are both *applications,* in particular directions, of a fundamental conviction" remains one of the most insightful and elegant characterizations of the relationship between these facets of Ruskin's thought (*Culture and Society* 135).

5. For discussions of the 1847 Act and its aftermath, see Gray 190–212; and J. T. Ward 346–77.

6. See Gray 23–37; and Gallagher, *Industrial Reformation,* 3–35.

7. Cole's diary entry for 28 November 1878 includes a newspaper cutting noting that Whistler had quoted this remark in his libel case against Ruskin, as evidence of Ruskin's propensity for personal attacks.

8. See also Bizup, "Walter Pater."

9. For an analysis of this dichotomy, see Adams, "Philosophical Forgetfulness."

10. See Sypher 99.

11. The proposition that "every Jack may have his Jill" does not logically require that every Jill may also have her Jack. Morris's utopia is not predicated upon the harmonious reconciliation of supply and demand but, like Ruskin's economic theory, upon the inversion of the presumption of scarcity that grounds capitalist ideology. See Sherburne.

12. See, for example, Spear 217; Sussman, *Victorians and the Machine* 133–34; Thompson, *William Morris* 649–50.

13. See, for example, Coleman.

14. See also Williams, *Keywords* 87–92.

15. G. R. Searle argues that during the Edwardian period, the technocratic and militaristic goal of "National Efficiency" served as a "cohering ideology," capable of appealing to different segments of society but incapable of sustaining real political change (xx). For a more general survey of the political, social, and cultural ramifications of the Edwardian efficiency movement, see Jonathan Rose's chapter "The Efficiency Men."

16. For a survey of Shaw's statements on efficiency, see Couchman.

WORKS CITED

Abrams, M. H. *Natural Supernaturalism: Tradition and Revolution in Romantic Litera-ture*. New York: W. W. Norton, 1971.

Adams, James Eli. *Dandies and Desert Saints: Styles of Victorian Masculinity*. Ithaca: Cornell UP, 1995.

———. "Philosophical Forgetfulness: John Stuart Mill's 'Nature.'" *Journal of the History of Ideas* 53.3 (1992): 437–54.

Adas, Michael. *Machines as the Measure of Men: Science, Technology, and Ideologies of Western Dominance*. Ithaca: Cornell UP, 1989.

Alfred [Samuel H. G. Kydd]. *The History of the Factory Movement*. 1857. 2 vols. New York: Augustus M. Kelley, 1966.

Alison, W. P. *Observations on the Management of the Poor in Scotland, and Its Effects on the Health of the Great Towns*. Edinburgh: William Blackwood and Sons; London: Thomas Cadell, 1840.

Armstrong, Tim. *Modernism, Technology, and the Body: A Cultural Study*. Cambridge: Cambridge UP, 1998.

Arnold, Matthew. *Culture and Anarchy*. 1869. Vol. 5 of *The Complete Prose Works of Matthew Arnold*. Ed. R. H. Super. Ann Arbor: U Michigan P, 1965.

The Art-Journal Illustrated Catalogue: The Industry of All Nations. London: G. Virtue, 1851. Rpt. as *The Crystal Palace Exhibition; Illustrated Catalogue; London, 1851*. Introd. John Gloag. New York: Dover Publications, 1970.

Ashworth, William J. "Memory, Efficiency, and Symbolic Analysis: Charles Babbage, John Herschel, and the Industrial Mind." *Isis* 87 (1996): 629–53.

Auerbach, Jeffrey A. *The Great Exhibition of 1851: A Nation on Display*. New Haven: Yale UP, 1999.

Babbage, Charles. Papers. British Library.

———. *The Works of Charles Babbage*. Ed. Martin Campbell-Kelly. 11 vols. New York: New York UP, 1989.

Baines, Edward. *History of the Cotton Manufacture in Great Britain*. London, 1835.

Bell, Quentin. *The Schools of Design*. London: Routledge and Kegan Paul, 1963.

Benjamin, Walter. *Illuminations*. Ed. Hannah Arendt. Trans. Harry Zohn. New York: Schocken Books, 1968.

Berg, Maxine. *The Machinery Question and the Making of Political Economy, 1815–1848*. Cambridge: Cambridge UP, 1980.

Bizup, Joseph. "Architecture, Railroads, and Ruskin's Rhetoric of Bodily Form." *Prose Studies* 21.1 (1998): 74–94.

———. "Walter Pater and the Ruskinian Gentleman." *English Literature in Transition, 1880–1920* 38.1 (1995): 51–69.

Black, Barbara J. *On Exhibit: The Victorians and Their Museums.* Charlottesville: UP of Virginia, 2000.

Bøe, Alf. *From Gothic Revival to Functional Form: A Study in Victorian Theories of Design.* New York: Humanities Press, n.d.

Bonython, Elizabeth. *King Cole: A Picture Portrait of Sir Henry Cole, KCB, 1808–1882.* London: Victoria and Albert Museum, n.d.

Boos, Florence S., and William Boos. "*News from Nowhere* and Victorian Socialist-Feminism." *Nineteenth-Century Contexts* 14.1 (1990): 3–32.

Bourdieu, Pierre. *Distinction: A Social Critique of the Judgement of Taste.* Trans. Richard Nice. Cambridge, MA: Harvard UP, 1984.

Brantlinger, Patrick. "Household Taste: Industrial Art, Consumerism, and Pre-Raphaelitism." *Journal of Pre- Raphaelite Studies* 9 (2000): 83–100.

———. "'News from Nowhere': Morris's Socialist Anti-Novel." *Victorian Studies* 19.1 (1975): 35–49.

Braverman, Harry. *Labor and Monopoly Capital: The Degradation of Work in the Twentieth Century.* New York: Monthly Review Press, 1974.

Brett, David. "The Interpretation of Ornament." *Journal of Design History* 1.2 (1988): 103–11.

Briggs, Asa. *Victorian Things.* Chicago: U Chicago P, 1988.

Carlyle, Thomas. *The Works of Thomas Carlyle.* Centenary Edition. Ed. H. D. Traill. 30 vols. New York: AMS Press, 1980.

Carr, Stephen Leo. "The Ideology of Antithesis: Science versus Literature and the Exemplary Case of J. S. Mill." *Modern Language Quarterly* 42.3 (1981): 247–64.

Cole, Henry. *Diary of Henry Cole.* Transcribed by Elizabeth Bonython. National Art Library, Victoria and Albert Museum.

———. *Fifty Years of Public Work of Sir Henry Cole, K.C.B., Accounted For in His Deeds, Speeches and Writings.* 2 vols. London: George Bell and Sons, 1884.

———. Introduction. *Official Descriptive and Illustrated Catalogue of the Great Exhibition.* Vol. 1. London: Spicer Brothers, 1851. 1–35.

———. "What Is Art Culture? An Address Delivered to the Manchester School of Art, 21st December 1877, by Sir Henry Cole, K.C.B." Reprinted for private distribution from the Report on the Manchester School of Art. National Art Library, Victoria and Albert Museum.

Coleman, Roger. "Design and Technology in 'Nowhere.'" *Journal of the William Morris Society* 9.2 (1991): 28–39.

Coleridge, Samuel Taylor. *On the Constitution of Church and State.* Ed. John Colmer. Vol. 10 of *The Collected Works of Samuel Taylor Coleridge.* London: Routledge and Kegan Paul; Princeton, NJ: Princeton UP, 1976.

Collini, Stefan. "From 'Non-Fiction Prose' to 'Cultural Criticism': Genre and Disciplinarity in Victorian Studies." *Rethinking Victorian Culture.* Ed. Juliet John and Alice Jenkins. London: MacMillan, 2000. 13–28.

Cooke Taylor, William. *Factories and the Factory System; From Parliamentary Documents and Personal Examination.* London: Jeremiah How, 1844.

———. *Notes of a Tour in the Manufacturing Districts of Lancashire; in a Series of Letters to His Grace the Archbishop of Dublin.* 1842. Cass Library of Industrial Classics, no. 12. London: Frank Cass, 1968.

Cooper, Ann. "For the Public Good: Henry Cole, His Circle and the Development of the South Kensington Estate." Diss., The Open University, 1992.

Couchman, Gordon. "Bernard Shaw and the Gospel of Efficiency." *The Shaw Review* 16 (1973): 11–20.

Dale, Peter Allan. *In Pursuit of a Scientific Culture: Science, Art, and Society in the Victorian Age.* Madison: U Wisconsin P, 1989.

Driver, Cecil. *Tory Radical: The Life of Richard Oastler.* New York: Oxford UP, 1946.

Eagleton, Terry. *The Ideology of the Aesthetic.* Oxford: Basil Blackwell, 1990.

Edmond, A. *A Reminiscence of the Great Exhibition of 1851.* New ed. London, 1853.

Engels, Frederick. *The Condition of the Working Class in England.* Ed. and trans. W. O. Henderson and W. H. Chaloner. Stanford: Stanford UP, 1968.

Fauconnier, Gilles, and Mark Turner. "Conceptual Integration Networks." *Cognitive Science* 22.2 (1998): 133–87.

Flinn, M. W. Introduction. *Report on the Sanitary Condition of the Labouring Population of Great Britain.* By Edwin Chadwick. Edinburgh: Edinburgh UP, 1965.

Forbes, Edward. "The Vegetable Kingdom, As Illustrated in the Exhibition." *The Art-Journal Illustrated Catalogue.*

Foucault, Michel. *Discipline and Punish: The Birth of the Prison.* Trans. Alan Sheridan. New York: Pantheon, 1977.

Frye, Northrop. *Anatomy of Criticism: Four Essays.* Princeton, NJ: Princeton UP, 1957.

Gallagher, Catherine. "The Body versus the Social Body." *The Making of the Modern Body: Sexuality and Society in the Nineteenth Century.* Ed. Catherine Gallagher and Thomas Laquer. Berkeley and Los Angeles: U California P, 1987. 83–106.

———. *The Industrial Reformation of English Fiction: Social Discourse and Narrative Form, 1832–1867.* Chicago: U Chicago P, 1985.

Gaskell, Elizabeth. *North and South.* Ed. Angus Easson. London: Oxford UP, 1973.

Gaskell, Peter. *Artisans and Machinery.* 1836. London: Frank Cass, 1968.

———. *The Manufacturing Population of England, Its Moral, Social, and Physical Conditions, and the Changes Which Have Arisen from the Use of Steam Machinery; with an Examination of Infant Labour.* London: Baldwin and Cradock, 1833.

Giedion, Siegfried. *Mechanization Takes Command: A Contribution to Anonymous History.* 1948. New York: W. W. Norton, 1969.

Gloag, John. Introduction. *The Crystal Palace Exhibition; Illustrated Catalogue; London, 1851.* New York: Dover Publications, 1970.

———. *Victorian Taste: Some Social Aspects of Architecture and Industrial Design, from 1820–1900.* New York: Macmillan, 1962.

Gordon, Lewis D. B. "The Machinery of the Exhibition: As Applied to Textile Manufactures." *The Art-Journal Illustrated Catalogue.*

Gray, Robert. *The Factory Question and Industrial England, 1830–1860.* Cambridge: Cambridge UP, 1996.

Haley, Bruce. *The Healthy Body and Victorian Culture.* Cambridge, MA: Harvard UP, 1978.

Herbert, Christopher. *Culture and Anomie: Ethnographic Imagination in the Nineteenth Century.* Chicago: U Chicago P, 1991.

Himmelfarb, Gertrude. *The Idea of Poverty: England in the Early Industrial Age.* New York: Knopf, 1984.

Hobsbawm, E. J. *Labouring Men: Studies in the History of Labour.* New York: Basic Books, 1964.

Holloway, John. *The Victorian Sage: Studies in Argument.* New York: Norton, 1953.

Hume, David. *An Enquiry Concerning the Principles of Morals.* Vol. 4 of *The Philosophical Works.* 1886. Ed. Thomas Hill Green and Thomas Hodge Grose. Darmstadt: Scientia Verlag Aalen, 1964. 169–287.

Hunt, Robert. "The Science of the Exhibition." *The Art-Journal Illustrated Catalogue.*

Hunter, Ian. *Culture and Government: The Emergence of Literary Education.* London: Macmillan, 1988.

Hyman, Anthony. *Charles Babbage: Pioneer of the Computer.* Princeton, NJ: Princeton UP, 1982.

Jameson, Fredric. *The Political Unconscious: Narrative as a Socially Symbolic Act.* Ithaca: Cornell UP, 1981.

Jones, Gareth Stedman. *Languages of Class: Studies in English Working Class History, 1832–1982.* Cambridge: Cambridge UP, 1983.

Jones, Owen. *The Grammar of Ornament, Illustrated by Examples from Various Styles of Ornament.* 1856. London: Studio Editions, 1986.

Joyce, James. *Ulysses.* 1922. New York: Vintage Books, 1986.

Joyce, Patrick, ed. *The Historical Meanings of Work.* Cambridge: Cambridge UP, 1987.

———. *Visions of the People: Industrial England and the Question of Class, 1848–1914.* Cambridge: Cambridge UP, 1991.

Kay, James Phillips [see also Kay-Shuttleworth]. *The Moral and Physical Condition of the Working Classes, Employed in the Cotton Manufacture in Manchester.* 2nd ed. London: James Ridgway, 1832.

Kay-Shuttleworth, Sir James. *Ribblesdale; or, Lancashire Sixty Years Ago.* London: Smith, Elder, 1874.

———. *Scarsdale; or, Life on the Lancashire and Yorkshire Border.* 3 vols. London: Smith, Elder, 1860.

———. *Thoughts and Suggestions on Certain Social Problems Contained Chiefly in Addresses to Meetings of Workmen in Lancashire.* London: Longmans, Green, 1873.

Kent, Christopher. "Victorian Social History: Post-Thompson, Post-Foucault, Postmodern." *Victorian Studies* 40.1 (1996): 97–133.

Landow, George. *The Aesthetic and Critical Theories of John Ruskin.* Princeton, NJ: Princeton UP, 1971.

———. *Elegant Jeremiahs: The Sage from Carlyle to Mailer.* Ithaca: Cornell UP, 1986.

Lawrence, Christopher. "The Nervous System and Society in the Scottish Enlightenment." *Natural Order: Historical Studies of Scientific Culture.* Ed. Barry Barnes and Steven Shapin. London: Sage, 1979. 19–40.

Lectures on the Results of the Great Exhibition of 1851, Delivered before the Society of Arts, Manufactures, and Commerce, at the Suggestion of H.R.H. Prince Albert, President of the Society. 2 vols. London: David Bogue, 1852.

Levine, A. S. "The Journalistic Career of Sir Henry Cole." *Victorian Periodicals Newsletter* 8 (1975): 61–65.

Lloyd, David, and Paul Thomas. *Culture and the State.* London: Routledge, 1998.

Lubbock, Jules. *The Tyranny of Taste: The Politics of Architecture and Design in Britain, 1550–1960.* New Haven: Yale UP, 1995.

Lutchmansingh, Larry D. "Commodity Exhibitionism at the London Great Exhibition of 1851." *Annals of Scholarship: Studies in the Humanities and Social Sciences* 7.2 (1990): 203–16.

Macaulay, Thomas Babington. "Southey's Colloquies on Society." *Critical and Historical Essays Contributed to the Edinburgh Review.* Vol. 1. 12th ed. London: Longman, Green, Longman, Roberts, and Green, 1865. 217–69.

Malthus, Thomas Robert. *Essay on the Principle of Population.* 1798. Reprints of Economic Classics. New York: Augustus M. Kelley, 1965.

Marx, Karl. *Capital: A Critique of Political Economy.* Vol. 1. Trans. Ben Fowkes. New York: Penguin, 1990.

———. "The Communist Manifesto." *Karl Marx: Selected Writings.* Ed. David McLellan. Oxford: Oxford UP, 1977. 221–47.

McCulloch, J. R. *The Principles of Political Economy: With Some Inquiries Respecting Their Application, and a Sketch of the Rise and Progress of the Science.* Edinburgh: William Tait, 1843.

Meek, Ronald L. *Social Science and the Ignoble Savage.* Cambridge: Cambridge UP, 1976.

Merrifield, Mrs. "The Harmony of Colours, As Exemplified in the Exhibition." *The Art-Journal Illustrated Catalogue.*

Mill, John Stuart. *Collected Works of John Stuart Mill.* Ed. J. M. Robson et al. 33 vols. Toronto: U Toronto P, 1963–91.

———. *Principles of Political Economy, with Some of Their Applications to Social Philosophy.* 1848. Ed. Sir William Ashley, 1909. Fairfield, NJ: Augustus M. Kelley, 1976.

Miller, Andrew H. *Novels behind Glass: Commodity Culture and Victorian Narrative.* Cambridge: Cambridge UP, 1995.

Miller, Gordon L. "Charles Babbage and the Design of Intelligence: Computers and Society in 19th-Century England." *Bulletin of Science, Technology, and Society* 10 (1990): 68–76.

Minihan, Janet. *The Nationalization of Culture: The Development of State Subsidies to the Arts in Great Britain.* New York: New York UP, 1977.

Morrell, Jack, and Arnold Thackray. *Gentlemen of Science: Early Years of the British Association for the Advancement of Science.* Oxford: Clarendon, 1981.

Morris, May. *William Morris: Artist, Writer, Socialist.* 2 vols. Oxford: Basil Blackwell, 1936.

Morris, William. *The Collected Works of William Morris.* 24 vols. London: Longmans, Green, 1910–15.

———. "The Worker's Share of Art." *William Morris: "News from Nowhere" and Selected Writings and Designs.* Ed. Asa Briggs. London: Penguin, 1984. 140–43.

O'Connor, Erin. *Raw Material: Producing Pathology in Victorian Culture.* Durham: Duke UP, 2000.

Official Descriptive and Illustrated Catalogue of the Great Exhibition. 3 vols. London: Spicer Brothers, 1851.

Paley, William. *Natural Theology: or, Evidences of the Existence and Attributes of the Deity, Collected from the Appearances of Nature.* London, 1802.

Pecora, Vincent. "Arnoldian Ethnology." *Victorian Studies* 41.3 (1998): 355–79.

Pevsner, Nikolaus. *High Victorian Design: A Study of the Exhibits of 1851.* London: Architectural Press, 1951.

Poovey, Mary. *Making a Social Body: British Cultural Formation, 1830–1864.* Chicago: U Chicago P, 1995.

Purbrick, Louise. "Ideologically Technical: Illustration, Automation and Spinning Cotton around the Middle of the Nineteenth Century." *Journal of Design History* 11.4 (1998): 275–93.

Rabinbach, Anson. *The Human Motor: Energy, Fatigue, and the Origins of Modernity.* New York: Basic Books, 1990.

Redgrave, Richard. "Supplementary Report on Design." *Reports by the Juries on the Subjects in the Thirty Classes into Which the Exhibition Was Divided.* London: William Clowes & Sons, 1852.

Richards, Jeffrey. "The Role of the Railways." *Ruskin and Environment: The Storm-Cloud of the Nineteenth Century.* Ed. Michael Wheeler. Manchester: Manchester UP, 1995. 123–43.

Richards, Thomas. *The Commodity Culture of Victorian England: Advertising and Spectacle, 1851–1914.* Stanford: Stanford UP, 1990.

Rifkin, Adrian. "Success Disavowed: The Schools of Design in Mid-Nineteenth-Century Britain (an Allegory)." *Journal of Design History* 1.2 (1988): 89–102.

Roach, Joseph. *Cities of the Dead: Circum-Atlantic Performance.* New York: Columbia UP, 1996.

Romano, Richard M. "The Economic Ideas of Charles Babbage." *History of Political Economy* 14.3 (1982): 385–405.

Rose, Jonathan. *The Edwardian Temperament, 1895–1919.* Athens: Ohio UP, 1986.

Ruskin, John. *The Complete Works of John Ruskin.* Ed. E. T. Cook and Alexander Wedderburn. 39 vols. London: George Allen, 1903–12.

Sala, George Augustus. *The House That Paxton Built.* London: Ironbrace, Woodenhead and Co. [Adolphus Ackermann], 1851.

Scarry, Elaine. *The Body in Pain: The Making and Unmaking of the World.* New York: Oxford UP, 1985.

Schaffer, Simon. "Babbage's Intelligence: Calculating Engines and the Factory System." *Critical Inquiry* 21.1 (1994): 203–27.

Searle. G. R. *The Quest for National Efficiency: A Study in British Politics and Political Thought, 1899–1914.* London: Ashfield, 1990.

Sedgwick, Eve Kosofsky. *Between Men: English Literature and Male Homosocial Desire.* New York: Columbia UP, 1985.

Select Committee on Art and the Connexion with Manufactures. *Report.* London, 1835–36.

Selleck, R. J. W. *James Kay-Shuttleworth: Journey of an Outsider.* Newbury Park, Ilford, Essex; and Portland, OR: Woburn Press, 1994.

Seltzer, Mark. *Bodies and Machines.* New York: Routledge, 1992.

Senior, Nassau. *An Outline of the Science of Political Economy.* 1836. London: George Allen and Unwin, 1938.

Shaw, George Bernard. *Collected Letters.* 4 vols. New York: Viking, 1985–88.

———. *Complete Plays with Prefaces.* 6 vols. New York: Dodd, Mead, 1962.

Sherburne, James Clark. *John Ruskin and the Ambiguities of Abundance: A Study in Social and Economic Criticism.* Cambridge, MA: Harvard UP, 1972.

Shuttleworth, Sally. *George Eliot and Nineteenth-Century Science: The Make-Believe of a Beginning.* Cambridge: Cambridge UP, 1984.

Smith, Adam. *An Inquiry into the Nature and Causes of the Wealth of Nations.* 1776. 2 vols. Indianapolis: Liberty Fund, 1981.

———. *The Theory of Moral Sentiments.* 1759. Ed. D. D. Raphael and A. L. Macfie. Oxford: Clarendon Press, 1976.

Smith, Jonathan. *Fact and Feeling: Baconian Science and the Nineteenth-Century Literary Imagination.* Science and Literature. Madison: U Wisconsin P, 1994.

Southey, Robert. *Sir Thomas More: or, Colloquies on the Progress and Prospects of Society.* 2 vols. London: John Murray, 1829.

Spear, Jeffrey L. *Dreams of an English Eden: Ruskin and His Tradition in Social Criticism.* New York: Columbia UP, 1984.

Stocking, George W. *Race, Culture, and Evolution: Essays in the History of Anthropology.* New York: Free Press, 1968.

———. *Victorian Anthropology.* New York: Free Press, 1987.

Sussman, Herbert L. *Victorian Masculinities: Manhood and Masculine Poetics in Early Victorian Literature and Art.* Cambridge: Cambridge UP, 1995.

———. *Victorians and the Machine: The Literary Response to Technology.* Cambridge, MA: Harvard UP, 1968.

Sypher, Eileen. "The 'Production' of William Morris' *News from Nowhere.*" *Minnesota Review* 22 (1984): 84–104.

Tenger, Zeynap, and Paul Trolander. "Genius versus Capital: Eighteenth-Century Theories of Genius and Adam Smith's *Wealth of Nations.*" *Modern Language Quarterly* 55.2 (1994): 169–89.

Thompson, E. P. *The Making of the English Working Class.* New York: Vintage Books, 1966.

———. "Time, Work-Discipline, and Industrial Capitalism." *Past and Present* 38 (1967): 56–97.

———. *William Morris: Romantic to Revolutionary.* New York: Pantheon Books, 1977.

Turner, Mark. *The Literary Mind.* New York: Oxford UP, 1996.

Ure, Andrew. *The Philosophy of Manufactures: Or, An Exposition of the Scientific, Moral, and Commercial Economy of the Factory System of Great Britain.* London: Charles Knight, 1835.

Ward, J. T. *The Factory Movement, 1830–1855.* London: Macmillan, 1962.

Ward, James. *The World in Its Workshops: A Practical Examination of British and Foreign Processes of Manufacture, with a Critical Comparison of the Fabrics, Machinery, and Works of Art Contained in the Great Exhibition.* London: William S. Orr, 1851.

Wells, H. G. *A Modern Utopia.* London: Chapman and Hall, 1905.

Welsh, Alexander. *George Eliot and Blackmail.* Cambridge, MA: Harvard UP, 1985.

———. "Writing and Copying in the Age of Steam." *Victorian Literature and Society: Essays Presented to Richard D. Altick.* Ed. James R. Kincaid and Albert J. Kuhn. Columbus: Ohio State UP, 1983.

Wilde, Oscar. "The Soul of Man under Socialism." 1891. *The Artist as Critic: Critical Writings of Oscar Wilde.* Ed. Richard Ellmann. New York: Random House, 1968.

Williams, Raymond. *Culture and Society, 1780–1950.* 1958. New York: Columbia UP, 1983.

———. *Keywords: A Vocabulary of Culture and Society.* Revised edition. New York: Oxford UP, 1983.

Wing, Charles. *Evils of the Factory System, Demonstrated by Parliamentary Evidence.* 1837. Reprints of Economic Classics. London: Frank Cass, 1867.

Winner, Langdon. *Autonomous Technology: Technics-Out-of-Control as a Theme in Political Thought.* Cambridge, MA: MIT Press, 1977.

Wordsworth, William. *Lyrical Ballads, and Other Poems, 1797–1800.* Ed. James Butler and Karen Green. The Cornell Wordsworth. Ithaca: Cornell UP, 1992.

Wornum, Ralph Nicholson. "The Exhibition as a Lesson in Taste." *The Art-Journal Illustrated Catalogue.*

Wortley, Lady Emmeline Stuart. *The Great Exhibition. Honour to Labour, a Lay of 1851.* London: N. Wright, n.d.

Wyatt, M. Digby. *The Industrial Arts of the Nineteenth Century: A Series of Illustrations of the Choicest Specimens Produced by Every Nation at the Great Exhibition of Works of Industry, 1851.* London: Day and Son, 1851.

Yeo, Richard. *Defining Science: William Whewell, Natural Knowledge, and Public Debate in Early Victorian Britain.* Cambridge: Cambridge UP, 1993.

Young, Robert J. C. *Colonial Desire: Hybridity in Theory, Culture, and Race.* London: Routledge, 1995.

INDEX

manufactures (as things) (*continued*)
"meretricious," 75–77, 171, 175–76; free trade
and, 23, 46–47, 123–25, 208 n. 19; versus
handicrafts, 158–59, 184–85; role in fostering
taste, 125–26, 169–70, 175–76; science of, 53,
150–51; as signs of processes, 14, 55–56, 57–59,
66, 71, 75–76, 85, 150; ugliness of, 84–85,
158–59, 171, 185. *See also* commodity or
commodities; value (commercial)

manufacturing population, 28–29, 33, 38, 41, 45.
See also factory labor; operatives; working
class

Maoris, 111–14

Marx, Karl: on alienation, 18, 100, 119; on
"Bourgeoisie" versus "Proletariat," 190; on
commodities, 55, 58; on factory labor, 18, 188;
on "manufacture" versus "automatic
factory," 189; on Ure, 23, 31, 189, 206 nn. 8, 12.
Works: *Capital*, 23, 31, 55, 58, 189, 206 nn. 8,
12; "The Communist Manifesto," 190

masculinity or men: as alternative to self-
interest, 177, 191–92, 194; autonomy and, 177,
183–86, 194, 201–2, 203–4; displacement of
adult male labor, 92, 102–4, 177, 182; effects
of factory labor on, 106–7; efficiency and,
203–4; versus mechanism, 177, 179, 183–84,
202. *See also* gentleman, ideal of; Morris,
William, on manliness; Ruskin, John, on
men or manliness

mathematics. *See* Babbage, Charles; *and under*
science

McCulloch, J. R., 88, 103

medical profession, 31–32, 90. *See also*
Alison, William Pulteney; Gaskell, Peter;
Kay-Shuttleworth, James Phillips; Ure,
Andrew; Wing, Charles

Meek, Ronald L., 86–88

Merrifield, Mrs., 165

middle class: and correspondence of physical
beauty and morality, 106; and discourse of
culture, 7, 148–49; education of, 13, 128;
improvement of, 108; respect for property,
29; as source of revolutionary desire, 192,
199–200. *See also* class or classes

Mill, John Stuart, 67, 68, 88–89, 11, 193–94

Miller, Andrew H., 208 n. 19

Miller, Gordon L., 55

mills. *See* factories; manufacturers

modernity and modernism: aesthetic
terminology, 120; and efficiency, 14, 56, 65,
160–61, 200–204; material creation as act of
semiosis, 71; preoccupations with bodily
waste and prostheses, 210 n. 5; technological
aesthetics, 56, 65, 116

Morris, William, 3, 5, 16–17, 166, 177–80, 188–202,
203; on capitalism, 179–80, 189–95, 197, 199;

on class distinctions, 190–92, 195; on desire
as revolutionary force, 191–92, 193–94, 197–98;
on manliness: —versus commercial
self-interest or competition, 177, 190, 191–92;
—versus effeminacy, 190, 196; —ideal of, 17,
177–80, 188–92, 194, 195–96, 201–2; —versus
mechanism, 17, 177–79, 189; Ruskin and
Marx as influences, 188–89; on socialism,
179–80, 189, 191, 192, 196–99; use of romance
genre, 179, 192–94, 195, 198–99; on utopia:
—machines in, 189, 199–202; —sexual desire
in, 196–98, 201–2, 211 n. 11; —women in,
195–96, 197–98; on work and pleasure,
188–89, 194. Works: "How We Live and How
We Might Live," 193–94, 199; preface to
"The Nature of Gothic," 16, 188–89;
News from Nowhere, 179–80, 195–200, 210 n.
6; "The Society of the Future," 189–92;
"Useful Work *versus* Useless Toil," 194

Native Americans, 86–87

nature: and factory system, 20–21, 25–30, 37–38,
155–56; manufacturing population's
separation from, 109–10; mastery over, 66–67,
94–95, 148, 191, 193–94; savage and, 103,
109–10, 112–14, 185; as source of aesthetic or
design principles, 85, 109; as source of design
principles, 111–14, 119, 137–39, 170, 174; as
source of moral or religious principles, 73–74,
81, 109; as source of scientific or technical
principles, 66, 148, 150–51, 165–66

Norton, Charles Eliot, 82

novel: industrial, 56, 92–93; sensation, 197

novelty. *See under* design and design theory;
taste

Oastler, Richard, 18–20, 24, 182, 206 n. 1

*Official Descriptive and Illustrated Catalogue of
the Great Exhibition*, 76–77, 147, 165

operatives: autonomy or freedom of, 33–34,
103–4, 177–79, 181–84, 189–90; compared to
other kinds of workers, 41–42, 48, 183;
compared to slaves, 18–19, 23, 41–42, 43–44,
137, 180–82; as components of factory, 31–34,
189; discipline of, 33–34, 36–37, 42, 114,
154–55; education of, 12–13, 128–29, 109–10,
128–30; factory system as benefit to, 34,
36–38, 43–44, 47–48, 59; and gender, 45, 102–3,
106–8, 182; and gentlemen, 186–87; health
(physical or moral) of, 22, 25, 34–36, 37–44,
96, 106–7, 179, 182; intelligence or vigilance
of, 12, 34, 107; mechanization of, 18–19, 25, 41,
43–44, 104, 179–80, 183–84, 189–90; morals
of, 29, 34–36, 42, 48, 103, 109–10; respect for
property, 29, 36–37. *See also* factory labor;
workers; working class

Victorian Literature and Culture Series

Daniel Albright
Tennyson: The Muses' Tug-of-War

David G. Riede
Matthew Arnold and the Betrayal of Language

Anthony Winner
Culture and Irony: Studies in Joseph Conrad's Major Novels

James Richardson
Vanishing Lives: Style and Self in Tennyson, D. G. Rossetti, Swinburne, and Yeats

Jerome J. McGann, Editor
Victorian Connections

Antony H. Harrison
Victorian Poets and Romantic Poems: Intertextuality and Ideology

E. Warwick Slinn
The Discourse of Self in Victorian Poetry

Linda K. Hughes and Michael Lund
The Victorian Serial

Anna Leonowens
The Romance of the Harem
Edited by Susan Morgan

Alan Fischler
Modified Rapture: Comedy in W. S. Gilbert's Savoy Operas

Emily Shore
Journal of Emily Shore
Edited by Barbara Timm Gates

Richard Maxwell
The Mysteries of Paris and London

Felicia Bonaparte
The Gypsy-Bachelor of Manchester: The Life of Mrs. Gaskell's Demon

Peter L. Shillingsburg
Pegasus in Harness: Victorian Publishing and W. M. Thackeray

Angela Leighton
Victorian Women Poets: Writing against the Heart

Allan C. Dooley
Author and Printer in Victorian England

Simon Gatrell
Thomas Hardy and the Proper Study of Mankind

Jeffrey Skoblow
Paradise Dislocated: Morris, Politics, Art

Matthew Rowlinson
Tennyson's Fixations: Psychoanalysis and the Topics of the Early Poetry

Beverly Seaton
The Language of Flowers: A History

Barry Milligan
*Pleasures and Pains: Opium and the Orient in
Nineteenth-Century British Culture*

Ginger S. Frost
Promises Broken: Courtship, Class, and Gender in Victorian England

Linda Dowling
The Vulgarization of Art: The Victorians and Aesthetic Democracy

Tricia Lootens
Lost Saints: Silence, Gender, and Victorian Literary Canonization

Matthew Arnold
The Letters of Matthew Arnold, vols. 1-6
Edited by Cecil Y. Lang

Edward FitzGerald
Edward FitzGerald, Rubáiyát of Omar Khayyám: *A Critical Edition*
Edited by Christopher Decker

Christina Rossetti
The Letters of Christina Rossetti, vols. 1-3
Edited by Antony H. Harrison

Barbara Leah Harman
The Feminine Political Novel in Victorian England

John Ruskin
The Genius of John Ruskin: Selections from His Writings
Edited by John D. Rosenberg

Antony H. Harrison
Victorian Poets and the Politics of Culture: Discourse and Ideology

Judith Stoddart
Ruskin's Culture Wars: Fors Clavigera *and the Crisis
of Victorian Liberalism*

Linda K. Hughes and Michael Lund
Victorian Publishing and Mrs. Gaskell's Work

Linda H. Peterson
Traditions of Victorian Women's Autobiography: The Poetics and Politics of Life Writing

Gail Turley Houston
Royalties: The Queen and Victorian Writers

Laura C. Berry
The Child, the State, and the Victorian Novel

Barbara J. Black
On Exhibit: Victorians and Their Museums

Annette R. Federico
Idol of Suburbia: Marie Corelli and Late-Victorian Literary Culture

Talia Schaffer
The Forgotten Female Aesthetes: Literary Culture in Late-Victorian England

Julia F. Saville
A Queer Chivalry: The Homoerotic Asceticism of Gerard Manley Hopkins

Victor Shea and William Whitla, Editors
Essays and Reviews: The 1860 Text and Its Reading

Marlene Tromp
The Private Rod: Marital Violence, Sensation, and the Law in Victorian Britain

Dorice Williams Elliott
The Angel out of the House: Philanthropy and Gender in Nineteenth-Century England

Richard Maxwell, Editor
The Victorian Illustrated Book

Vineta Colby
Vernon Lee: A Literary Biography

E. Warwick Slinn
Victorian Poetry as Cultural Critique: The Politics of Performative Language

Simon Joyce
Capital Offenses: Geographies of Class and Crime in Victorian London

Caroline Levine
The Serious Pleasures of Suspense: Victorian Realism and Narrative Doubts

Emily Davies
Emily Davies: Collected Letters, 1861-1875
Edited by Ann B. Murphy and Deirdre Raftery

Joseph Bizup
Manufacturing Culture: Vindications of Early Victorian Industry